STEAK LOVER'S COOKBOOK

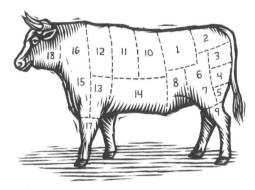

BY WILLIAM RICE

Illustrations by M. KATHRYN THOMPSON

WORKMAN PUBLISHING • NEW YORK

Rice, William.
Steak lover's cookbook / by William Rice
p. cm. Includes index.
ISBN 0-7611-0631-6 (alk. paper).—ISBN 0-7611-0080-6 (pbk.: alk. paper)
1. Cookery (Beef) I. Title.
TX749.5.B43R53 1996
641.6'62–dc20
Cover and book design by Paul Gamarello
Cover photograph by Louis Wallach

Workman Publishing Company, Inc.
708 Broadway
New York, NY 10003-9555

Manufactured in the United States of America
First printing February 1997
10 9 8 7 6 5 4 3 2 1

To my mother, and to Jill, living proof that a marriage can have a better half.

ACKNOWLEDGMENTS

For helping to shape a raw concept into a ready to serve book, Suzanne Rafer, Paul Gamarello, Susan Ramer, Barry Bluestein and Kevin Morrissey, and Susan Derecskey.

For their invaluable contributions in researching steak cookery and steak lore, Diane E. Haglund; Marlys Bielunski, Susan Lamb Parenti, Irene Yeh, Debbie Baughman and B.J. Valenziano of the National Cattlemen's Beef Association; Betty Hughes and Carol Moeller of Weber-Stephen; Cate Erickson; Jerry Lekan of Paulina Market, and John Scimca of John's Finer Foods; Ellard "Butch" Pfaelzer of the Bruss Company; and Chuck Jolley and Jerry Lyons of Cryovac.

For their passion about steak, their friendship, and for making the steak house all that it can be, Pat Cetta of Spark's Steak House and Bern Laxer of Bern's.

For sharing steaks, including some improbable experiments, Pam, Roy, and Irma Van Cleave, Judy and Joe Fell, Debbie and Bob Cummins, Ivan and Janet Kaplan, Jo and Tony Terlato, Vikki and Elliot Brown, Elaine and Mitch Khosrova, Mary and Jim Burns, Betsey and Johnny Apple, Susan and David Brinkley, and from the past, Bobby and Jim.

Finally, thanks to those cooks, professional and amateur, who shared recipes with me, and to my colleagues at the *Chicago Tribune* for their professionalism and inspiration.

CONTENTS

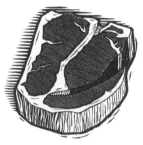

DOWNTOWN CUTS...117

ALL AROUND THE TOWN .181

GREAT STEAK!

Hello. I am here to serve you steak. Not just one steak, but lots of steaks, cooked and presented in lots of different ways.

I'm also happy to report these steaks are hot. The 1990s has witnessed the re-appreciation of the pleasure of eating a food that everyone can understand and that just tastes good. Once again, the steak dinner is the feast of choice for special occasions and a symbol of American well-being and prosperity. Once again, people speak with real enthusiasm about the excitment of confronting a "big, juicy, succulent" steak. We say we "crave" a steak, and we mean it. For me, there is the pleasure and the extra seductive element of pleasure delayed.

Steak, I confess, did not play a large part in my childhood. My mother was a good cook, celebrated within our family for her terrific desserts. But her approach to steak was to buy one that was no more than half an inch thick and cook it until she was sure it was brown all the way through. As a result, steak was not much in demand Chez Rice.

It wasn't until my first year in college that I tasted a steak that was crisp, almost crunchy, on the surface and thick enough to be gloriously pink in the center. And juicy. Ah, how I loved that juice!

For that matter, how I loved the outsized, richly dressed salad that came before the steak, the equally outsized baked potato on the plate with the steak—indeed the entire experience of dining at a restaurant aptly named "The Steak House."

Gifted with an uncommonly good appetite, the thinness of my wallet was the only impediment as I pursued steaks of record sizes over the next few years. I also ate steak raw, marinated, and chicken-fried. Gradually I discovered a wider horizon that included garlic-anointed sirloins swimming in fragrant pizzaiola sauce beside a big portion ot pasta. They ranked right up there with the thin, chewy but incredibly flavorful steak served at second-rank French restaurants. A gob of heavenly butter on top, distributed bits of chopped shallot and parsley over the steak as it melted.

About this time, happily, my chauvinist notion that Americans had the monopoly on preparing great steak was erased. It took only a single visit to the tappen yaki room of a Japanese restaurant. The light-ning-fast cutting and cooking on the flat-top grill around which we were seated was wonderfully theatrical. The steak was supremely tender. But what impressed me most was the impact of soy sauce and less familiar seasonings on the meat, and the crunch of the barely cooked vegetables served with it.

Eating steaks in restaurants was fun, and, it turned out, a wonderful preparation for what came next—cooking them. As a novice, bachelor cook in the pre-pasta 1960s, when fancy carry-out food came from a deli and was a pastrami sandwich, it was inevitable I'd become familiar with steak. There weren't many options and it was what everyone wanted to eat.

I progressed from burgers to *bavette,* the superior version of flank steak sold at Washington's French Market. A pair of fellow journalists, with whom I shared quarters, were willing collaborators in demolishing my experiments. My Japanese dining experience opened a whole new world, and the delight I've taken since in using Asian techniques and flavorings to cook steak is reflected in recipes such as Asian Beef Salad with Cucumbers and Thai Red Beef Curry.

As I cooked on, there were opportunities to make side dishes and experiment with sauces. I'd doctor a barbecue sauce until it became my own. Copying the French chefs, I'd turn a simple pat of butter into a repository for garlic and herbs and more. Making *beurre composé,* as the French call it, is an invitation to almost limitless innovation.

Composed butters are, I learned eventually, but child's play. With the encourage-ment of Craig Claiborne, as I neared age thirty, I resigned from the *Washington Post,* took my meager savings, and enrolled in Paris's famed Le Cordon Bleu.

Talk about the steak-and-potatoes American diet! The French semed to order steak and potatoes even more often than we did, but they make both in so many different ways that the combination never becomes monotonous. At the school, I learned the difference between filet and entrecôte, garnishes for such classics as *filet à la forestière* (with morel mushrooms), entrecôte bordelaise (with poached bone marrow), and a remarkable array of sauces. The opportunity to travel led me to Florence, where I devoured the famous T-bone called *fiorentina.* I found fascinating steak preparations, too, in such disparate environments as Scandinavia and Spain.

Back home and back in journalism, working at the *Washington Post,* then *Food & Wine* magazine, and most recently the *Chicago Tribune,* I've had occasion to discover the diversity of great steak in the great steak houses, from such down-home classics as the Ranchman's Cafe in tiny Ponder, Texas, Jess & Jim's in Kansas City and Doe's Eat Place in Greenville, Mississippi, to upscale Peter Luger and Sparks in New York City, Bern's in Tampa, and the unparalleled array in Chicago.

My main objective in this book is to share practical information about buying, cooking, and serving steak at home. Using my book in your kitchen, you can include steak in your weekly diet with recipes using what I think of as "downtown cuts" that are relatively low in cost and easy to prepare. Other recipes, calling for more expensive "uptown cuts," are perfect for entertaining and special occasions.

The book is organized by cuts of steak because it's not enough simply to ask a butcher for steak for dinner. Inevitably, you must decide which steak you want. You must say "sirloin" or "flank." Knowledge of these cuts and how best to cook each of them also is vital to preparing a steak properly and enjoying it fully. There's a reason a chuck steak costs less than a T-bone. It is less tender and cooking it will require more attention and time. But the reward is in the taste and flavor.

Much of what is offered to you in this personal celebration of dining on steak will be new. The best and brightest of our restaurant chefs have been expanding the use of steak on their menus and introducing some very inventive dishes. In New York City, Larry Forgione of An American Place makes a rich beer sauce for chuck steaks. In Chicago, David Schy of the Hubbard Street Grill plays magician and turns eighteen ingredients into one dynamite sauce for skirt steak. At San Francisco's popular Lulu, Reed Hearon garnishes a succulent bone-in rib steak with arti-chokes, potatoes, and black olive butter. I've adapted these recipes—and more from other chefs I know—for the home kitchen, revised old favorites to take into account the way we eat today, and developed others to take advantage of the extraordinary range of ingredients available in our markets.

There's more: appetizers to serve before your steak, side dishes to serve with it, dreamy and unabashedly rich desserts for after; there are also drink recipes, and my thoughts on wine to serve with various steak preparations. Those of you who love the outdoor grill will find elements of an entire meal—vegetables, steak of course, and even a dessert pizza. In addition, there's a listing of some of my favorite steak houses and mail-order sources for steaks that are restaurant-quality or from specialty-beef cattle.

Tender American steak from corn-fed cattle is one of the taste treats of the modern world. The French, Greeks, and Asians agree. Most often this opinion is formed during a meal in a restaurant. But stick with me and you'll learn the ways to prepare great steak at home.

—William Rice
Chicago, February 1997

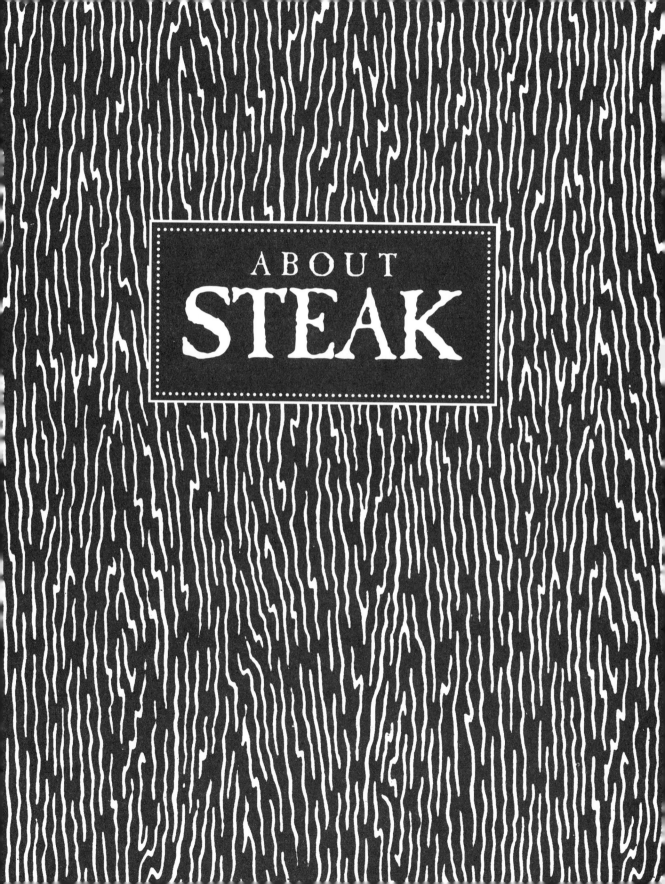

ABOUT
STEAK

MAKING, BUYING, AND COOKING STEAK

C attle have changed a great deal in the United States since ranchers in the last century began crossbreeding the Spanish immigrant longhorn, a lean animal with great endurance, with fatter cattle from England. Today's calf probably is a genetically engineered Angus, Hereford, French Charolais, or a crossbreed. Hereford is popular with some steak house chains because it yields bigger steaks, but Angus is the best seller.

MAKING A STEAK

M aking a steak may take up to two years and involve as many as half a dozen different stages.

A calf is born in the spring weighing about 80 pounds. Most likely the locale is a farm in the Midwest, but it could be in Texas, Florida, California, or several other states that have beef cattle industries. The animal destined to provide high quality steaks spends about six months on the farm or ranch, being weaned to solid food. During that time, the steer will grow to more than four hundred pounds and become a steer by virtue of castration. In the fall it is either sold as a "feeder calf" or kept to graze until the following spring.

Once sold, the steer is placed in a feed lot. Most of these are located in grain-producing states such as Colorado, Kansas, Nebraska, Iowa, Illinois, and Texas. Fed a diet of corn, sorghum, oats, barley, and vitamins, a steer's weight increases to between one thousand and fifteen hundred pounds in three to six months. But today's cattle do not become as fat as they once did. They have been redesigned genetically over several generations to produce meat that is leaner, yet still flavorful.

"Natural" beef can come from steers that are fed grain grown with pesticides, but the animals must not have received hormone implants, which are given to as much as 80 percent of the nation's cattle. Held longer on the range, up to fourteen months, steers destined to provide natural beef eat a feed lot diet of alfalfa, corn silage, and fresh hay. Over four months they gain about four hundred pounds.

This steak on the hoof is composed of about 18 percent protein, 22 percent fat, and 60 percent water. But the cattle buyers employed by beef packing companies, who come regularly to the feed lots, are thinking about texture, fat content, and connective tissue, the qualities of meat that determine its tenderness and the way in which it should be cooked. The harder and more prevalent the connective tissue, the tougher that flesh is likely to be.

The muscle fibers of a young animal are smaller and have been used less, therefore it is less tough. More use, as with legs and neck, equal more toughness. An oft-quoted generality is the closer the meat is to a hoof or horn, the tougher it will be. Therefore there are variations in tenderness even within cuts.

The National Cattlemen's Beef Association lists nine sub-primal cuts: chuck, fore shank, brisket, rib, short plate, short loin, sirloin, flank, and round. The least exercised of these is the short loin, in the middle of the back, followed by the sirloin and rib.

As for fat, even though younger animals, veal for example, are more tender, their meat seems drier because it has less fat. As fat develops in a steer, it makes the meat's texture more moist, but also increases the level of calories and cholesterol.

Another element in this world of tradeoffs is that more activity tends to create more flavor. Less expensive leg and shoulder cuts have more flavor than more expensive loin cuts. Indeed, beef has more flavor than veal. The development of connective tissue tends to be cumulative. The animal's exercise time adds up and tissue becomes firmer as the animal ages.

With all the above in mind, along with fluctuations in demand and price, the cattle buyers choose steers for their companies.

The packer is responsible for processing the animal and dividing, or "dressing," about eight hundred pounds of meat into the primal cuts. Some of those are vacuum-packed and sent to wholesale butchers, others are cut further into sub-primal cuts. Most of these are vacuum-packed, too, and may be sent to wholesale butchers or directly to supermarket chains. An increasingly small percentage will be sent on without being vacuum-packed. In any event, the aging process has begun.

AGING BEEF

Aging beef is a chemical change that occurs slowly under a controlled temperature during the first ten days after slaughter, perhaps longer. It heightens flavor and tenderizes meat; on that everyone agrees.

While some aspects of aging still are a mystery to scientists, the dominant theory is that freed enzymes attack cell proteins, causing the meat to break down and become softer. Separately, proteins are reduced to strongly flavored amino acids. For beef, the ideal aging cycle is ten days to three weeks hanging unwrapped at a temperature in the mid to high 30°F with controlled humidity. A limiting factor on aging is the susceptibility of fat to oxidation, which, in turn, may lead to off-flavors and spoilage.

In the rush of modern life, it seems butchers no longer can afford the luxury of giving beef some time to just hang out. Citing the shortage of meat locker storage space, the cost of holding the beef back from market, and so-called consumer preference for the less pronounced taste of unaged or barely aged beef, the industry allows most beef to age for only the period of time needed to transport it from the packer to the supermarket. This may be as short as four days. What arrives at perhaps 90 percent of America's supermarkets and restaurants is not sides or quarters, but precut, vacuum-packed "boxed beef." The meat has been wrapped and hermetically sealed in polyethylene bags that promote the aging effect. Since some juice coats and moistens the surface of the meat, this process is known as "wet-aging." As with Kleenex and facial tissue, the brand name of the company that developed the process, Cryovac, has become synonymous with vacuum-packing meat.

Boxed beef was introduced in the late 1950s and early 1960s as a service for restaurants and hotels that couldn't justify buying a half-carcass. Supermarket chains soon demanded this service, too, and when a firm called Iowa Beef Processors was founded in the early 1970s specifically to produce boxed beef, the old, dry-aging method was doomed. In time, Iowa Beef became the nation's dominant meat-packer and the old-line firms that didn't adapt went out of business.

Beef intended for retail sale goes directly from the processor to the supermarket company. A restaurant's beef may go from the processor to a middle man, a wholesale packer, where it will be portion cut, repackaged, and aged before being delivered to the restaurant.

These days, dry-aged beef is more talked about than seen. Once no great restaurant or hotel, especially in New York City, would sell a prime steak that hadn't spent time hanging in a meat locker. And visitors to Manhattan's theater district still stop to peer through a window at Gallagher's on West 52 Street, into a refrigerated aging room containing fresh meat being aged.

NOT AGING STEAK AT HOME

A warning! Do not try to dry-age steak in your home. Only large primal and sub-primal cuts are suitable to the process. The bacteria that will collect on a single steak could cause illness. Keep fresh steak in the refrigerator, well wrapped, for no more than four days. If you choose to freeze uncooked steak, do it under the coldest temperature possible because the faster it freezes the less fluid loss there will be when you thaw it.

Dry-aged beef lovers insist that the meat has a better texture and that its flavor is complex and fascinating. While both dry- and wet-aged beef are mild and soft to the tooth, a dry-aged steak will have an earthy, slightly musty aroma and may be a little drier and firmer. Dry-aging also deepens the red color of the flesh and causes shrinkage, which, some experts believe, is the reason dry-aged beef seems to have a more intense flavor.

There is, however, considerably less yield from dry-aged meat. Dry-aging a two hundred pound cut for fourteen days will result in as much as 20 percent loss due to evaporation and shaving mold from the meat's surface. (In wet-aging there is little moisture loss because the bag adheres so tightly to the meat.)

A restaurant such as Gallagher's may choose to age its own meat and recoup the investment by pricing prime steaks at prime prices. But rare is the retail butcher with the courage to charge $20 a pound for raw meat.

In response, advocates of "wet-aging" say their method is easier to control, costs far less, and wins taste test after taste test. Wet-aging in Cryovac produces less aging effect, but also less shrinkage, and some aging does occur to meat in transit. However, the retailer is unlikely to hold the meat any longer than the time it takes to tray it and put it on display. Advocates cite the advantages of standardized cuts, consistency of product, and better quality control.

The science of wet-aging has not changed much over the years, but the packaging and strength of the vacuum has improved. So has the distribution system. It promises the retailer that he can buy specific cuts according to his needs, promoting broader selection, more efficient inventory control, and—we hope—a better price for the consumer.

As for the great debate over dry- versus wet-aged steak, a Cryovac official sums it up with all the magnanimity of a winner: "It's what you're used to that tastes best," he says, "and fewer and fewer Americans have an opportunity to become used to dry-aged beef."

BUYING A STEAK

Most of us buy our steak from a supermarket self-serve counter. Usually, there's a butcher within call. While there has been considerable wringing of hands in recent years that true butchers are disappearing—along with all manner of skilled craftspeople in other disciplines—that butcher is all you have in a supermarket to provide information and an assurance of quality. Try to get to know him by showing interest and by praising when praise is due.

The steaks in the supermarket or in the butcher's display case are precut for convenience. Ideally, there are flecks of fat throughout the meat and the fat around the border is close-trimmed and white—unless the meat is from free-range lean beef. Then it should be slightly yellow. Avoid steaks with clumps of fat because the fat will only be cut away and discarded. If you want a steak you don't see or one cut to a specific diameter or a tenderloin cut to a specific weight, ask for it. In addition, it's good to develop a contact at a butcher shop for special purchases while continuing to use the supermarket for everyday needs.

Wherever I shop, two decisions that I have to make are: What steak should I buy and how much of it do I need? It's worthwhile educating yourself to some degree about the configuration of cuts of beef. Recognizing the shape and bone structure of a steak will reassure you that it is labeled properly. And you will know, for example, that since sirloin steaks with a small pin bone are cut nearer to the loin, they are more tender than sirloins with a long, flat bone that are cut nearer to the round. Choice is by far the most common of the quality grades. If a steak is graded "select," be prepared for quicker-cooking but less-tender meat. If it is

super-rich prime, both the butcher or label and the price will let you know.

James Beard, a large man with a lusty appetite, recommended some years ago that for the "average appetite, one-half to one pound of steak is not too much to allow." Contemporary appetites and sensibilities dictate something less except at steak house feasts. In my house, a boneless strip or sirloin steak of twelve ounces provides enough meat for two, and even three, if it is sliced thin. An inch-thick T-bone or porterhouse weighing a pound serves the same, and a filet for one need not weigh more than five to six ounces.

Once you arrive home with your purchase, refrigerate it. A well-wrapped steak should be fine up to four days. If you plan to freeze it, do so immediately. Remove the steak from the butcher paper, wrap it tightly in plastic wrap, and seal it in a heavy-duty freezer bag labeled with the cut and date. It should be fine for six months, but the meat gradually loses flavor and in time will be flabby when thawed.

COOKING A STEAK PERFECTLY

(formerly Cooking the Perfect Steak)

I renamed this section when I realized that you and I can play no role in "making" a perfect steak. That process culminates at the meat packer or in an aging locker. At best, we can only hope to pick one up or point one out at the meat counter.

But when it comes to cooking, everything

is up to us. The chef-philosopher Wolfgang Puck once told me his job as chef "is to buy the best ingredients I can, then try not to screw them up."

So it is with cooking steak. If you or I screw up, everyone will notice. Furthermore, the steak or steaks represent a sizable investment in food. But the real reason we want this to come out right is the pleasure a perfectly cooked steak brings to those who eat it.

There are those who insist the only place to find a perfect steak cooked perfectly is in a steak house. My answer is that while you cannot duplicate the intense heat of a restaurant grill, 800°F or more, you can prepare steak at home that is just as enjoyable. As for the meat, if you enjoy prime beef and are willing to pay the price, you can mail order great restaurant steaks (see page 232).

Why do we cook meat in the first place? To make it taste better and easier to eat and digest. We respond to cooked meat because heat actually creates flavor in meat. First, by damaging the cell membranes, it helps create a gazpacho of fat, water-soluble compounds, enzymes, sugars, minerals, and free amino acids. Second, the high temperatures cause browning on the surface of the meat and that crust is very intensely flavored and aromatic.

DONENESS

The most critical point in preparing a great steak isn't when you start cooking, it's when you stop. The degree of doneness is absolutely essential to a steak's success.

As soon as you cut into a steak, well before you've tasted it, your eyes are flashing "go at it!" or "caution" signals to the brain. This early warning system is reacting to the color of the meat. The red pigment in raw meat is myoglobin. At 135°F (rare) it is still mostly red; at 145°F (medium rare) it is pink in the center, but the color is noticeably brown toward the surface; at 155°F (medium) there is only a

THE TOUCH METHOD

It will take some practice to turn the following ritual into a practical skill, but soon the touch system will be your number-one guide to judging doneness.

For Rare

Let one hand hang limp. With the index finger of the other hand push gently into the soft triangle of flesh between the thumb and index finger of the hanging hand. It will offer very little resistance, give way very easily, and feel soft and spongy. That is the feel of rare steak.

For Medium-rare

Extend the hand in front of you and spread the fingers. Press the same spot with the index finger of the other hand. The flesh will be firmer but not hard, springy, and slightly resistant. This is the feel of medium-rare steak.

For Medium

Make a fist and press the spot. It will feel firm and snap back quickly, offering only a minimum of give, as does meat cooked to medium.

No need for a further comparison. Cook your steak any more and it will be a lost cause.

trace of pink at the center, and while the meat still should be moist, the grain will be more apparent; and at 160°F (well done), the fiber proteins will be hard, dense, and the surface an unappetizing brown.

Marlys Bielunski, the National Cattlemen's Beef Association's astute test kitchens director and the reigning authority on how consumers cook steak at home, says: "The most common mistake when preparing steak at home is to overcook it. Unlike chefs, home cooks do not work with steak every day and they play it safe. Even if a meat thermometer is used, the cook tends to wait until the reading hits medium-rare or medium, but the meat goes on cooking. Steaks are usually at their most flavorful cooked to no more than medium doneness."

Nothing in the process is more given to variables than cooking a steak to a specific point of doneness. These include thickness, cut, whether the oven or pan has been preheated, and the internal temperature of the meat when cooking begins. The Beef Association recommends cooking steak directly from the refrigerator, and you can also cook them straight from the freezer (see page 90). I prefer to allow steak to come to room temperature before cooking. Not surprisingly, my steaks cook more quickly. While I will suggest cooking times in each steak recipe that should give you a medium-rare or medium steak, these can be no more than approximations. To do yourself, and your steak, justice, I insist—and I'm not really an insistent guy on most subjects—you learn and practice the touch method of judging doneness (see page 7).

Another way to see how far a steak has progressed on the doneness scale when grilling or panbroiling, is to keep an eye out for the first blood-red tears that appear on the top. They are a sign that the steak, with the heat coming from underneath, has reached the medium-rare stage on one side. When the drops are pink, the steak has reached medium. Turn it at once, depending on your preference.

Do I hear someone say, "What about using a thermometer?" A standard meat thermometer, with its bulky probe and its need to be in the meat throughout the cooking process, is impractical for steaks. Even with an instant-read thermometer in hand, the thinner a steak, the more difficult it becomes.

METHODS OF COOKING

Steak can be cooked by dry heat or by moist heat.

The dry-heat cooking methods are broiling, panbroiling, panfrying, roasting, and grilling. Dry heat is just dandy for the tender uptown, more expensive cuts, so in the pages ahead you'll find I broil porterhouse and strip steaks, panfry filets and T-bones, and grill just about anything that comes to hand. The moist-heat cooking methods, good for softening the connective tissue in the tougher downtown cuts, are boiling, steaming, braising, and stewing. Flank steak, though it has that downtown address, is best cooked by dry heat—broiling or grilling—and now costs as much as some of the uptown cuts. Searing, a technique that often is used with steaks cooked by either method, rates a separate description (see page 24). So does grilling (see page 26).

GRADING BEEF

When it comes to keeping track of the beef supply, inspection is mandatory while grading is voluntary. To complicate matters at the very beginning, there are two programs of grading beef, not one. The program familiar to very few of us not in the industry is called yield grading, that is, "an estimate of the relative amount of lean, edible meat" a steer will provide. The wholesale trade pays a lot of attention to yield grades. Quality grading, on the other hand, is something consumers hear a lot about.

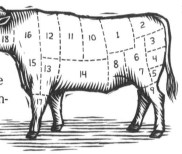

When an inspector from the U.S. Department of Agriculture grades a steer at a packing plant, he provides a reality check for the buyer and at least the promise that beef graded prime or choice will provide steaks that are tender and flavorful. The factors the inspector looks for are: "ample marbling, white fat, bright fresh flesh color and firm, fine flesh texture." The grade is also a signpost as to how much the butcher can charge and the customer might expect to pay.

Standards have eroded over the years, most notably in new grading regulations issued in 1976, though consumer activists and a good many nutritionists will say that the less fatty beef now sold as prime and choice is not a sign of lowering quality standards once the term "quality" is broadened to encompass more than fat.

Of the eight quality grades, only "choice" and "select" are used for retail steaks in mainstream markets with nearly 70 percent carrying the "choice" designation. Packers and retailers who do not use the grading system may use their own brand names, such as Excel Sterling Silver or Safeway Lean. Lesser grades disappear into ground beef and processed meat products.

"Prime" beef does not play a large part in this book because it does not play a large part in our lives. Only about 5 percent of America's beef is graded prime and that percentage is not expected to increase. Prime steaks are offered in some specialty markets, but the overwhelming majority of the meat of this grade is directed to restaurants, hotels, and private clubs.

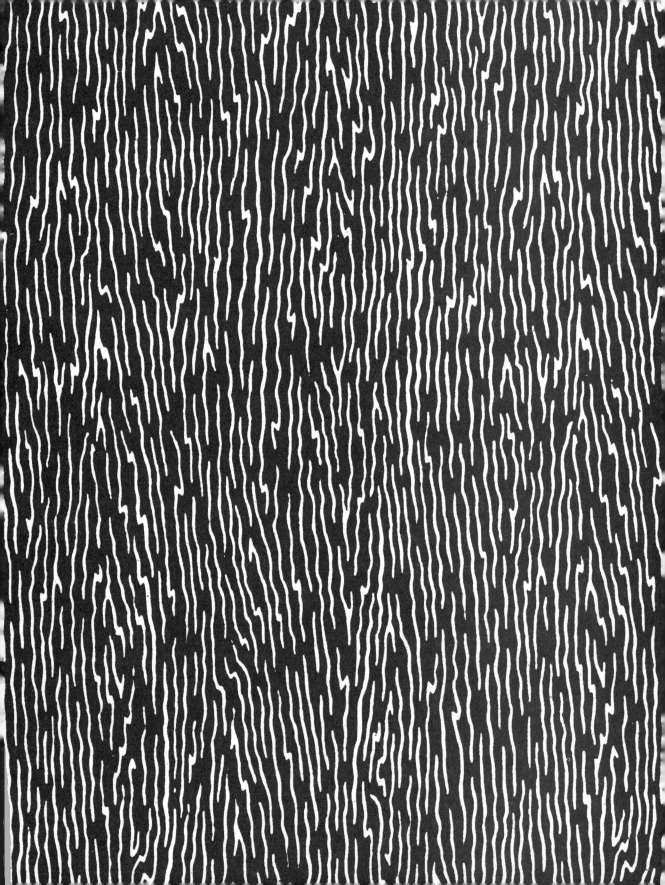

UPTOWN
CUTS

TENDERLOIN

True to its name, the tenderloin is unsurpassed for tenderness, a shining asset. Also, there is no bone in a tenderloin. It's all meat—which accounts in part for this cut's high price. If a chef or a butcher brags that his beef is tender enough to be cut with a butter knife, you can be sure he is talking about a tenderloin cut. The other great asset the tenderloin offers is versatility. Trimmed and left whole, the tenderloin will weigh 4 to 6 pounds and be about 18 inches long with a conical shape. It can be cooked whole or cut into individual steaks of differing size and thickness. These steaks may be called tenderloin steaks, filet steaks, filets mignons, and tenderloins, names that are used interchangeably by retailers. Size and weight of individual steaks vary, though most are cut between ¾ and 1½ inches thick, must be at least 1 inch in diameter, and weigh from 6 to 12 ounces. The classic cut known as Chateaubriand, from the center of the tenderloin, is 2 to 3 inches thick, as it is intended to provide two servings.

Because a steak from the tenderloin is so easy to cut, it becomes a perfect vehicle for sauces and garnishes that get in the way if the diner is faced with cutting up a steak on the bone.

A whole tenderloin or a Chateaubriand steak can be grilled or roasted and the meat carved into fairly thick slices. Individual tournedos or filets mignons (sometimes wrapped in bacon) are often grilled or broiled. But my favorite method for cooking these steaks is panfrying.

Known also as sautéing, panfrying is about the quickest and most effective way to brown meat with a flat surface. The steak is cooked with just enough fat to prevent it from sticking, at a temperature considerably lower than for broiling. The pan must be hot enough to sear the meat so quickly it will *sauter,* or jump, yet not so hot that the fat starts to smoke. Since butter burns at 250°F and vegetable oil at about 450°F, it's best to sauté with half butter and half oil or to skip the butter altogether and use only oil.

My Best Ever recipe for panfrying a tenderloin steak is the French classic The True Steak au Poivre. Other recipes that use this cut vary from the exotic Asian Beef Salad with Cucumbers to an Uptown Cheese Steak.

THE TRUE
STEAK AU POIVRE

Here is a dish that is among the most famous in the French classic culinary repertory, yet it is far less complex than most. The flavors of black pepper, Cognac, and cream form a fragrant but lively coating that gives the tender but bland filet a new allure. Sometimes Steak au Poivre is prepared with the firmer, more flavorful strip steak, but, like Fred dancing with Ginger, the sauce and the filet are the perfect match. Let a Zinfandel or Barbera provide the background music.

■■■■■■■■■■■■■■■■■■■■■■■■

*2 filets mignons (6 to 8 ounces each),
     cut 1¼ inches thick
1½ tablespoons black peppercorns
1 tablespoon unsalted butter
2 tablespoons vegetable oil
Salt, to taste
2 tablespoons Cognac
⅓ cup crème fraîche or heavy
     (or whipping) cream*

1. About 30 minutes before cooking, remove the steaks from the refrigerator and pat them dry. Coarsely crush the peppercorns in a mortar with a pestle or in a peppermill and spread them on a plate. Coat the filets on both sides with the pepper. Set aside at room temperature.

2. Melt the butter and oil in a large heavy-bottomed skillet with a long handle. When very hot, add the filets. Cook until seared and well-crusted on one side, about 4 minutes. Turn and cook the second side, 4 minutes more for medium-rare or 5 minutes more for medium. Baste the filets with pan drippings and salt them after turning.

3. Remove the skillet from the heat. Transfer the filets to a plate and pour off the cooking fat. Do not wash or wipe out the skillet. Return the filets to the skillet. In a small saucepan, heat the Cognac over medium heat. When it boils, pour the Cognac over the filets (make sure your hair is tied back and your sleeves are rolled up before you do this). Carefully light the Cognac with a long kitchen match. It will flare up momentarily. Gently shake the skillet over the hot burner until the flames die. (This procedure accomplishes two objectives: All the alcohol burns off and residual fat in the skillet

burns as well.) Transfer the steaks to 2 plates or a platter and keep warm.

4. Add the crème fraîche to the skillet and bring it to a boil, scraping the bottom with a wooden spoon to deglaze the meat juices. Gently whisk the sauce until it has thickened slightly, about 2 minutes. Add salt.

5. Pour the sauce over the filets and serve at once.

SERVES 2

STEAK AND POTATO SALAD

S teak and potatoes not only make a great team, both can be as tasty the second time around as when freshly cooked. So don't hesitate to use left-overs to make this salad. Serve it as a weekend lunch or light supper main course with a Côtes du Rhône.

■■■■■■■■■■■■■■■■■■■■■■■

1 filet mignon (7 to 8 ounces), cut 1
   inch thick
1 tablespoon cracked black
   peppercorns
1½ teaspoons vegetable oil
1 cooked red potato (about 6 ounces)
4 medium, white button mushrooms,
   stems trimmed
4 scallions, white and 2 inches of
   green
6 ounces mesclun (mixed baby greens)

Vinaigrette
1 teaspoon Dijon mustard
1 tablespoon red wine vinegar
4 tablespoons extra virgin olive oil
Salt, to taste

1. Coat the steak with pepper on all sides by pressing the cracked pepper into the meat.

2. Heat the oil in a small skillet over medium heat. Add the steak and cook until seared and nicely browned on one side, 4 minutes. Turn and cook the second side 4 minutes more for

a medium-rare steak, 5 minutes more for medium. Remove the meat from the pan and set aside to cool to room temperature. (A leftover cooked steak au poivre may be substituted. Bring to room temperature before serving.)

3. Cut the potato into chunks. Thinly slice the mushrooms and scallions. Cut the steak into ¼-inch-thick slices and set aside.

4. Place the mesclun in a large bowl. Whisk the vinaigrette ingredients together. Add the vinaigette to the bowl and toss until the greens are coated lightly with dressing. Divide between 2 dinner plates or 4 salad plates.

5. Scatter the potato chunks and mushroom slices over the greens. Fan the steak slices onto the center of the salad. Spoon any remaining dressing over the steak. Sprinkle the scallions over the meat and serve.

SERVES 2 AS A MAIN COURSE OR 4 AS A FIRST COURSE

ODE TO BEEFSTEAK

After the soup, we had what I do not hesitate to call the very best beefsteak I ever ate in my life.... As I write about it now, a week after I have eaten it, the old, rich, sweet, piquant, juicy taste comes smacking on my lips again; and I feel something of that exquisite sensation I then had. I am ashamed of the delight which the eating of that piece of meat caused me. G_ and I had quarreled about the soup; but when we began on the steak, we looked at each other, and loved each other. We did not speak— our hearts were too full for that; but we took a bit, and laid down our forks, and looked at one another, and understood each other. There were no two individuals on this wide earth—no two lovers billing in the shade—no mother clasping baby to her heart, more supremely happy than we. Every now and then, we had a glass of honest, firm, generous Burgundy, that nobly supported the meat. As you may fancy, we did not leave a single morsel of the steak, but when it was done, we put bits of bread into the silver dish, and wistfully sopped up the gravy. I suppose I shall never in this world taste anything so good again."
—William M. Thackeray, "Memorials of Gourmandizing" (as reproduced in *A Food Lover's Companion*)

SURF AND TURF
ASIAN STYLE

On a visit to Chicago to publicize one of his books, my friend Ken Hom spoke of a Chinese Trinity of flavoring ingredients—green onions, garlic, and ginger. I remembered Ken's Trinity combination one night when I wanted to give filet steaks a flavorful East-West personality. This is what I cooked up—a delicious combination of steak and seafood.

- -

4 filets mignons (about 4 ounces each; see Note)
2½ tablespoons vegetable oil
⅓ cup plus ¼ cup minced scallions
1 tablespoon plus 2 teaspoons peeled and minced fresh ginger
1 tablespoon plus 2 teaspoons minced garlic
1 tablespoon cornstarch
2 tablespoons rice wine or water
¾ cup low-sodium chicken or vegetable broth
¼ cup oyster sauce
1 tablespoon plus 2 teaspoons soy sauce
½ tablespoon sesame oil
6 ounces medium shrimp, peeled and chopped
1 teaspoon Szechuan peppercorns, ground

1. Preheat the broiler.

2. Pat the meat dry on both sides, then coat with 2 tablespoons of the vegetable oil. Set aside.

3. To help speed the last-minute preparation of the sauce, combine the ¼ cup scallions, 1 tablespoon ginger, and 1 tablespoon garlic in a small bowl. In another bowl, combine the cornstarch and rice wine. Combine the broth, oyster sauce, 1 tablespoon soy sauce, and the sesame oil in a 2-cup measure. Place the bowls and measuring cup near the stove.

4. Prepare the topping by combining the chopped shrimp, Szechuan pepper, ⅓ cup scallions, 2 teaspoons ginger, 2 teaspoons garlic, and 2 teaspoons soy sauce in a small bowl. Mix well and set aside.

5. Broil the steaks until seared and nicely browned on one side, 4 minutes. Turn and broil 3 minutes more. Spread the shrimp topping evenly over each filet, then continue to broil the meat until the topping is opaque and has begun to brown, about 1 minute. (The steaks will be medium-rare.) Transfer the steaks to a warm platter or 4 warm plates.

6. While the steaks are cooking, heat a wok or skillet. Add the remaining ¹/₂ tablespoon of vegetable oil and the scallion-ginger-garlic mixture to the wok. Stir until the scallions soften, about 30 seconds, then add the liquids in the measuring cup. Bring to a boil, stir up the cornstarch mixture and stir in. When the sauce thickens, about 1 minute, spoon 2 tablespoons of it onto each filet steak. Pass the remainder of the sauce in a sauce boat.

SERVES 4

Note: Most supermarket filets mignons weigh 7 or 8 ounces. Either ask the butcher to cut 4-ounce filet steaks 1 to 1¹/₄ inches thick for you or cut two 8-ounce filet steaks in half crosswise at home.

BARBARA POOL FENZL'S
STUFFED FILETS
WITH ANCHO SAUCE

Barbara Fenzl, a cooking teacher and food writer based in Phoenix, has helped to popularize contemporary Southwestern cooking. In this recipe she uses three different chilies—fresh Anaheims and poblanos and dried anchos. As the sweetest of the dried chilies, the anchos add a fruity as well as a spicy note to the sauce. Veteran grill cooks might use hot-burning mesquite wood for added flavor. Lacking a grill or faced with bad weather, broil the steaks instead. Pour beer, not wine, with these filets.

■ ■

2 heads garlic, unpeeled
1 tablespoon olive oil
3 dried ancho chilies
3 poblano chilies, roasted, peeled, and
*   seeded (page 88)*
Salt and freshly ground black pepper,
*   to taste*

¹/₄ cup heavy (or whipping)
*   cream*
6 filets mignons (about 6 ounces each)
*   cut 1 inch thick*
1 tablespoon minced fresh oregano
*   leaves*
2 Anaheim chilies, roasted, peeled,
*   seeded (page 88) and sliced into*
*   6 pieces*

1. Preheat the oven to 350°F.

2. Rub the heads of garlic with olive oil, wrap them in aluminum foil, and bake on a rack until soft, about 1 hour. Set aside to cool.

3. Place the ancho chilies in a bowl, cover with very hot water, and let soak for 45 minutes. Drain, reserving ½ cup of the soaking water. Place the ancho and poblano chilies in a blender with the reserved water and purée until smooth, about 45 seconds. Strain the purée into a small saucepan, season with salt and pepper, and add the cream. Heat, taste, and adjust seasoning, adding more water or cream if the sauce is too thick or too spicy. Set aside. (The sauce may be made ahead. Cover and refrigerate until ready to use. Reheat before serving.)

4. Prepare coals for grilling or preheat the broiler.

5. Slice a horizontal pocket in each steak and set aside.

6. Squeeze the softened garlic from each clove into a small bowl. Add the oregano, salt, and pepper, and mash the mixture into a paste with a fork. Spoon a generous amount of the garlic mixture into the pocket in each steak. Add a piece of Anaheim chili and press to seal the pockets. Season the steaks with salt and pepper.

7. Cook the steaks until seared and well-crusted on the bottom, 5 minutes. Turn and cook 4 minutes more for medium-rare or 5 minutes more for medium.

8. Meanwhile, reheat the sauce. Place the steaks on 6 warm plates and top each steak with 1 to 2 tablespoons sauce.

SERVES 6

ASIAN BEEF SALAD
WITH CUCUMBER

This wonderfully fresh-tasting salad is a very pleasing first course and can be served as a light entrée. Because the elements can be prepared ahead and final assembly is so quick, it's good to serve immediately after coming home from an event. Pour beer or a sparkling wine from Spain.

1 to 2 jalapeños, split, seeded, and
    coarsely chopped
1½ teaspoons salt
2 teaspoons Thai fish sauce (nam pla;
    see Note)
2 tablespoons sugar
2 tablespoons Japanese rice wine or
    dry sherry
2 tablespoons white vinegar
2 teaspoons fresh lime juice
2 scallions, white and some green,
    thinly sliced
2 tablespoons chopped fresh mint
    leaves
2 tablespoons chopped fresh cilantro
    leaves
1 tablespoon very thinly sliced peeled
    lemongrass (see Note)
2 filets mignons (about 6 ounces
    each), cut ¾ inch thick
1 tablespoon vegetable oil
1 cucumber, peeled and cut lengthwise
    into very thin slices

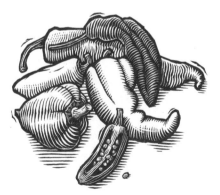

1. Preheat the broiler.

2. Combine the jalapeños, salt, fish sauce, sugar, rice wine, vinegar, and lime juice in a food processor or blender. Purée the mixture and set aside.

3. Combine the scallions, mint, cilantro, and lemongrass in a small bowl. Mix well and set aside.

4. Pat the steaks dry and coat lightly with oil. Broil the steaks for 4 minutes, or until brown and crusty on one side. Turn and broil 3 minutes more for medium-rare or 4 minutes more for medium. Transfer the steaks to a cutting board and let rest for 5 minutes. Carve each steak into ¼-inch-thick slices. (The recipe may be done ahead to this point. Cover and refrigerate the sauce, herbs, and meat separately. Return to room temperature before serving.)

5. Make a bed of cucumber slices on a platter or 2 or 3 plates. Arrange the steak over the cucumber, spoon the sauce over the steak, and scatter the herb mixture over all.

SERVES 2 OR 3

Note: Thai fish sauce (*nam pla*) and lemongrass are available in Asian markets, specialty food stores, and some supermarkets.

COLD FILET

WITH MONIQUE KING'S
ORANGE-CUMIN VINAIGRETTE

Monique King, chef of Chicago's funky and fun Soul Kitchen restaurant, had her taste buds tickled early, working for the dynamic duo of Susan Feniger and Mary Sue Milliken at City restaurant in Los Angeles. I like to use one of her favorite salad dressings on slices of filet served at room temperature on a bed of greens. For the most effective presentation, do not cook the steaks beyond medium-rare. Accompany the steaks with sangria in the summer, Rioja in the winter.

■ ■

2 filets mignons (about 8 ounces
    each), cut 1 inch thick
1 tablespoon vegetable oil, preferably
    corn oil
1½ teaspoons minced shallots or
    scallions
¼ teaspoon ground cumin
1 teaspoon grated orange zest
1 tablespoon fresh orange juice
1 tablespoon sherry vinegar
3 tablespoons extra virgin olive oil
Salt and white pepper, to taste
8 cups mesclun (mixed baby greens)
    or torn romaine, washed and very
    well dried (about 8 ounces)

1. Preheat the broiler or prepare coals for grilling.

2. Allow the steaks to come to room temperature, pat dry and lightly coat with vegetable oil. Cook until seared and nicely browned on one side, about 4 minutes. Turn the steaks and cook 4 minutes more for medium-rare. Set aside until cool. (Steaks may be prepared ahead to this point. Refrigerate the steaks, but let them return to room temperature before continuing.)

3. Combine the shallots, cumin, orange zest, orange juice, and vinegar in a small bowl. Slowly whisk in the olive oil. Adjust the seasoning with salt and pepper, to taste. Pour all but 1 tablespoon of this dressing over the greens in a large bowl. Toss to coat and arrange the greens on 4 medium-size plates.

4. Carve the steaks into ¼-inch-thick slices and arrange them on top of the greens. Spoon the remaining dressing over the meat and serve immediately.

SERVES 4

CHATEAUBRIAND
WITH BEARNAISE SAUCE

This steak, cut from the thickest part of the tenderloin, merits a very special occasion. It is served with béarnaise, to me the most lavishly sensual of all steak sauces. While this recipe is meant, in spirit, to be served to two hungry persons in the full thrall of love, there is, in fact, enough meat to feed three. The sauce can be prepared ahead and rewarmed over—but not touching—simmering water. The wine should definitely come from Bordeaux and be as old and as expensive as possible. Refrigerate any leftover béarnaise and, as my wife advises, "just let it melt on things."

■■■■■■■■■■■■■■■■■■■■■■■■

1 center-cut beef tenderloin (about 1¼ pounds), cut 1½ to 2 inches thick
2 tablespoons vegetable oil, preferably corn oil
Salt

Béarnaise Sauce
2 tablespoons dry white wine
1 tablespoon white wine vinegar, preferably tarragon flavored
1 tablespoon chopped fresh tarragon leaves
1 tablespoon minced shallots (optional)
White pepper, to taste
2 egg yolks (see Note)
1 tablespoon fresh lemon juice
Salt, to taste
2 or 3 drops hot pepper sauce, preferably Tabasco Jalapeño Sauce
1 cup melted unsalted butter, hot

1. At least 45 minutes before cooking, remove the steak from the refrigerator, and let it come to room temperature. Pat it dry, coat lightly with vegetable oil, and set aside.

2. Preheat the oven to 450°F.

3. Heat a large ovenproof skillet, preferably cast iron, over medium-high heat. Sear the tenderloin until browned on one side, about 3 minutes. Turn, season with salt, and sear the second side for 3 minutes more. Transfer the skillet to the oven and roast the steak about 12 minutes for medium-rare and 14 minutes for medium. Transfer the steak to a cutting board and let it rest for 4 to 5 minutes before carving.

4. While the steak is resting, prepare the béarnaise sauce. Combine the white wine, vinegar, $1/2$ tablespoon of the tarragon, shallots, if using, and a pinch of white pepper in a very small saucepan. Bring to a boil and reduce until only 2 teaspoons of liquid are left, about 2 minutes. Set aside.

5. Put the egg yolks, lemon juice, a pinch of salt, a pinch of white pepper, and the hot pepper sauce into a blender jar. Have the hot butter close at hand. Cover the jar, turn the blender on to medium-low speed, and pour the butter in through the feed hole in a thin but steady stream. When the sauce has thickened, add the wine reduction and the remaining $1/2$ tablespoon tarragon. Blend briefly, taste, and adjust seasoning as desired. To keep the sauce warm while carving the meat, set the jar in a pan filled with 3 to 4 inches of hot water.

6. Carve the steak into $1/2$-inch-thick slices. Arrange the steak slices on plates. Lightly coat the meat with béarnaise and pass the remainder in a sauce boat.

SERVES 2 OR 3

Note: The eggs in the béarnaise sauce do not get fully cooked by the heat of the other ingredients. Be sure to buy only farm-fresh, best-quality eggs before preparing a dish in which they aren't cooked through.

SEARING

To sear! It's an action verb, traumatic even. We read or hear of searing pain, seared hearts, searing rebuttals. In cooking the meaning is slightly less intense, since the cook who slaps a steak onto a very hot pan or grill does allow the meat to sear and change color but stops short of actually burning the surface.

This action, done on both sides, is widely, if mistakenly, thought to be crucial to producing a moist and juicy steak. Even so, it remains a dramatic and useful ritual. Laboratory experiments prove that the crust does not form a waterproof jacket around the meat. The juices remain because, due to the rapidity of the cooking, they don't have time to get out.

The juices that come to the surface and evaporate give off the perfumed aroma that puts appetites into overdrive. More important, they leave behind solid substances that brown easily, including protein and natural sugar. These harden to give the surface exciting texture, color, and flavor. If the pan is deglazed, even the juices that escape can be used to contribute flavor and color to a sauce.

By the mid-1960s, *Joy of Cooking* had set things right and endorsed searing in the name of taste, not nutrition. Yet the myth persists.

BEEF TENDERLOIN
WITH ARUGULA

Slicing beef tenderloin into medallions is the simplest trick to producing a very tender and quick-cooking steak dinner. Here, the beef is seared and served on top of wilted arugula in the Italian manner. Fresh minced herbs are an optional garnish for the meat, and the drink, Chianti Classico.

■ ■

1½ pounds center-cut beef tenderloin, sinew removed
8 ounces arugula
5 tablespoons olive oil
1½ tablespoons balsamic vinegar
Salt and freshly ground black pepper, to taste
1 tablespoon mixed minced fresh rosemary and sage leaves (optional)

1. Cut the tenderloin into 12 slices, each ¾ inch thick. Flatten the medallions slightly with the flat side of a chef's knife or a cleaver. Set aside.

2. Stem the arugula, wash the leaves, and pat dry. Set aside.

3. Heat 1 tablespoon of the oil in a large skillet, preferably nonstick, over medium-high heat. Add as many of the beef medallions as fit in a single layer without overcrowding. Cook until seared, 1½ to 2 minutes. Turn the meat and cook until nicely browned but still with red juices, 1½ to 2 minutes more. Transfer the cooked meat to a plate and cover loosely with aluminum foil to keep warm. Repeat with the remaining medallions.

4. Add the remaining 4 tablespoons oil and the vinegar to the same skillet. Immediately add the arugula, cook, stirring over medium-high heat until all the leaves are wilted, about 1 minute.

5. Make a bed of arugula on each of 4 to 6 plates. Place 3 or 2 beef medallions on top of each. Sprinkle the meat with salt and pepper, and, if desired, with the herbs. Pour any remaining cooking juices from the skillet over the meat. Serve immediately.

SERVES 4 TO 6

BILL'S SIX-STEP GUIDE TO GREAT GRILLING

Before you start, realize that no self-respecting manufacturer would sell a grill unit without attaching detailed operating instructions. If you won't read those, you won't read this. If you read those, you probably don't need to read this—so I'll be brief.

1. Be sure the grill is outdoors (unless you are using a stovetop grilling unit) and on level ground.

2. Open the vents and pile about two dozen top-of-the-line briquets on the grate. Using hickory or apple wood as fuel and a flavoring for the steak is appealing, but wood is expensive and takes quite a while to reduce to coals. Wood chips on charcoal may be the best course. Since I rarely venture far from the house, I use an electric coil starter. (Ask someone to remind you to unplug it once the coals are burning.) If using a liquid starter, the one absolute prohibition is: Never, never squirt fuel onto a burning fire. If using a gas grilling unit, none of this matters.

3. For well-trimmed steaks 1½ inches thick or less, chops, and burgers, there's no need to set up a drip pan and cook over indirect heat. An activist cook equipped with a squirt pistol and a willingness to tend closely to the meat and move and turn it as often as needed will do just fine working over direct heat.

4. There will be about half an hour of warm-up time. Pace yourself in consuming liquid refreshments. Once the coals are ready (covered with gray ash and glowing), flirt with pain and place your hand, palm down, over the fire at grill height. If you can hold it there for 4 seconds, the coals are hot and ready for the steak. (Gadget lovers with a grill thermometer can skip this ritual and start grilling when the temperature reaches 360°F). If you are making Tuttaposto's Grilled Dessert Pizza (see Index), allow the coals to get a little less hot. If you can hold your hand over them for 6 seconds, they are ready.

(continued)

26

5. Don't put the meat on the grill, however, without checking you have an apron on, and a mitt or mitts, tongs or a spatula, and the afore-mentioned squirt bottle close at hand. (You'll notice no pronged fork and no sharp knife are in the vicinity. Piercing the steak will do irreparable harm.) I subscribe to the "sear one side, turn, and sear the second side, then let the meat cook" school of grilling unless the steak is an extra-thick monster. For planning purposes, allot 10 to 12 minutes to cook a 1-inch-thick steak to medium-rare and 12 to 14 minutes to medium. If the steak is 1½ inches thick, add 2 minutes to the calculation. But due to the variables, using the touch system to gauge doneness (see page 7) is essential.

6. As you prepare to snatch the perfectly cooked steak from the grill, it's very disconcerting to realize you neglected to arrange for the presence of a cutting board or platter ready to receive the meat. Tell yourself to do this under Step 5 the next time. In the interest of coordinated dining, it's equally important to alert those responsible for other parts of the meal of your progress. That done, you can take your bows.

JOHN PISTO'S
GRILLED BEEF ROLLS
ON A SKEWER

L iving and cooking on the coast in Monterey, California, restaurateur and television personality John Pisto has mastered virtually every type of seafood cookery. But there's a taste for beef, too, in his Italian heritage, and he often prepares beef rolls stuffed with raisins and pine nuts in the Sicilian fashion at home for friends. To accompany the rolls, John usually makes tubular pasta such as ziti with a fresh tomato sauce and pours a red wine made in Monterey County.

1 cup bread crumbs, toasted (see Note)
Olive oil
2 cloves garlic, minced
¼ cup plus 2 tablespoons chopped fresh flat-leaf parsley leaves
2 tablespoons freshly grated Parmesan cheese
2 tablespoons pine nuts
2 tablespoons raisins, soaked in warm water until plump and drained
Salt and freshly ground black pepper, to taste
1 pound beef tenderloin, cut into 8 slices, chilled
10 bay leaves, soaked in water to soften
1 medium red onion, cut into 8 chunks
4 to 5 cloves garlic, chopped
1 tablespoon chopped fresh oregano leaves or 1½ teaspoons dried oregano
1 cup water

1. Pour the bread crumbs into a small bowl and stir in 1 to 2 tablespoons of oil, just enough to slightly dampen them. Add the minced garlic, 2 tablespoons parsley, Parmesan, pine nuts, raisins, salt and pepper. Set aside.

2. Place a piece of chilled steak between 2 sheets of wax paper or plastic wrap and pound with a meat pounder, the side of a cleaver, or a rolling pin to flatten it to a thickness of ¼ inch. Flatten the remaining pieces. (If you wish, ask the butcher to flatten the meat when you buy it.)

3. Rub a light coating of olive oil over one side of each slice of steak. Season with salt and pepper, then add a light coating of the bread crumb mixture. Roll each slice tightly around the filling. (Reserve excess filling for use on pasta or vegetables.)

4. Rub 2 long metal skewers with olive oil. Thread a bay leaf on a skewer, pierce a beef roll crosswise through the center, then thread a chunk of onion. Repeat, ending with a bay leaf, until each skewer holds 5 bay leaves, 4 beef rolls, and 4 chunks of onion. Set aside.

5. Prepare coals for grilling or preheat the broiler. Preheat the oven to warm.

6. Combine ⅓ cup olive oil, the chopped garlic, the remaining ¼ cup parsley, the oregano, and water in a small saucepan. Bring to a boil, simmer for 2 minutes, and remove from the heat. Set aside.

7. Just before cooking, brush the meat and onions with olive oil and season with salt and pepper. Cook until the meat is seared and nicely browned on one side, about 2 minutes. Turn and cook the other side 2 minutes more for rare or 3 minutes more for medium. Transfer the skewers to a deep platter and pour the olive oil-water mixture over them. Place in a warm oven until ready to serve.

SERVES 8

Note: To toast bread crumbs, preheat the oven to 350°F. Sprinkle the crumbs on a baking sheet and heat until golden, 8 minutes.

SCANDINAVIAN-STYLE
OPEN-FACE TENDERLOIN SANDWICHES

The Scandinavians excel at producing cold salads and sandwiches, at least I've yet to come upon a Scandinavian buffet table I could walk past without collecting several items to sample. The one link among most of these creations is that mayonnaise is used lavishly. So I fashioned a mayonnaise with Scandinavian ingredients to dress up open-face sandwiches to be displayed on a party buffet or passed at a reception. The sauce is equally appealing served with cold lobster or shrimp. (If you have a bottle of aquavit, the caraway-flavored liquor drunk throughout Scandinavia, incorporate some in the sauce.)

■ ■

1 beef tenderloin (about 4½ pounds)
2 tablespoons vegetable oil
Salt and freshly ground black pepper,
    to taste
1 cup mayonnaise
2 tablespoons Dijon mustard
1 teaspoon fresh lemon juice
½ teaspoon caraway seeds, ground
½ teaspoon sugar
¼ teaspoon white pepper
1 tablespoon aquavit (optional)
¼ cup chopped fresh dill
Up to 27 slices light rye bread

1. The morning before serving, prepare the tenderloin. Preheat the oven to 425°F.

2. Lightly coat the meat with oil and season liberally with salt and black pepper. Roast 12 to 15 minutes per pound for rare to medium-rare. Transfer to a platter, cool, cover with plastic wrap and refrigerate.

3. Spoon the mayonnaise into a small mixing bowl. Add the mustard, lemon juice, caraway, sugar, ½ teaspoon salt, white pepper, and aquavit, if using. Whisk until well blended, taste, and correct the seasoning. Stir in the dill. Set aside to mellow for at least 30 minutes at room temperature. (Flavored mayonnaise may be made ahead. Cover and refrigerate for up to 3 days.)

4. Use a cookie cutter to cut 2½-inch circles in up to 18 slices of the bread. Cut up to 9 more slices into 3-inch squares, trimming away the crusts. Cover with a damp towel to keep the bread fresh.

5. Carve the tenderloin into ¼- to ½-inch-thick slices, then trim the slices to fit the bread circles and squares. (Save the tenderloin scraps to garnish a salad or to mix into scrambled eggs.)

6. Spread 1 teaspoon sauce on each circle and 2 teaspoons sauce on each square. Place a slice of tenderloin on top of the sauce. Cut the squares in half on a diagonal. Place a ½-teaspoon dollop of sauce in the center of each sandwich. Arrange sandwiches on a platter and serve.

SERVES UP TO 36

UPTOWN

CHEESE STEAK SANDWICH

T he Philadelphia cheese steak is the *ne plus ultra* of downtown steak sandwiches. Uptown, one might use white bread and sliced tenderloin and draw inspiration from that old standby Welsh rarebit to create a perfect weekend lunch dish or a treat for a late-evening supper. Serve this sandwich with a flavorful ale.

■■■■■■■■■■■■■■■■■■■■■■■■■

*4 ounces Mimolette or Edam cheese,
    cut into ¼-inch dice*
½ teaspoon dry mustard
2 teaspoons Dijon mustard
*2 tablespoons unsalted butter, cut into
    ¼-inch dice*
1 tablespoon Worcestershire sauce
¼ teaspoon cayenne pepper
6 slices day-old white bread
*12 ounces beef tenderloin, cooked
    (page 22, steps 1 and 2), cooled, and
    cut on the bias into 12 thin slices*

1. Place the cheese, dry mustard, Dijon mustard, butter, Worcestershire, and cayenne in a food processor. Pulse to reduce the cheese pieces to the size of small pebbles, then process until the mixture forms a paste, about 1 minute. You should have about ¾ cup.

2. Spread 2 tablespoons of the cheese paste on each slice of bread. Top the bread slices with 2 slices of meat, leaving a border of cheese visible around the edges. Arrange the bread slices side by side on a baking sheet or broiler pan and cover with plastic wrap and refrigerate if making in advance.

3. About 15 minutes before serving, preheat the broiler.

4. Remove the plastic wrap, if used. Place the open-face sandwiches under the broiler and cook until the cheese is bubbling and begins to brown, 2 to 2½ minutes. Serve at once.

SERVES 6

Note: For a party, use a cookie cutter to cut the bread into eighteen 2½-inch rounds, top each with 2 teaspoons of cheese paste and 1½-inch round of meat. Broil the sandwiches just before serving.

PHILADELPHIA CHEESE STEAK SANDWICH

The Philly Cheese Steak is not so much a recipe as a way of life. Take the same round steak you would use for The Italian Beef Sandwich (page 137), sauté up a mess of onions, heat something with the same color and texture as Cheez Whiz. Arrange the onions, meat, and cheese spread inside a roll and eat away. Or try an equally earthy cheese steak sandwich, such as the one starting on the facing page, made with an uptown cut of steak.

GERMAINE SWANSON'S
SHAKING BEEF CUBES

When Germaine Swanson came to the United States from Vietnam and established Germaine's, which became one of Washington, D.C.'s best-known restaurants, she also launched what has become known as Pacific Rim cuisine by offering a pan-Asian menu. This full-flavored, easy-to-prepare dish shows why her cooking became so popular. (This recipe's popularity will soar among cooks on a budget when they learn that Germaine also prepares it using flank steak.) Serve this with steamed rice. The only secret is to be sure the oil is really hot. Cook the beef in two batches rather than one, so as not to overcrowd the pan.

1 beef tenderloin (about 4 pounds)

1 tablespoon plus 1 teaspoon chopped garlic

3 tablespoons chopped shallots or scallions

¼ cup beef broth

¼ cup soy sauce

White pepper, to taste

3 heads Boston lettuce, cored, washed, and drained

2 tablespoons distilled white vinegar

¼ teaspoon salt

½ cup plus ⅓ cup vegetable oil

1 large red onion, thinly sliced

1 large white onion, thinly sliced

4 tablespoons (½ stick) unsalted butter, cut into pieces (optional)

1. Cut the tenderloin into ¾-inch cubes, trimming any fat. Combine 1 tablespoon of garlic, the shallots, broth, soy sauce, and white pepper in a large bowl. Add the beef cubes, toss, and set aside at room temperature for 20 to 30 minutes.

2. Arrange the lettuce leaves on a large platter. Whisk together the remaining 1 teaspoon garlic, white pepper, vinegar, salt, and ⅓ cup oil in a medium-size bowl. Add the red onion slices, toss, and pour over the lettuce.

3. Heat the remaining ½ cup oil over high heat in a wok or large skillet. As soon as the oil begins to smoke, add the steak cubes and the white onion slices in batches. Stir and shake the pan rapidly until the meat is crisp and browned on the outside, about 3 minutes for rare, 3½ minutes for medium-rare, and 4 minutes for medium.

4. Turn the contents of the wok into a colander set over a bowl to drain. Arrange the beef and onions on the bed of lettuce. Or, if using the butter, return the beef and onions to the cleaned wok, add the butter, and toss over medium-high heat until the butter has melted and coated the meat. Arrange the beef mixture on the bed of lettuce and serve at once.

SERVES 8 TO 10

T-BONE

Somehow, I've always associated T-bone steaks with the West and cowboy cookouts. The steak in my memory is cut thin, but it need not be. People who like steak on the bone like the T-bone. So do people like me who can't make up their minds because the T-bone is two steaks in one. The leg of the T separates an oval soft tenderloin from an oblong, firm top loin.

Maybe it's more of that western romance, but I swear the best-tasting T-bones come from the grill. The bone makes this cut easy to manipulate on the grill and the steak can be served as is to one person or be sliced off the bone to serve two or more. Try either method with the astonishingly simple Famous Fiorentina, my Best Ever, or have a western night party, panfry some T-bones, and serve up Cowboy Beans (page 196) from the chuck wagon.

THE FAMOUS
FIORENTINA

It's only a T-bone, but it put Florence on the steak map. The Tuscan region of Italy is justly famous for its wine, olive oil, beef, and an austere and simple approach to cooking—all of which come into play in making and serving a proper Fiorentina. The T-bone should not be very thick. The fire should be hot and made from wood or vine cuttings. The guests should be in their places before the cooking begins, armed with glasses of Chianti. Usually the steak is served in solitary splendor, with only bread at hand for mopping up the juices. You may have to remind yourself to include the lemons the first time you make a Fiorentina, but once you've tasted the lemon-accented steak, you'll never forget again.

■■■■■■■■■■■■■■■■■■■■■■■■■■■

4 T-bone steaks (about 12 ounces each), cut ¾ inch thick
¼ cup olive oil
Salt and freshly ground black pepper, to taste
2 lemons, each cut into 8 wedges

1. Prepare coals for grilling, allowing at least 30 minutes for the coals to become properly hot.

2. Remove the steaks from the refrigerator and allow them to come to room temperature. Trim any excess fat, pat dry, and coat lightly with olive oil.

3. Place the steaks over the coals. Cook to sear one side, 2 minutes. Turn and season the cooked side with salt and pepper. Sear the second side for 3 minutes. Turn, season the second side with salt and pepper, and continue cooking until the steak is well-crusted and is medium-rare, about 3 minutes more. (A Tuscan never would cook Fiorentina to medium, but if you must, lengthen the final stage to 4 or 5 minutes.) Transfer the steaks to large plates or platters, garnish with lemon wedges, and serve at once.

SERVES 4

34

T-BONE STEAK
WITH TOMATO-GREEN PEPPERCORN BUTTER

Here's a composed butter for steak-lovers who crave really intense flavors. The tomatoes provide a rich, concentrated sweetness, the peppercorns aroma and bite, while rosemary is certainly the least shy of the aromatic herbs. I prefer to use this butter with a T-bone because the steak has plenty of flavor of its own and the butter and steak juices marry to make the taste even better. Choose an earthy, fruity wine such as Taurasi, the greatest Southern Italian red, or Barbera, or a Côtes du Rhône.

■ ■

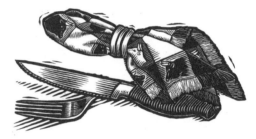

1 medium clove garlic, minced

*2 sun-dried tomatoes packed in oil,
    drained and minced*

*2 teaspoons canned green pepper-
    corns, drained and minced*

*1½ teaspoons fresh rosemary leaves,
    minced*

*4 tablespoons (½ stick) unsalted
    butter, at room temperature*

¼ teaspoon salt

2 teaspoons fresh lemon juice

*2 T-bone steaks (about 1 pound each),
    cut 1 inch thick*

1½ tablespoons vegetable oil

1. Combine the garlic, sun-dried tomatoes, peppercorns, and rosemary in a small mixing bowl. Cut the butter into 4 chunks and add to the bowl. Add the salt and lemon juice. Beat until the mixture is well blended and smooth. (This may also be done in a food processor.)

Transfer the tomato-peppercorn butter to a 4-inch-wide sheet of plastic wrap. Roll the plastic wrap around the butter, then shape the package with your fingers into a log-shape roll the diameter of a 25-cent piece. Refrigerate.

2. Preheat the broiler or prepare coals for grilling.

3. Remove the log of butter from the refrigerator and cut eight ¼-inch-thick rounds. Return the remaining butter to the refrigerator or freeze. It can be used with pasta or grilled fish.

4. Pat the steaks dry, then coat lightly with oil on both sides. Broil or grill until seared and well-crusted on one side, 5 minutes. Turn and

cook on the other side 3 minutes more for medium-rare or 4 minutes more for medium. Transfer the steaks to a cutting board and let rest for 5 minutes, loosely covered.

5. Place a steak on each of 2 warm plates and top

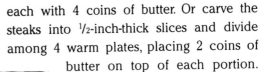

each with 4 coins of butter. Or carve the steaks into ½-inch-thick slices and divide among 4 warm plates, placing 2 coins of butter on top of each portion. Serve at once.

SERVES 2 OR 4

T-BONE STEAK
WITH SIX-SHOOTER RUB AND COWBOY BEANS

The giant T-bone, weighing 1½ pounds or more, was—and still is—a favorite cut in cowboy country steak houses. I choose a smaller cut and liven it up with my six-shooter rub, which also peps up the beans. With the beans and steak, drink Lone Star or a beer from your favorite brewery.

■ ■

*2 T-bone steaks (about 1 pound each),
    cut 1 inch thick
1 tablespoon Six-Shooter Spice Rub
    (recipe follows)
2 tablespoons vegetable oil
1 recipe Cowboy Beans (page 196)*

1. Thirty minutes before cooking, remove the steaks from the refrigerator, pat dry, and press the spice rub into both sides of each steak. Coat lightly with the oil and set aside.

2. Heat a large heavy frying pan, preferably cast iron, over medium-high heat. When hot, add the steaks and sear on one side to a rich brown crust, about 4 minutes. Turn and sear the second side for 4 minutes more for medium-rare or 5 minutes more for medium.

3. Transfer the steaks to a cutting board. Let rest for 5 minutes while rewarming the beans. Carve each steak into ½-inch-thick slices and serve on warm plates with the beans.

SERVES 4

SIX-SHOOTER SPICE RUB

Six ingredients, each one packing a flavor punch, are assembled to provide a western flair to steaks that will be grilled, broiled, or panfried. Use the mixture generously, rubbing it into the meat. The purpose is to flavor the meat rather than tenderize it, so there's no need to wait before cooking.

1 tablespoon ground cumin
1 tablespoon chili powder
1 tablespoon paprika, preferably hot
    Hungarian
1 tablespoon dried marjoram
1 tablespoon dry mustard
1½ teaspoons freshly ground black
    pepper

Combine the cumin, chili powder, paprika, marjoram, dry mustard, and pepper in a small bowl and stir until blended. Pour into a small jar, cover, label, and set aside until needed.

MAKES ABOUT ⅓ CUP

T-BONE STEAK
DRESSED IN THE POSTO STYLE

Beans and bacon are happy together, so are steak and red wine. But these classic pairings are elevated to elegance when a creative talent such as chef Luciano Pellagrio of the stylish Los Angeles restaurant Posto introduces the two couples in a dish that is both simple and sophisticated. Owner Piero Selvaggio, a connoisseur of Italian and California wines and one of the world's great hosts, suggests cooking with and drinking either Chianti Classico or a Napa Valley Merlot.

2 T-bone steaks (about 1¼ pounds
   each), cut 1 inch thick
4 strips thinly sliced smoked bacon
1 cup fresh fava beans, blanched and
   peeled, or thawed frozen baby lima
   beans
1½ teaspoons finely chopped fresh
   sage leaves
1½ teaspoons finely chopped fresh
   rosemary leaves
2 cloves garlic, thinly sliced
1½ tablespoons butter
1 tablespoon olive oil
1½ cups dry red wine
½ cup beef broth
Salt and freshly
   ground black
   pepper, to
   taste

and the olive oil. Place the steaks in the skillet
and sear until well-crusted on one side, about 3
minutes. Turn and sear the second side for 3
minutes. Turn again and cook 3 minutes more
for medium-rare or 4 minutes more for medium. Transfer the steaks to a cutting board. Cover
with aluminum foil to keep warm.

4. Pour off the cooking oil, return the skillet to
the heat, and add the wine. Bring to a boil over
high heat and reduce by half, about 5 minutes.
Add the broth and reduce 3 minutes more.
Meanwhile, warm the beans over medium
heat and season with salt and pepper.

5. Carve the steaks and arrange the slices in
the center of 4 warm plates. Top with a sprin-
kling of crumbled bacon. Pour the meat juices
into the wine sauce and stir in the remaining
½ tablespoon of butter. Spoon the fava beans
around the steak and spoon sauce over all.

SERVES 4

1. Pat the steaks dry and set aside to come to
room temperature. Cook the bacon in a skillet
over medium heat until crisp. Drain on paper
towels, crumble, and set aside. Discard all but
1 tablespoon of the bacon fat from the pan.
Add the beans, sage, and rosemary and stir
together.

2. Cook the garlic in a small dry skillet until
golden and crisp and add to the beans. Set
aside.

3. Heat a large heavy skillet over medium-high
heat. When hot, add 1 tablespoon of the butter

CLOSING THE GAP

Use bamboo skewers or wooden
toothpicks softened in water to
close gaps created by the removal of
fat or bone from an uncooked steak
or to hold together dangling pieces,
the so-called tail of porterhouse and T-
bone steaks, for instance. The idea is
to make the steak as compact as possible so it will cook evenly.

SLICED T-BONE
WITH ASIAN-FLAVORED
WATERCRESS

Watercress has been sitting beside steak on platters and plates, largely ignored, for ages. To bring some deserved attention to this peppery garnish, I stir-fry it, dress it in Asian oyster sauce and sesame oil, and present it with beautifully pink sliced T-bone on unadorned plates. In the spirit of fusion, serve Shiraz, a dry Australian red wine made from the French Syrah grape.

■ ■

1 T-bone steak (about 1½ pounds), cut
    1¼ inches thick
2 tablespoons soy sauce
1 tablespoon rice wine or sherry
2½ tablespoons vegetable oil
1 tablespoon oyster sauce
1 teaspoon sesame oil
3 scallions, white and 2 inches of
    green, finely chopped
12 ounces watercress, large stems
    removed

1. Pat the steak dry and place it on a plate. In a small bowl, combine 1 tablespoon of the soy sauce, the rice wine, and 1 tablespoon of the vegetable oil. Stir the mixture well, then use a brush to paint it all over the steak. Set the steak aside for 30 minutes.

2. Preheat the broiler.

3. In a clean small bowl, combine the remaining 1 tablespoon of soy sauce, the oyster sauce,

and sesame oil; place the bowl near the stove.

4. Broil the steak until seared and nicely crusted on one side, about 5 minutes. Turn and cook the other side 4 minutes more for medium-rare or 5 minutes more for medium. Transfer the steak to a cutting board and let rest for 5 minutes, loosely covered.

5. While the steak is resting, heat a wok or large skillet over medium-high heat. Add the remaining 1½ tablespoons vegetable oil and the scallions and toss until they soften, about 30 seconds. Add the watercress and stir until it wilts and softens, 2 to 3 minutes. Add the oyster sauce mixture and toss just until the watercress is coated, 20 to 30 seconds.

6. Cut the meat away from the bone, slice it crosswise into ³/₄-inch-thick slices, and divide among 2 or 3 warm plates. Use a slotted spoon to transfer the watercress from the wok to plates and serve at once.

SERVES 2 OR 3

CONDIMENTS

Often, I suspect, I add seasoning or a condiment to a steak not so much to give it flavor as to put something on that steak that will make it my own. The following is a compendium of a dozen of my secret weapons that make even a good-tasting steak taste better—fast.

Salt: To me, salt is invaluable in bringing out the flavor and juice of a broiled, panfried, or grilled steak. A good cook will salt a steak after it is seared but often overlooks lightly salting freshly cut slices of steak before serving them. Don't forget.

Pepper: Some years ago I made up my mind to use a peppermill or nothing. The volatile oil in a peppercorn, which carries much of the flavor, evaporates quickly, leaving behind only dry, dusty grains with a bitter bite. Think of that when you next pick up a pepper shaker in a diner! The reigning king of journalistic gourmands, R.W. (Johnny) Apple of *The New York Times,* actually gave me a pocket peppermill some time ago. But, I draw it only when truly provoked. When loading your peppermill, seek out a distinctive pepper such as Tellicherry from Madagascar.

Mustard: As you will see from mustard's use as an ingredient in recipes scattered through this book, I don't rely on only one style. My still-incomplete voyage of culinary enlightenment began the day I realized French mustard was different from French's mustard. But when serving steak, especially cold steak, an array of mustards is in order—not just the Grey Poupon. They are easy to obtain. In specialty food stores, the flavored mustards all but jump into your cart, and the Inglehoffer people in Beverton, Oregon, have an extensive line.

Barbecue Sauce: If proof is needed that I—a certified judge for the annual Memphis in May World Barbecue Championship—believe in the restorative and healing powers of barbecue sauce, see the lavish expenditure of this magic potion in my recipe for Butt Steak Braised in Barbecue Sauce (page 106). See also my recommendations for making a barbecue sauce of your own (page 175). In lieu of a recipe, I offer the following advice to saucemakers: Cheat only when necessary and never, never share your

40

formula or it won't be a secret recipe anymore.

Hot Pepper Sauces: I'm devoted to Tabasco Sauce (the newer, milder green Jalapeño sauce from Tabasco as well as the red) and—in addition to the recipes in which it is recommended—find it especially useful on breakfast steak and eggs to help the taste buds awaken. Look, too, for Busha Browne's Spicy and Hot Pepper Sherry to use in soup, Bloody Marys, and more.

Steak Sauce: From the French-inspired Sauce Robert to the American champion, A.1., bottles containing the dark, concentrated, palate-stimulating lava called steak sauce stand ready to provide a quick fix to a steak deficient in flavor. Formulas vary, but most play sweet, sour, and salty elements against one another and therefore are more intriguing to taste than ketchup or hot pepper sauce. In fact, with hot peppers such a prevalent ingredient, it's sometimes a relief to have a sauce to turn to that is hot pepper–free. Occasionally, I will use a teaspoon or two of steak sauce to flavor a dressing for a composed salad containing steak, but usually I prefer to take it straight.

Cajun Power Garlic Sauce: The name tells you all you need to know, except that this sauce has a thin consistency that makes it well-suited to coat steaks or be stirred into a sauce or soup. I think of it as a liquid rub that will provide a hit of hot

spice with a lingering aftertaste. (Bottled sauces from Thailand and China containing garlic, soy, and hot peppers perform a similar function.)

Balsamic Vinegar: This is one of the most intriguing of Italy's endless culinary gifts to the New World. Aged in wood barrels like wine, it emerges with a sweet-sour taste rightly called pungent and, if it has been aged for many years, a very high price tag. But no more than a few drops atop a steak or in a salad dressing are sufficient to leave a significant impression. Genuine "balsamico" comes from Modena. The Monari Federzori brand is widely available.

Horseradish: How can you love something that can make you cry and your nose run? I guess it's part of the pleasure-pain principle. In any event, horseradish has been providing people with both since Biblical times. Its particular affinity for beef is easy to comprehend. The bite of the horseradish enlivens the sweet meat while cutting the richness of fat. In addition to creamy and white horseradish in jars, I recommend making your own Infused Horseradish Oil (page 108).

Worcestershire Sauce: This condiment evolved from tastes acquired during the English occupation of India. Soy, molasses, anchovy, and tamarind contribute to a piquant flavor that heightens the taste of both steak and sauces served with steak.

PORTERHOUSE

This is my favorite cut of steak, a view that is reinforced whenever I have the opportunity to dine at Peter Luger's in Brooklyn, which serves no other. It contains soft and rich tenderloin as well as firm-textured and juicy sirloin strip separated by a T-shaped bone. (The T-bone steak has the same configuration but a smaller amount of tenderloin.) Why settle for one type when you can sample both?

In addition to the more complex preparations of porterhouse that follow, let me share one that is simple and effective. It's called pan-broiling, a technique the National Cattlemen's Beef Association calls "frying without fat" in an attempt to entice calorie-conscious cooks. The steak is cooked in a preheated skillet, or better yet, if it is a single steak, in a ridged grill pan over medium-high heat. Turn it only once and—here's the gimmick—pour off the fat as it accumulates.

I like the results of this method very much. It produces the best possible crust on a conventional stove, but there are drawbacks: You need good ventilation since the pan is likely to smoke and you need to be relatively strong to pour fat from a heavy pan. Also, I cheat and apply a thin film of oil to the pan and the meat to prevent sticking.

As for cutting up the cooked steak, James Beard took a delightfully self-serving approach: "Carve the bone completely out of the steak with a sharp knife and hide it for yourself, then cut the meat in diagonal slices as thick as you wish. Slice right across the filet and the contra filet [sic]

43

A MIGHTY PORTERHOUSE STEAK

Mark Twain has just described a European beefsteak as "the size, shape and thickness of a man's hand with the thumb and fingers cut off."

Imagine a poor exile contemplating that inert thing and imagine an angel suddenly sweeping down out of a better land and setting before him a mighty porter-house steak an inch and a half thick, hot and sputtering from the griddle; dusted with fragrant pepper; enriched with little melting bits of butter of the most unimpeachable freshness and genuineness; the precious juices of the meat trickling out and joining the gravy, archipela-goed with mushrooms; a township or two of tender, yellowish fat gracing an outlying district of the ample country of beefsteak; the long white bone which divides the sirloin from the tenderloin still in its place; and imagine that the angel also adds a great cup of American home-made coffee, with the cream a-froth on the top, some real butter, firm and yellow and fresh, some smoking hot biscuits, a plate of hot buckwheat cakes, with transparent syrup—could words describe the gratitude of this exile?

so that everyone gets a fine piece of each part of the steak."

Simple Pan-Broiled Porterhouse is my Best Ever preparation of this cut, though I'm easily tempted to grill a giant porterhouse or put a smaller one under the broiler while making Nicole Bergere's Garlic Butter Sauce.

PAN-BROILED
PORTERHOUSE

The "secrets" to the sensational taste of a great restaurant steak are the quality of the meat and the magical seared crust that locks in juices and flavor. Home broilers cannot reach the temperature (as high as 800°F) that causes meat to char so rapidly, so I obtain that essential crust by another method. I panbroil the steak on top of the stove in a cast-iron pan. All that's needed is a very hot pan and enough strength to lift it easily, careful attention to time, and good ventilation. Garlic lovers might want to substitute garlic-flavored oil for the vegetable oil. Match great flavor with great flavor and drink a Zinfandel or Barolo with your porterhouse.

■ ■

1 porterhouse steak (about 1¾ pounds), cut 1¼ inches thick
½ teaspoon freshly ground black pepper
2 tablespoons chopped fresh thyme leaves
2 tablespoons vegetable oil, plus some for the pan
Pan Sauce (optional; recipe follows)

1. Pat the steak dry. Coat one side of the steak with half the pepper and half the thyme, patting the seasonings into the meat. Coat a plate with 1 tablespoon of the oil and place the steak, seasoned side down, on the plate. Pat the remaining pepper and thyme into the top side of the steak and coat lightly with the remaining 1 tablespoon of oil. Set the steak aside for 30 minutes.

2. Use a paper towel to very lightly coat the surface of a ridged or plain cast-iron skillet with vegetable oil. Heat the pan until the oil coating begins to smoke. Place the steak in the pan and cook until seared and nicely browned on one side, about 5 minutes. Turn the steak and cook 5 minutes more for medium-rare or 6 minutes more for medium.

3. Transfer the steak to a cutting board and let it rest for 5 minutes. While the steak is resting, make the Pan Sauce, if desired. Carve the steak into ½-inch-thick slices and serve.

SERVES 3 OR 4

PAN SAUCE

Next to simply placing a tablespoon of butter on top of a hot steak and letting it melt, pan sauce is the easiest all-purpose way to make a panfried steak even more juicy and flavorful. In many classic kitchens, this procedure would involve starting by making a roux with flour and whisking in a little butter at the end to provide a glamorous sheen. But this isn't a party sauce. This one's for you, or maybe two of you.

Steak pan with drippings
½ cup beef broth or ¼ cup broth and
*   ¼ cup red or white wine*
Salt and freshly ground black pepper
*   (optional)*

1. Remove the steak from the pan to a cutting board and let it rest before slicing or serving. Pour off as much of the fat from the pan as you can.

2. Return the pan to medium-high heat, add the broth, and bring it to a boil, scraping up the brown bits clinging to the bottom of the pan with a wooden spoon. Boil until the liquid is reduced by half, about 4 minutes.

3. Meanwhile, slice or plate the steak and any side vegetables or garnish. Pour the sauce through a strainer into a cup. Taste and season with salt and pepper, if desired. Pour over the steak and serve at once.

SERVES 1 OR 2

COMPOSED BUTTERS

Softened butter can be flavored with almost any combination of herbs, spices, and condiments. Such composed butters are wonderfully convenient to have at hand. I often make them with at least a stick of butter so there will be some left over. They freeze beautifully and thaw quickly to provide an instant flavored butter sauce for a steak or vegetables. My problem is that I quickly forget what ingredients these plastic-wrapped butter logs contain, so I've learned to label and date them. This smacks of Home Ec 101, I know, but you'll soon realize it's worthwhile.

Note: Elaborations tend to suggest themselves. Those I've tried more than once include ¼ teaspoon of mustard, Worcestershire sauce, or balsamic vinegar stirred into the sauce.

PORTERHOUSE
WITH SHALLOT-LEMON BUTTER

I f there is anything in the spectrum of composed butters that could be called both assertive and elegant, the butter for this recipe is it. Don't cook the steaks over charcoal or wood. Broil them so the pure sweetness of the meat and its juices can intermingle with the appealing tartness of the butter. Serve green beans on the same plate, topped with a little of the butter. The wine should have some finesse. A Merlot from France, Les Jamelles or Georges Duboeuf, will do very well.

■ ■

4 porterhouse steaks (12 ounces each),
*   cut 1 inch thick*
2 tablespoons vegetable oil
1 tablespoon finely chopped shallots
1 teaspoon finely chopped fresh flat-
*   leaf parsley leaves*
¼ teaspoon freshly ground black
*   pepper*
¾ teaspoon minced lemon zest
4 tablespoons (½ stick) unsalted butter,
*   at room temperature, cut into*
*   4 pieces*
Salt, to taste

1. Preheat the broiler.

2. Pat the steaks dry, coat them lightly with oil, and set aside.

3. Combine the shallots, parsley, pepper, and lemon zest in a small bowl and whisk together. Add the butter and continue to whisk until

the mixture is homogenous. Refrigerate for 10 to 15 minutes if the butter is very soft. (Composed butter may be made ahead and stored, covered, in the refrigerator. Return to room temperature before serving.)

4. Broil the steaks until seared and well-crusted on one side, about 5 minutes. Turn, salt the meat, and broil 3 minutes more for medium-rare or 4 minutes more for medium.

5. Transfer the steaks to a cutting board and let rest for 5 minutes. Slather a tablespoon of the composed butter on each steak and serve.

SERVES 4

SLICED PORTERHOUSE
WITH NICOLE BERGERE'S GARLIC BUTTER SAUCE

This is the perfect choice for a big-deal dinner involving intimate friends. Beautiful slices of meaty porterhouse (be sure everyone gets slices of both tenderloin and top loin) are presented on a silken pillow of a garlic-scented butter sauce I learned from Chicago bakery owner and cooking teacher, Nicole Bergere. The combination is both robust and sophisticated. Garnish the plate with zucchini or another green vegetable that can be coated easily with the butter sauce, then shoot the moon by pouring a wine from Pomerol or a Napa Valley Cabernet Sauvignon, such as Robert Mondavi Reserve or Opus One.

■■■■■■■■■■■■■■■■■■■■■■■■■

2 porterhouse steaks (about 1½
    pounds each), cut 1 inch thick
2 tablespoons vegetable oil
1 tablespoon ketchup
1 tablespoon Worcestershire sauce
1 teaspoon paprika, preferably sweet
    Hungarian
½ teaspoon dry mustard
2 teaspoons cider vinegar
3 medium cloves garlic, pushed
    through a garlic press
Salt and freshly ground black pepper,
    to taste
8 tablespoons (1 stick) unsalted butter,
    chilled, cut into 8 pieces

1. Pat the steaks dry. Lightly coat both steaks with oil and set aside at room temperature for 30 minutes.

2. Combine the ketchup, Worcestershire, paprika, mustard, and vinegar in a medium-size heavy skillet and whisk to blend. Place the skillet on a turned-off burner. Put the garlic in a small dish and cover with plastic wrap. (The recipe may be prepared ahead to this point.)

3. Preheat the broiler.

4. Broil the steaks until seared and well-crusted on one side, about 5 minutes. Turn the steaks, season with salt and pepper, and broil 3 minutes more for rare or 4 minutes more for medium. Transfer the steaks to a cutting board and let rest for 5 minutes.

5. While the steaks are cooking, warm the ketchup mixture over very low heat. When the steaks are resting, add the butter to the warm sauce, 1 or 2 pieces at a time, whisking constantly. The butter should melt but not liquefy. If it is melting too fast, remove the pan from the heat and continue to whisk. Once all the butter has been incorporated, stir in the garlic and season with salt.

6. Carve the steaks into 1/2-inch-thick slices and divide among 4 to 6 warm plates. Spoon 2 tablespoons of the sauce over each portion and serve immediately.

SERVES 4 TO 6

TONY TERLATO'S
PORTERHOUSE STEAK
WITH HERBS AND TOMATOES

No one turns down an invitation to the company dining room at Paterno Imports in Chicago. Not only does Paterno CEO Anthony J. (Tony) Terlato serve the best of his impressive Italian, French, and American wine selection, he does the cooking as well. The wine he poured for me with this steak and its herb-accented sauce was a California Cabernet Sauvignon, from Freemark Abbey's Bosche vineyard.

2 porterhouse steaks (about 1½ pounds each), cut 1¼ inches thick

⅓ cup plus 2 tablespoons olive oil, preferably extra virgin

3 cups peeled, seeded, and chopped ripe tomatoes or 1 can (28 ounces) plum tomatoes, drained, seeded, and finely chopped

1 large clove garlic, minced

Pinch of crushed red pepper flakes

1 tablespoon chopped fresh oregano leaves

1 tablespoon chopped fresh flat-leaf parsley leaves

6 to 8 basil leaves, rolled tightly and cut into thin ribbons

Salt and freshly ground black pepper, to taste

1. Preheat the broiler or prepare coals for grilling.

2. Allow the steaks to come to room temperature, pat dry, and coat lightly with 2 tablespoons olive oil. Set aside.

3. Combine the tomatoes, garlic, pepper flakes, oregano, parsley, basil, and salt and pepper in a medium-size bowl and stir well to blend. Stirring slowly, blend in the remaining $\frac{1}{3}$ cup olive oil. Set aside for at least 30 minutes, stirring occasionally.

4. Broil or grill the steaks until seared and well-crusted on one side, about 4 minutes.

Turn, season with salt, sear the second side for 4 minutes, and continue cooking for 4 minutes. Turn, season the second side, and cook 2 minutes more for medium-rare or 3 minutes more for medium.

5. Transfer the steak to a carving board, and let rest for 5 minutes. Cut away the bone and carve the steaks into $\frac{1}{2}$-inch-thick slices. Divide the slices among 4 warm serving plates. Spoon the sauce over the steak and serve at once.

SERVES 4

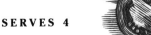

GRILLED
GIANT PORTERHOUSE
WITH SHERRY-SHALLOT VINAIGRETTE

Usually I leave the cooking of extra-thick cuts of steak to the experts at steak houses. But at least once a summer I find cooking a giant porterhouse or sirloin irresistible. It's a commitment, though. It takes longer to cook this cut than others and you can't just put the steak on the grill and turn it once. It needs frequent attention so the meat won't dry out and movement on the grill so the tenderloin section won't overcook while the sirloin section is reaching medium-rare. (It's easier to cook the steak by indirect heat, but not nearly as satisfying.) My preference is to have a big salad as a first course and nothing, except maybe some steak fries, with the porterhouse. I always treat myself to a fine Zinfandel, from Ridge if I'm lucky.

1 porterhouse steak (about 4 pounds),
cut 2½ inches thick
2 tablespoons olive oil
1 tablespoon Dijon mustard
2 shallots, chopped
1 tablespoon minced garlic
1½ tablespoons dry sherry
1½ tablespoons sherry vinegar
⅓ cup extra virgin olive oil
Salt and freshly ground black pepper,
to taste

1. Prepare coals for grilling.

2. Allow the steak to come to room temperature, pat it dry, and coat both sides with olive oil. Set aside.

3. Combine the mustard, shallots, and garlic in a small bowl. Whisk in the sherry and the sherry vinegar. Pouring slowly, whisk the extra virgin olive oil into the shallot mixture. Season with salt and pepper and set aside.

4. When the fire is hot enough for you to hold your hand at grill level for 4 seconds, place the steak on the grill and sear one side until nicely browned, about 3 minutes. Turn and sear the second side for 3 minutes. Move the steak, to keep the tenderloin away from the most intense heat, cover the grill, and cook for 4 minutes. Then turn and move the steak again. Season the steak with the salt and cover the grill. Cook for 5 minutes, turn it, season with salt. Cook, covered, for 5 minutes more for medium-rare or 7 minutes more for medium.

SALTING

I'm a firm believer in the ability of salt to enhance flavor. I also believe it should be used judiciously and at the appropriate time. While some argue that salt added before cooking will infuse the meat, many more are convinced salt draws out moisture, resulting in a drier, less tender steak. Furthermore, some scientists say juices leached out by the salt will boil and steam on the surface of the steak, resulting in a grayish color and mushy consistency. That image is enough to convince me to salt a steak only after it has been seared and turned. As for pepper, it becomes bitter when scorched, so I usually wait to add it until the meat has been removed from the heat.

5. Transfer to a cutting board and let the steak rest for 4 or 5 minutes. Remove the bone and carve the meat into ¾-inch-thick slices. Stir the sauce and, if desired, heat it briefly in a microwave oven. Divide the meat among 4 to 6 warm plates, spoon the sauce over, and serve.

SERVES 4 TO 6

THE ENDURING MAGIC OF THE STEAK HOUSE

To fully appreciate steak, it is as essential to dine in a great steak restaurant as it is to sip the classified growths of Bordeaux to understand the possibilities of red wine or to smoke the genuine Cuban product before claiming cigar connoisseurship. Not only are the steaks exceptional, due to the use of aged prime beef and expert preparation over heat far higher than that available to the home cook, the steak house—with its larger-than-life portions and customers—offers a distinctively American dining experience.

My own introduction to steak houses occurred in my late teens. A newly arrived student at the University of Virginia in Charlottesville, I was led to a now long-gone place near the grounds. There I discovered steak. Pink and thick and juicy, firm in texture, this was meat that mattered. From that evening forward, I've been a steak fan.

I'm not alone. The steak house is riding a wave of popularity that may prove unprecedented, if only because no one takes it for granted any more. Even in my town, Chicago, a mecca for steak-lovers, three major steak houses have opened and become fixtures during this decade: Gibsons, the Chicago Chop House, and the Saloon. All three offer a relaxed, clubby (and noisy) atmosphere and owe their success not just to superlative steak, but also to an intimacy between staff and regular customers that is rarely so strong in other types of restaurants.

Indeed, one of the appeals of the steak house is its chameleonlike character. One will be as stiff and formal as a posh men's club, the next as relaxed and vibrant as an Italian taverna, a third loose-kneed and folksy as a country hoedown. It can be a gathering place for the family or one of the priciest dining spots in town, the last bastion of the three-martini lunch crowd or a haven for wine connoisseurs. Competition is stiff, however, and the day is long gone when an athlete could open a restaurant by putting up a sign with his name on it along with the words "Steaks and Chops" and draw a crowd.

The prototype began to emerge in big cities in the aftermath of Prohibition. The dominant styles are Italian (of which the purist example is New York City's Palm), country rustic (I point you to the Hereford House in Kansas City), and

TODAY'S SPECIALS

1½ LB. SIRLOIN FOR TWO
12 OZ. STRIP STEAK
1 LB. T-BONE

FAMILY STYLE
MASHED POTATOES
CREAMED SPINACH

MISSISSIPPI MUD PIE
BREAD PUDDING
STRAWBERRY SHORTCAKE

urban elegant (Morton's of Chicago has successfully franchised this concept).

In smaller towns, the steak house often represents your best hope of dining above the subsistence level. I still hold vivid memories of eating a giant sirloin and cooked-to-order steak fries at Doe's Eat Place in Greenville, Mississippi, some years before it opened in Little Rock, and downing a juicy T-bone and rustic ambiance at the Ranchman's Cafe in Ponder, Texas, a town whose only other claim to fame is that it was featured in the movie *Bonnie and Clyde.*

Another reason offered for the boom in steak house dining is that the generation now in its late thirties and forties, the infamous Baby Boomers, has come to appreciate—after the endless elaborations of new American cuisine—the comfort of eating food everyone can understand. A steak dinner, complete with lavish portions of salad, potato, and a whipped cream-topped dessert, is a real treat.

Furthermore, no matter how different their ambiance, the great steak houses share a similar approach to portions, personnel, and price. Any steak house worth its A.1., serves outsized, even outlandish, portions of steak, as well as salad, potatoes, and even vegetables. The great steak house does not employ ciphers as servers. Be he (or she) gruff or amiable, your server has a personality and shows it. (Rumor has it that the Palm sends its most sharp-tongued New York City waiters to train new hires in other cities.) Finally, a great steak house meal does not come cheap. Most individual steaks, in major cities at least, sell for $20 to $30 or even more. But that's not gravy. If the beef is prime and aged, the owner would make a much higher percentage profit by selling you a slab of lasagne.

Incidentally, a classic steak house never has a chef in the French sense. The broiler man is a craftsman, a skilled technician, but the last thing an owner wants in his kitchen is a creative artist. The great steak house holds its clientele with quality ingredients and consistency in cooking. Steady customers are not looking for variety. They tend to order the same cut time and again, and if they order it medium-rare, it better not be served medium or rare.

Not all steak restaurants broil their steaks. Some use the grill method. My favorite place to watch a grill man show off his skill is at a vintage gem in St. Louis, the Tenderloin Room. The open grill is located in the eye of the Tenderloin, so it is easy to watch the cook keep an order of several different steaks in nearly constant motion to bring each one to the desired degree of doneness at the same moment.

A TOUR OF STEAK HOUSES

The volume leader of the prestige steak house pack is Ruth's Chris. Founded by Ruth Fertel in New

(continued)

Orleans almost forty years ago, the chain now owns or franchises thirty restaurants across the nation. Her secret, other than centralized purchase of specially fed and cut vacuum-packed beef from a single Chicago firm, is a coating of hot butter that covers each sizzling steak. Beef loves butter and the Ruth's Chris approach produces the juiciest (and thereby, for me, the best) filet mignon of them all.

The "good ol' boy" mood that hangs in the air at Ruth's Chris, the way cigarette smoke once did, takes on a decidedly country tinge in the old stockyard towns of the Heartland. In Kansas City, the Hereford House and the Golden Ox are both Western (steer horns mounted on the wall and cowboy boots on the customers), sparsely furnished, and dimly lit. The steaks are big. So are the drinks. No hype, no sizzle. Sad to say, according to the Zagat Survey, affluent locals prefer to eat their steaks in a posh Marriott Hotel restaurant.

Another prime example of this genre is Johnny's Cafe in Omaha. Elsewhere in the Midwest, St. Elmo Steak House in Indianapolis, nearly a century old, offers—along with a great shrimp cocktail and giant steaks—the contrast of a stark and worn setting and a classy, up-to-date wine selection.

Ambiance has been almost as important as the food in creating the aura that surrounds the Palm in Manhattan. It was established in the 1920s as a hole-in-the-wall under the Second Avenue El. The El (outdoor, elevated subway tracks) is long gone, but the Palm remains, cramped, worn, and seemingly uncared for, with cartoon drawings of favored customers on the walls, sawdust on the floor, and not a menu in sight.

This is a men's club. Only insiders are meant to know very good southern Italian fare is available (plus prime rib that some feel is the true culinary triumph of the kitchen) as well as the strip steaks, chops, and monster lobsters that everyone orders. (One way to deal with the huge portions is for two persons to split a lobster or shrimp salad and a single steak.) The twelve Palms outside New York retain the cartoon drawings and the macho mood. But they lack the patina of age, are tidier, and do offer menus.

THE ITALIAN CONNECTION

Gene and Georgetti in Chicago is another worn antique of the Italian school. Don't expect, as a first-time diner—or even as a second- or third-timer—that you will be offered one of the coveted tables in the room that houses the always crowded bar or the one directly behind it. It's likely you'll be shown to an upstairs table instead. While you won't go wrong ordering a strip steak here, my first choice is the T-bone. It weighs about a pound, comes hot from the broiler along with some lovely juices, and provides an intriguing contrast between the soft-as-butter tenderloin and the more textured sirloin on either side of the T.

There are other winning formats within the Italian tradition. Consider Sparks in Manhattan. Here's a steak restaurant for the person who wants a grown-up dining experience complete with such amenities as carpeting, tablecloths, a world-class wine list, and a polite and efficient staff. The attitude is inclusionary, not exclusionary.

As for the steak, the owners, the Cetta brothers, worked as butchers before they became restaurateurs. They claim a special aging process they will not describe fully gives their steaks—especially the strip sirloin—a flavor edge. But it is the wine, visibly displayed and expertly served, that brings in customers who are not regular steak house habitués. Pat Cetta, a passionate romantic, has several thousand cases aging in the basement. My advice is to pair your steak with a California Zinfandel, Italian Chianti, or a wine from France's Rhône valley. But why settle for my advice when you can have Pat Cetta's?

Wine is a big draw as well at Bern's in Tampa, which may be the most distinctive (or eccentric) steak house in the nation. Consider the wine list. It's a book that weighs four-and-a-half pounds and it's chained to your table! The restaurant itself is a crazy-quilt of dining rooms added over the years, topped—literally—with seating upstairs for desserts, dessert wines, and spirits and cigars. The decor has been described at "haute bordello."

Bern's adds up to a grand expression of another steak house trait: Have a theme or gimmick that elevates the experience beyond mere dining into the realm of show business. The ringmaster here is Bern Laxer, an intense former New Yorker who is personable, quirky, and quality obsessed. He shares his obsessions through the menu, which also contains the best one-page primer on steak and steak cookery I've seen anywhere.

A detailed chart presents the six cuts of beef served at Bern's along with the thickness, weight, servings, and price. The diner learns that aging filet makes it "more flavorful and sweeter," that by ordering a strip sirloin for two or more (same price per person), "you'll get far more flavor from the slower, longer exposure to the coals." There's also a warning for those who order steak well done. "Aged meat is already tender," Laxer writes, "(and never bloody) . . . it becomes tougher the longer you cook it."

For all Laxer's dedication, his is not my favorite steak house trophy. The steak of my dreams is the porterhouse served at Peter Luger in Brooklyn. Cut from sides of beef hand-selected by the (female) owner, it emerges from the furious flames of a

(continued)

basement broiler remarkably crusty and moist. It is quickly sliced into serving pieces and presented with the bone in a pool of juice. The relative handful of Luger nay-sayers complain the sliced meat loses juice and cools off too quickly. The standard answer is to tell them to stop talking and eat faster.

The turn-of-the-century decor at Peter Luger is German and genuine, while many of the convivial waiters appear to date from the same era. Do not ignore the bread (German rye from a nearby neighborhood bakery) or the thick-cut fried potatoes (surely anointed with a little beef fat). On my most recent visit, a friend won a bet from me by ordering—and getting—a rack of beautifully tender lamb chops. The lamb, of course, was served as a warm-up course before the steak.

Nostalgia does not have a role in the Morton's of Chicago concept. Instead, each of the thirty-four Morton's could be the setting for a *Lifestyles of the Rich and Famous* telecast. Elegance is the keynote, but there's nothing understated about the way in which famous-name wines are positioned to catch the eye as you enter. Lights are low, colors are primary, and banquet seating adds a touch of formality. The tuxedo-clad waiters push silver carts that display the richness of excess: gleaming cuts of beef, an outsized potato, the spearlike asparagi. The servers are restrained, the food as good as it looks in the uncooked state,

with the strip sirloin and porterhouse offering unparalleled tenderness. A meal here is a pricy but very soothing massage.

Al's in St. Louis is a similarly classy place, while Chops in Atlanta and The Grill in Beverly Hills—both stylish, bright and brassy—express a more contemporary vision of luxury. Finally, I would point those seeking not just a perfect steak but an all-around expression of the steak house ethos to Gibsons in Chicago. It has become the most popular of the city's steak palaces by combining an appeal to the past (Gibson girls, the Gibson cocktail, art deco decor, and antique photographs) with a vibrant (meaning noisy) and diverse bar crowd, "outsized but not overpriced" drinks and portions, a menu that offers genuine, tasty options for those who choose to skip the steak, and an attentive wait staff. As for the choice of steak, I'm partial to an off-the-menu special, a bone-in rib steak called "W.R.'s Chicago Cut."

Whatever the cut, however, and wherever the setting, the most beguiling aspect of a great steak house is its pride in product. No matter how much "sizzle" is provided by the decor, the staff, or celebrity customers, management knows it's the taste of the steak that counts, that lingers in the memory and prompts diners to return. So the question asked at the end of the meal, "Wasn't that the best steak you ever tasted?" is always rhetorical.

STEAK HOUSE LIST

Here are names and addresses of significant and reliable steak houses across the nation, including those I have cited in the foregoing pages. Many cities also now offer a clone of one or more of the three leading upscale steak house chains—Morton's of Chicago, Ruth's Chris, and the Palm—but I have listed each only in its home city. In suburban locations, look for very satisfactory casual-dining chain steak houses such as Outback and Lone Star.

ATLANTA:

Bones
3130 Piedmont Road
(404) 237-2663

Chops
70 West Paces Ferry Road
(404) 262-2675

BALTIMORE:

Polo Grill (The Inn at the Colonnade)
4 West University Parkway
(410) 235-8200

BOSTON:

Grill 23 & Bar
161 Berkeley Street
(617) 542-2255

Hilltop Steak House (the largest volume steak house in the country, serving 30,000 customers a week)
Route 1
Saugus
(617) 233-7700

CHICAGO:

Chicago Chop House
60 West Ontario Street
(312) 787-7100

Gene & Georgetti
500 North Franklin Street
(312) 527-3718

Gibsons
1028 North Rush Street
(312) 266-8999

Morton's
1050 North State Street
(312) 266-4820

The Saloon
200 East Chestnut Street
(312) 280-5454

CINCINNATI:

The Precinct
311 Delta Avenue
Columbia-Tusculum
(513) 321-5454

(continued)

DALLAS:
Del Frisco's Double Eagle
4300 Lemmon Avenue
(214) 490-9000

Chamberlain's Prime Chop House
5330 Belt Line Road
(214) 934-2467

DENVER:
The Buckhorn Exchange
1000 Osage Street
(303) 534-9505

DETROIT:
Carl's Chop House
3020 Grand River
(313) 833-0700

FORT LAUDERDALE:
Raindancer
3031 East Commercial Boulevard
(305) 772-0337

GREENVILLE, MISSISSIPPI:
Doe's Eat Place
502 Nelson
(601) 334-3315

HOUSTON:
Brenner's
10911 Katy Freeway, 1-10W
(713) 465-2901

INDIANAPOLIS:
St. Elmo Steak House
127 South Illinois Street
(317) 637-1811

KANSAS CITY:
Hereford House
2 East 20 Street
(816) 842-1080

Jess and Jim's
135 and Locust
(816) 942-9909

LOS ANGELES:
The Grill
9560 Dayton Way
Beverly Hills
(310) 276-0615

MADISON, WISCONSIN:
Smokey's Club
3005 University Avenue
(608) 233-2120

MIAMI:
Christy's
3101 Ponce de Leon Boulevard
Coral Gables
(305) 446-1400

Schula's
15400 NW 154 Street
Miami Lakes Golf Resort
(305) 822-2324

MILWAUKEE:
Sally's
1028 East Juneau Street
(414) 272-5363

MINNEAPOLIS:
Murry's (home of the "silver butter-knife steak" for two, so tender you can cut it with a you-know-what)
26 South 6 Street
(612) 339-0909

Manny's Steakhouse (huge portions served by huge waiters)
Hyatt Regency Hotel
1300 Nicollet Mall
(612) 339-0201

NEW ORLEANS:
Ruth's Chris original location
711 North Broad Street
(504) 486-0810

NEW YORK CITY:
Palm
837 Second Avenue
(212) 687-2953

Peter Luger
178 Broadway
Brooklyn
(718) 387-7400

Sparks Steak House
210 East 46 Street
(212) 687-4855

Smith & Wollensky
201 East 49 Street
(212) 753-1530

OMAHA:
Johnny's Cafe
4702 South 27 Street
(402) 731-4774

PONDER, TEXAS:
Ranchman's Cafe
(817) 479-2221

PORTLAND, OREGON:
The Ringside
2165 West Burnside Boulevard
(503) 223-1513

ST. LOUIS:
Al's
1200 North First Avenue
(314) 421-6399

Tenderloin Room
212 North Kings Highway
(314) 361-0900

SALT LAKE CITY:
The New Yorker Club
60 West Market Street
(801) 363-0166

(continued)

59

SAN DIEGO:
Rainwater's on Kettner
1202 Kettner Boulevard
(619) 233-5757

SAN FRANCISCO:
Harris'
2100 Van Ness Avenue
(415) 673-1888

Vic Stewart's Steak House
850 South Broadway
Walnut Creek
(510) 943-5666

SEATTLE:
Metropolitan Grill
820 Second Avenue
(206) 624-3287

TAMPA:
Bern's
1208 Howard Avenue
(813) 251-2421

WASHINGTON, DC:
Sam & Harry's Steak House
1200 19 Street NW
(202) 296-4333

STRIP OR TOP LOIN

This is a traveling cut, having gained fame as both the New York strip steak and the Kansas City strip steak. It's also called the boneless loin, and by the French, *contre-filet*. What's behind the name is a short loin minus its filet and bone. (It's possible to find bone-in strip steaks, but both consumers and restaurateurs prefer the boneless version.)

The strip is the second most popular steak house cut, second to tenderloin, in part because it is of a convenient shape and size to cook under a broiler or on a grill, has a great texture—grainy and somewhat chewy—and is very juicy. This steak should be cut 1 to 1½ inches thick.

Broiling is my cooking method of choice. In my conventional gas oven, I broil an inch-thick strip 2 inches from the heat. The steak browns quickly, although I can't match the fabulous crust the supercharged broilers of a steak house produce. To encourage browning, I always preheat the broiler and coat the steak with oil. While broiling such relatively thin steaks, I usually turn them only once because opening the broiler lowers the temperature and slows the cooking process. I don't baste either, for the same reason—and because it's a nuisance.

Conventional wisdom calls for the use of a broiling pan so the fat drains under the metal shield and is protected from the flame, but I find flare-ups are rare when I cook a closely trimmed supermarket steak. So I cover the broiler pan with aluminum foil, which I carefully bundle up and discard after the steak is cooked, thus avoiding the need to clean the broiler pan.

For me, the Best Ever preparation of strip steak comes from my memories of restaurants in Little Italy in Manhattan, where a broiled strip would be served with a more than generous amount of tomato-based sauce. Try my version of Strip Steak with Italian Tomato Sauce. There's a

recipe, too, for strip steak with onions and pimientos from the Palm steak houses. Sometimes the top loin is left intact to be roasted in my Strip Roast with Horseradish Cream Sauce.

STRIP STEAK
WITH ITALIAN TOMATO SAUCE

The role of Italian-Americans in creating the steak house tradition in this country cannot be overstated. And it was inevitable that they would find ways to combine their tomato sauces from the Old Country with rich and tender American beef. This recipe is my variation on one of the most popular of these combinations, steak pizzaiola. To create an Italian ambiance, set the table with a red-and-white checked tablecloth, serve the steak with a side of spaghetti topped with the pizzaiola sauce, and pour Chianti from a ceramic pitcher.

■ ■

2 strip steaks (about 12 ounces each),
   cut 1 inch thick
3 tablespoons olive oil
1 strip bacon, diced
¼ cup chopped onion
2 teaspoons minced garlic
1 small rib celery, chopped
¼ cup grated carrot
2 fresh basil leaves, chopped, or
   ¼ teaspoon dried basil
1 can (14½ ounces) plum tomatoes,
   drained and chopped
½ teaspoon salt
¼ teaspoon freshly ground black
   pepper

1. Pat the steaks dry and lightly coat with 2 tablespoons of the oil. Set aside to come to room temperature.

2. Heat the remaining 1 tablespoon of oil with the bacon, onion, garlic, celery, and car-rot over low heat in a heavy skillet large enough to hold the steaks. Cook, stirring occasionally, until the bacon begins to crisp and the vegetables are soft, 8 to 10 minutes.

3. Add the basil, tomatoes, salt, and pepper. Raise the heat to medium and bring the mixture to a simmer. Lower the heat and cook, uncovered, for 15 minutes to reduce the sauce and blend the flavors. Taste and correct seasoning as desired. (The sauce may be made ahead.)

4. Preheat the broiler.

5. Broil the steaks until just browned on one side, about 3 minutes. Turn and sear the other side for 2 minutes. Meanwhile, bring the sauce to a simmer, if necessary. Transfer the steaks to the pan with the sauce. Spoon some sauce over the meat, cover the pan, and cook for 5 minutes at a bare simmer.

6. Transfer the steaks to a cutting board. Let rest briefly, then cut into ½-inch-thick slices. Spread ¼ cup of the sauce on each of 4 warm plates. Arrange the steak on top of the sauce, spoon additional sauce over the steak, and serve. Pass any remaining sauce at the table.

SERVES 4

STRIP STEAK
WITH SPANISH CHEESE SAUCE

Thanks to the tapas boom, Americans are becoming more familiar with Spanish food, and enjoying it in informal settings. Spanish wines, spirits, and cheese are found more readily in markets, too. This recipe makes use of the superb Spanish blue cheese cabrales, sharp and salty yet creamy as well, and the fruity smoothness of fine Spanish brandy. They contrast beautifully with the corn-fed sweetness of a tender strip steak. To expand on the Spanish theme, make a Spanish first-course salad, perhaps shrimp and tomatoes, and a flan for dessert. Pour a red wine such as Torres Coronas or Gran Coronas. Leftover cheese spread can be used on canapés, in omelets, or combined with rice as a filling for stuffed vegetables.

■ ■

4 ounces blue cheese, preferably Spanish cabrales, cut into chunks
2 tablespoons unsalted butter, cut into small pieces
1 tablespoon minced shallots
1 teaspoon minced garlic
1½ tablespoons brandy, preferably Spanish, such as Carlos I
¼ teaspoon freshly ground black pepper
2 tablespoons beef broth or water
1 strip steak (about 12 ounces), cut 1 inch thick
1 tablespoon vegetable oil

1. Combine the cheese, butter, shallots, garlic, brandy, and pepper in a food processor. Pulse 4 or 5 times to mix the ingredients, then process until the mixture is homogeneous, about 30 seconds. You should have about ¾ cup cheese spread. (The cheese spread may be made ahead and refrigerated until needed.)

2. Preheat the broiler.

64

3. Spoon ¼ cup of the cheese spread into a small saucepan. Add the broth and place the saucepan on a turned-off burner or near the stove. Refrigerate all but 1 tablespoon of the remaining cheese spread and save for another use.

4. Rub the steak lightly with oil. Broil the steak until seared and nicely crusted on top, 5 minutes. Turn the steak and broil about 3 minutes more for medium-rare or 4 minutes more for medium. Spread the reserved 1 tablespoon of cheese spread over the top of the steak. Cook until the cheese melts and begins to brown, about 30 seconds. Transfer the steak to a cutting board.

5. Whisk the cheese spread and beef broth together over medium-high heat until smooth and bubbling.

6. Cut the steak into ½-inch-thick slices and divide between 2 warm plates. Spoon the sauce over the steak and serve at once.

SERVES 2

THE PALM'S STEAK
A LA STONE

The Palm, the historic Manhattan steak house, sells its prime steaks by mail order in Palm Pak selections (page 232). I once ordered a Palm Pak of strip steaks, and when they arrived, bought an uncooked fresh steak from the restaurant. The frozen and fresh strips were very similar in shape and marbling. When cooked, the fresh steak was a little juicier, but the taste was identical. Investigation over, I went on to prepare and enjoy one of the Palm's most popular recipes, leaked to me by the Chicago Palm's genial general manager, John Blandino. Named for a favorite customer, this rich dish calls for a really rich wine such as Piero Antinori's Tignanello. (Incidentally, if you read the recipe and think, "This could serve a dozen people," you're right.)

■ ■

¼ cup vegetable oil, preferably corn

*3 medium onions (about 1½ pounds),
cut into ¼-inch-thick slices*

*1 jar (12 ounces) imported whole
pimientos, cut open, seeded,
and flattened or cut into large
sections*

*3 strip steaks (about 1 pound each),
cut 1½ inches thick, at room
temperature*

*Salt and freshly ground black pepper,
to taste*

*6 slices of white bread, crusts removed,
toasted, and cut in half on the
diagonal*

*8 tablespoons (1 stick) butter, melted
and warm*

*⅓ cup chopped fresh flat-leaf parsley
leaves*

1. Preheat the broiler.

2. Put the oil and onion slices in a large skillet and place over medium-low heat. Cook, stirring from time to time, until the onions are soft but not browned, about 15 minutes. Spread the pimientos over the onions in a single layer. Cover to keep warm. Set aside.

3. Broil the steaks until nicely browned on one side, 3 minutes. Turn, season the browned side with salt and pepper and cook the second side for 6 to 7 minutes. Turn, season, and cook 3 to 4 minutes more for medium-rare or 5 to 6 minutes more for medium. Transfer to a cutting board.

4. Place 2 toast triangles on each of 6 plates. Spoon onions and pimientos over the toast. Carve the steaks into ½-inch-thick slices and place them over the vegetables and toast. Season with salt and pepper, spoon melted butter over the steak slices, sprinkle with chopped parsley, and serve.

SERVES 6

THE CASE FOR FAT

Fat lubricates meat fibers, making them easier to pull apart, while the flavor compounds that fat carries help stimulate the flow of saliva. Juiciness, food scientists say, comes in two stages: first an initial impression of moistness on biting into the meat, then the actual moisture that is released as you chew. Cut away excess exterior fat, though. It's not needed for internal flavor; it may cause flare-ups in the broiler or on the grill, and it looks very unappetizing if it reaches the table still attached to the steak. Slash the fat layer around a steak every three-quarter inch because fat shrinks faster than meat and will cause the steak to curl or warp, cook unevenly, and look ugly.

THE SALOON'S
CHEESE STEAK SANDWICH
WITH BARBECUE MAYONNAISE

The original Philadelphia cheese steak sandwich doesn't travel well, according to friends from Philadelphia who devote considerable effort trying to convince people from elsewhere that their city is the gastronomic capital of America. They're making headway with me, so I won't replicate the Philly cheese steak (page 31), but offer instead this spicy Chicago creation as casual party fare. Serve it with coleslaw and beer.

■ ■

1 cup mayonnaise

*1 tablespoon McCormick's Barbecue
    Spice*

2 teaspoons fresh lemon juice

1 teaspoon minced garlic

1 teaspoon paprika

½ teaspoon minced jalapeño

Cayenne pepper, to taste

Salt, to taste

4 tablespoons olive oil

1 large onion, thinly sliced

*1 small red bell pepper, stemmed,
    seeded, and cut into julienne strips*

*1 small green bell pepper, stemmed,
    seeded, and cut into julienne strips*

*4 strip steaks (about 12 ounces each),
    cut 1 inch thick*

*8 submarine sandwich rolls, split and
    much of the interior pulled out*

*8 ounces sharp Cheddar cheese,
    shredded*

8 ounces Monterey Jack cheese, shredded

1. Combine the mayonnaise, barbecue spice, lemon juice, garlic, paprika, jalapeño, cayenne, and salt in a small bowl and whisk until well blended. Set aside. (Sauce may be prepared ahead. Refrigerate, covered, until needed.)

2. Preheat the broiler.

3. Heat 2 tablespoons of the oil in a large sauté pan over medium heat. Add the onion and both bell peppers and sauté until soft and starting to color, about 8 minutes. Remove pan from the heat and season vegetables with salt. Set aside.

4. Pat the steaks dry, then coat them with the remaining 2 tablespoons oil. Broil the steaks

until seared and well crusted on one side, about 4 minutes. Turn, season with salt, and cook the second side for 4 minutes more for medium-rare or 5 minutes more for medium. Transfer the steaks to a cutting board. Do not turn off the broiler.

5. Reheat the vegetables while cutting the steaks crosswise into ¹/₂-inch-thick slices.

Spread the barbecue mayonnaise on both sides of each roll. Add the steak slices, top with the vegetables, and sprinkle cheese over all. Place under the broiler, two at a time, until the cheese melts. Serve immediately.

SERVES 8

STEAK DIANA

I have memories—more from the movies than real life, I confess—of a time when maître d's and captains at hotel dining rooms and supper clubs prepared their specialties at the customers' tables. A classic from that era is Steak Diane. I took it back into my kitchen, made some changes to rein in the overwhelming presence of Worcestershire, and reemerged with Steak Diane's more flavorful cousin, which I call Steak Diana. Be sure all the ingredients are measured and close at hand before beginning or the meat will overcook. Serve it with a lush Cabernet Sauvignon from California's Napa Valley. Cuvaison and Silverado are personal favorites.

■■■■■■■■■■■■■■■■■■■■■■■■

2 tablespoons unsalted butter

1 tablespoon vegetable oil

4 strip steaks (about 6 ounces each), cut ¹/₂ inch thick

2 tablespoons Cognac

Salt and freshly ground black pepper, to taste

2 small cloves garlic, minced

2 tablespoons dry red wine, preferably Cabernet Sauvignon

¹/₂ cup beef broth

¹/₂ teaspoon Worcestershire sauce

¹/₂ teaspoon Dijon mustard

¹/₂ teaspoon tomato paste

¹/₃ cup heavy (or whipping) cream

1. Preheat the oven to warm.

2. Melt the butter with the oil in a large skillet over medium heat until the butter stops bubbling. Increase the heat to medium-high, add the steaks (cook only two at a time if four overcrowds the skillet) and sauté until brown, 2 minutes. Turn and cook 1 minute more for medium-rare or 1½ minutes more for medium.

3. Heat the Cognac in a small saucepan over medium heat. When it boils, remove it from the heat. Carefully light the Cognac with a long kitchen match. In a single smooth motion pour the burning Cognac over the steaks (make sure your hair is tied back and your sleeves are rolled up before you do this). It will flare up momentarily. Gently shake the skillet over the heat until the flames die. Transfer the meat to a warm platter, season with salt and pepper, and place the platter in the oven.

4. Pour off all but ½ tablespoon of the butter and oil from the skillet. Add the garlic and cook over medium heat until softened, about 45 seconds. Add the wine and scrape the bottom of the pan with a wooden spoon to deglaze it. Add the broth, Worcestershire, mustard, tomato paste, and the juices that have collected on the meat platter.

5. Turn the heat to high. Whisking to blend the ingredients, boil the sauce to reduce it by half, about 3 minutes. Add the cream and continue to boil until silken sauce is formed, 2 minutes more.

6. Turn the steaks in the sauce to coat well, transfer to warm plates, and spoon the remaining sauce over. Serve at once.

SERVES 4

STRIP ROAST
WITH HORSERADISH CREAM SAUCE

This is the centerpiece of a steak dinner to serve to special guests. Instead of being cut into steaks, the top loin is roasted intact, carved, and served with a creamy sauce enlivened with freshly grated horseradish root. A good accompaniment to this dish is More Than Mashed Potatoes (page 207). The wine with this dish should have character. A peppery Châteauneuf-du-Pape will fit the bill.

■■■■■■■■■■■■■■■■■■■■■■■ ■

1 boneless top loin strip roast
  (about 4 pounds)
Vegetable oil
Salt and freshly ground black pepper,
  to taste
¾ cup freshly grated horseradish
  (see Note)
2 tablespoons minced shallots
1 tablespoon Dijon mustard
2 teaspoons minced garlic
1½ cups heavy (or whipping) cream
½ cup dry white wine
White pepper, to taste

1. Preheat oven to 400°F.

2. Rub the strip roast with oil, then sprinkle with salt and black pepper. Place the roast, fat side up, on a rack, in a roasting pan. Roast the meat for about 1 hour for medium-rare. Check the inner meat temperature with an instant-read thermometer after 50 minutes. When the meat registers 120° to 130°F in the center, remove it from the oven to rest. (Large roasts, such as this, continue to cook out of the oven and increase in temperature by at least 10°F.) Let the roast rest on a cutting board, loosely covered with aluminum foil, for at least 5 minutes before carving.

3. While the meat is roasting, prepare the sauce. Combine the horseradish, shallots, mustard, garlic, cream and white wine in a medium-size saucepan over medium-high heat. Bring to a boil, stirring to mix, then reduce the heat to low. Simmer, stirring occasionally, until the sauce is somewhat thickened, about 15 minutes. Season to taste with salt and white pepper. Add any juices from the cooked roast that have collected on the cutting board.

4. Carve the roast into ¼-inch-thick slices. Spoon some warm horseradish cream sauce onto each serving plate. Lay 2 slices of the roast beef over the sauce for each serving. Pass any extra sauce separately.

SERVES 8

Note: You can substitute bottled horseradish for fresh. Place it in a strainer and rinse it under water. Press out the excess moisture. The resulting sauce may have a somewhat sharp taste to it due to the vinegar used in processing horseradish.

SHORT-ORDER
STEAK AND EGGS

I reserve steak and eggs for a weekend morning, a time when the pull of the market or the Sunday paper means I don't want to be in the kitchen much longer than it takes to brew and pour the coffee. Therefore I've honed my technique so that with some preparation, I spend no more than five minutes at the stove. Playing short-order cook really wakes me up. I add a few minutes if toast and grits or fried green tomatoes are on the menu. And if wine is in order, I willingly break the red-with-meat commandment and pour Champagne.

■■■■■■■■■■■■■■■■■■■■■■■■■

1 strip steak (about 12 ounces),
*   cut 1 inch thick*
1 tablespoon plus ½ teaspoon
*   Worcestershire sauce*
½ teaspoon fresh lemon juice
Freshly ground black pepper, to taste
4 large eggs
1 tablespoon minced chives or scallions
1 tablespoon milk
2 tablespoons unsalted butter
Salt, to taste

1. While the steak is still cold, slice it horizontally in half to create 2 thin steaks. Trim off all the exterior fat and gristle you can and pat the steak dry. Pound it lightly, in recognition of the hour. Mix 1 tablespoon of the Worcestershire, the lemon juice, and ¼ teaspoon of pepper in a small bowl. Paint this mixture onto both sides of each steak. Set aside.

2. Break the eggs into another bowl, add the chives, milk, and remaining ½ teaspoon Worcestershire and beat lightly. Set aside.

3. Melt 1 tablespoon of the butter in a large skillet over medium heat. Melt the remaining tablespoon butter in a smaller skillet over low heat. Add the steaks to the larger pan. Cook until one side is browned, about 2 minutes. Turn the steaks and season lightly with salt. Cook 2 minutes more for medium-rare and 3 minutes more for medium.

4. As soon as the steak is turned and salted, turn up the heat under the smaller pan to medium, add the egg mixture, and once the eggs start to set, stir vigorously to scramble them. When scrambled to your liking, remove from the heat. Season with salt and pepper and divide between 2 warm plates. Place a steak on each plate, take a deep breath, and serve.

SERVES 2

DOGGIE BAG

STEAK SALAD

Here's an example of how a relatively small amount of leftover steak can be recycled to make several people happy. The amounts given here should satisfy three healthy appetites as a main course or provide a first course for six. The salad is especially nice in summer when there's a chance fresh garden beets, beans, and corn will be at hand. On a hot day, consider chilling the salad plates and the greens.

■ ■

6 to 8 ounces cooked strip steak or
*   filet steak*
1 small red onion, cut into thin rings
²/₃ to ¾ cup (1 ear) cooked corn
*   kernels*
4 ounces cooked green beans, cut on
*   the diagonal into strips*
2 medium cooked beets, cut into
*   ¹/₂-inch cubes*
6 cups mesclun (mixed baby greens)
*   or other mixed greens*
1 tablespoon Dijon mustard
¹/₄ teaspoon salt
¹/₄ teaspoon freshly ground black
*   pepper*
1 tablespoon fresh lemon juice
4 tablespoons olive oil, preferably
*   extra virgin*
6 cherry or cocktail tomatoes,
*   halved*

2. Combine the onion, corn, green beans, beets, and greens in a large salad bowl. Combine the mustard, salt, and pepper in a small bowl. Using a whisk or a fork, slowly stir in the lemon juice, then the olive oil. Add all but 1 tablespoon of the dressing to the salad bowl. Toss until the greens and vegetables are well coated.

3. Divide the salad among 3 large or 6 small plates. Arrange the meat slices on top, drizzle the remaining dressing over the meat and garnish the salad with cherry tomatoes. Serve immediately.

SERVES 3 AS A MAIN COURSE OR 6 AS A FIRST COURSE

1. Cut the steak into 2 x ¹/₂-inch strips and set aside.

DOGGIE BAG

STEAK SANDWICH

I open the refrigerator and my eyes light up. There, temporarily forgotten, is the famous doggie bag, containing steak brought home from a restaurant meal. I can simply gnaw the meat off the bone or, the better option, recycle it into a salad, a sandwich, or hash. Try one of these recipes with the contents of your next doggie bag (see Index for page numbers): Cold Filet with Monique King's Orange-Cumin Vinaigrette, Short-Order Steak and Eggs, and Superior Steak Hash, or try this casual and unusual lunch time treat on family or friends. Those not mechanically inclined may want to chop the meat and whisk the sauce by hand. The sauce was taught to me by executive chef Azmin Ghahreman of the Four Seasons Resort Maui at Wailea. He uses it with seared tuna.

■ ■

*6 ounces cooked strip steak or sirloin
 steak, trimmed of fat*

2 tablespoons beer

*1 teaspoon spicy seasoning, such as
 Paul Prudhomme's Cajun Magic*

2 teaspoons soy sauce

1 tablespoon Dijon mustard

3 tablespoons olive oil

3 tablespoons vegetable oil

8 slices white bread

1 ripe tomato, cut into 4 slices

1. Cut the steak into $1/2$-inch pieces, place in a food processor, and pulse briefly until meat has been reduced to a coarse grind, about 15 pulses. You should have 1 to $1^{1}/_{4}$ cups. Transfer the meat to a small bowl and set aside.

2. Pour the beer and seasoning mix into the blender. Pulse once, then wait 1 minute. Add the soy sauce and mustard. Combine the olive and vegetable oils in a liquid measuring cup. With the motor running, pour the oils into the blender in a slow, steady stream. Pour the sauce back into the measuring cup. You should have about $1/2$ cup. Taste and, if desired, add more seasoning mix. (Sauce may be made ahead, covered, and refrigerated until needed.)

3. Pour $1/4$ cup of the sauce into the bowl with the meat and stir to mix. Divide and spread the meat mixture onto 4 slices of bread and place a tomato slice on top. Spread 1 tablespoon of the sauce on each of the remaining bread slices and cover each sandwich. Cut the sandwiches in half and serve.

SERVES 4

RIB

The primal (basic) rib cut (there are seven ribs to a side), can be subdivided into roasts or rib steaks, with or without the bone, rib-eye steaks, and baby back or short ribs. Although admired as perhaps the most satisfying of all beef cuts, the rib, which contains a generous proportion of fat and is a high-ticket item, no longer has the cachet it once did. In *The Complete Book of Outdoor Cookery,* written in the mid-1950s, James Beard even recommended cooking individual rib steaks on the bone, to be eaten without cutlery, for "an outdoor boys' party."

But these days the standing rib roast, the "joint" so envied in Dickensian England, is as out of favor as midday family dinners on Sunday. Nonetheless, in keeping with the scaled-down appetites of today, a well-trimmed rib steak (called *entrecôte* by the French), still is a marvelously satisfying treat for a pair of sensualists, especially when the bone is left on.

My Best Ever rib steak comes from San Francisco chef Reed Hearon. For Lulu's Oven-Roasted Rib Steak with Artichokes and Potatoes he sears the meat on both sides, then roasts it in a hot oven. Instead of the direct transfer of heat through the pan to the meat, in roasting, the heat is carried by the air inside the oven.

I sear and roast steaks 2 inches and thicker because if they are cooked over direct heat, the surface is likely to burn before the interior is sufficiently cooked. But just to prove there is an exception to every rule, French chef Roger Vergé cooks his rib steak (page 82) on top of the stove. The more meat and fat a steak has, the higher the roasting temperature can be. I'll roast a rib steak, for instance, at more than 400°F. But for cuts with more connective tissue, chuck and rump for example, 275° to 300°F is best, even though it takes much longer at that temperature to roast the meat to medium-rare or medium.

LULU'S
OVEN-ROASTED RIB STEAK
WITH ARTICHOKES AND POTATOES

Reed Hearon, chef-owner of the successful Lulu in San Francisco, believes in cooking big cuts of meat with bold flavorings. Originally intended for the outdoor grill, I have adapted his recipe for roasting in an indoor oven. (Outdoors, Reed grills the steak for 6 minutes on each side, lets it rest off the heat for 10 minutes, then returns it to the grill for 2 minutes on each side for very rare.) The quantities here are for three or four servings, but for a treat serve this recipe for two and use the leftovers to make Rib Steak Salad. The butcher will have to cut this chop from a standing rib roast. Marinate the meat and prepare the olive butter and braised vegetables ahead so there will be little last-minute work to do. This dish will make almost any Merlot wine seem like a prize-winner.

■■■■■■■■■■■■■■■■■■■■■■■■

1 tablespoon chopped fresh rosemary leaves

2 tablespoons chopped fresh thyme leaves

2 tablespoons chopped fresh flat-leaf parsley leaves

2 tablespoons fresh ground black pepper

2 teaspoons dried herbes de Provence

1/2 cup olive oil

1 rib steak with bone (about 2 pounds), cut 2 1/2 inches thick

8 tablespoons (1 stick) unsalted butter, softened

1 tablespoon pitted and chopped Niçoise olives or prepared tapenade

1 1/2 teaspoons minced anchovy fillets or anchovy paste

Braised Artichokes and Potatoes

1 package (9 ounces) frozen artichoke hearts, thawed

1/4 cup olive oil

1 pound red potatoes, washed and thinly sliced

2 cloves garlic, peeled and chopped

2 bay leaves

1 1/2 teaspoons chopped fresh thyme leaves

1 1/2 teaspoons chopped fresh flat-leaf parsley leaves

1/2 teaspoon salt, preferably coarse (kosher)

1/4 cup dry white wine

1/4 cup water

1. At least 8 hours before cooking, and preferably the day before, marinate the steak.

Combine the rosemary, thyme, parsley, pepper, and *herbes de Provence* in a small bowl. Stir in the oil until well blended. Place the steak on a plate with a rim and rub the meat with the marinade, coating it completely. Cover the plate with plastic wrap and refrigerate.

2. Combine the butter, chopped olives, and anchovies and mash until blended. Cover the olive butter with plastic wrap and refrigerate until 30 minutes before serving.

3. If desired, prepare the braised vegetables in advance as well. Cut each thawed artichoke heart vertically into 3 or 4 slices and set aside.

4. Heat the oil in a skillet with a tight-fitting lid over medium heat. Add the potatoes and turn to coat. Add the garlic, bay leaves, thyme, parsley, and salt. Stir for 1 minute; add the wine and water. Bring the liquid to a boil, cover, and lower the heat to a bare simmer. Cook for 10 to 12 minutes, then add the artichokes. Simmer, covered, for 10 minutes, or until the potatoes test tender. (If not serving at once, cool and refrigerate. Reheat, covered, for 10 minutes.)

5. Remove the steak from the refrigerator at least 30 minutes before cooking. Preheat the oven to 475°F.

6. Heat an ovenproof skillet, preferably cast iron, over medium-high heat. Transfer the steak directly from the marinade to the pan. Cook and turn until the steak is seared and nicely browned on both sides, 8 to 10 minutes total.

7. Transfer the skillet to the oven and cook for

12 minutes. Remove the skillet from the oven, pour off the accumulated fat, and turn the steak over. Return the skillet to the oven and cook for 10 minutes more for medium-rare.

8. Transfer the steak to a cutting board and cover loosely with aluminum foil. Let rest for 10 minutes. With the steak lying flat, cut 1-inch-thick slices perpendicular to the bone, then cut away the bone.

9. Spoon the vegetables onto warmed plates, then top with steak. Spoon a dollop of olive butter on top of each portion of steak just before serving (refrigerate leftover butter for use on grilled fish or another steak).

SERVES 3 OR 4

RESTING

Why let just-cooked steaks and roasts "rest" before carving? I recommend leaving steaks on the cutting board 5 minutes (10 to 15 minutes for roasts) because as the meat begins to cool, the juices redistribute themselves and settle and the meat becomes firmer. As a result, it can be cut more evenly and, if desired, thinner, and the juices will not run out so profusely. Some contend there is no need to let steak, a relatively thin cut of meat, rest. For them, I suggest a test: Cut a freshly cooked sirloin in half, slice one portion, allow the other to rest, then look at the accumulated juices of each.

RIB STEAK SALAD

This salad, an experiment inspired by leftovers from Lulu's Oven-Roasted Rib Steak, turned out to be a very elegant, herb-perfumed dish with a great balance of meat and vegetables. Eight ounces of leftover steak is just right for two portions. Serve the salad with red wine or beer.

■■■■■■■■■■■■■■■■■■■■■■■■

8 ounces cooked rib steak, carved from
   the bone
6 to 8 cooked broccoli florets or about
   20 cooked green beans
½ cup finely diced sweet onion, such
   as Vidalia
⅔ cup leftover Braised Artichokes and
   Potatoes (page 77; optional)
½ medium red bell pepper
½ head crisp lettuce, preferably
   romaine
¼ cup plain lowfat yogurt
1 teaspoon chopped Niçoise olives or
   prepared tapenade
1 teaspoon tomato paste
½ teaspoon anchovy paste
1 teaspoon chopped fresh thyme
   (optional)
1 teaspoon chopped fresh flat-leaf
   parsley leaves (optional)
2 tablespoons olive oil
Salt and freshly ground black pepper,
   to taste (optional)

1. Trim any pieces of fat from the steak and cut the meat into big bite-size pieces. Set aside.

2. Place the broccoli, onion, and braised artichoke mixture, if using, in a salad bowl. Core and seed the red pepper, cut it lengthwise into strips, then cut the strips in half. Add to the bowl. Add the steak pieces. Wash and dry the lettuce, then tear it into large bite-size pieces. Add it to the bowl.

3. To make the dressing, spoon the yogurt into a small bowl. Add the olives, tomato paste, anchovy paste, and the herbs, if using. Stir well with a whisk, then slowly stir in the olive oil. (Because the steak is highly seasoned, I use no salt and pepper at this point. If desired, add it individually at the table.)

4. Pour the dressing over the salad, toss until well blended, and serve.

SERVES 2

WINE WITH STEAK

Once it was easy to order wine to go with steak. After a customer ordered red meat, the waiter would ask "Red wine?" If the answer was "Yes," he would produce the single kind available, something called "burgundy" or "Chianti."

But as steak houses have prospered and become symbols of the good life, wine lists have grown longer and the selections pricier. Often, in addition, there are sub-lists of beers (imported and esoteric American microbrewery choices that are flavorful and full-bodied enough to accompany fine food), spirits (single-malt Scotch and single-barrel bourbons), and even bottled waters.

While no other steak house can match the four-pound book that contains the listing of wines sold at Bern's in Tampa, perusing the selection at even moderate-price restaurants can be time-consuming and befuddling. And it's even more difficult to choose at wine shops. I cannot propose a surefire formula for buying or ordering wine to accompany steak. I can, however, provide a quick, step-by-step outline of how I make my choices.

Step 1: Someone once wrote that wine's "first duty is to be red," and when it comes to steak, I agree. Let the wine be red. And since steak is a dense, full-flavored meat, I find a relatively heavy, full-bodied wine makes more of an impression than a light red or white wine. If the berry and spice or herbal flavor of the wine complement a steak, the meat will return the favor by softening tannins in young reds, making them seem rounder and more mature.

Step 2: How will the steak be cooked? If it is grilled, a robust red is called for. Broiled and panbroiled steaks have less insistent flavors and tolerate and support wines of some complexity. Braised steak usually has acquired flavors from the marinade and responds best to a hearty, spicy wine. Also, the type of steak makes a difference. A bite of chewy steak is going to be in my mouth longer than a piece of tender filet, so I will pick a sexy wine—one with considerable flavor and aftertaste—with downtown cuts. Temperature is another factor. I prefer light red wine or beer with steak served at room temperature.

Step 3: Is there a sauce? If there is and the sauce is linked to a nation or region, I look for a wine from the same place. Obviously this is easier to do if the sauce is European or American than if it's from Asia, where wine is an oddity. In this case, especially if the sauce or the dish is accented with lively spices, my fallback is to seek balance by choosing a wine that is not very complex and fairly fruity, one that will give an impression of sweetness.

Step 4: How much am I comfortable paying? No one will truly enjoy a wine he or she feels is too dear or overpriced. For me, taking price into consideration helps by narrowing the choice considerably, especially in restaurants. Here are the choices I make after skipping through this process:

♦ With sirloin or T-bone steak grilled over coals or hardwood: Zinfandel, Chianti Classico, Rioja.

♦ With broiled or panfried strip steak: California Cabernet Sauvignon, Merlot, Shiraz or Cabernet-Shiraz.

♦ With roasted or panfried rib or rib-eye steak: California Cabernet Sauvignon, Syrah, Rioja.

♦ With broiled flank or skirt steak: Syrah, Côtes du Rhône, Beaujolais.

♦ With braised round or chuck steak: Barolo, Petite Sirah, Zinfandel.

♦ With sliced cold filet or strip steak: Bordeaux, California Pinot Noir, Beaujolais.

The taste of broiled whole tenderloin or filet steak invariably is dominated by the sauce served with it. Therefore:

♦ With tomato sauce: Chianti or Zinfandel.

♦ With herb-flavored butter sauce: St. Emilion or Merlot.

♦ With mushroom sauce: full-bodied Burgundy, California or Australian Cabernet, Barbaresco or Barolo.

♦ With spicy Asian sauce: Côtes du Rhône, Cabernet Franc, or Barbera.

RIB STEAK
WITH SHALLOT SAUCE

This rather expensive treat was introduced to me by the great French chef Roger Vergé. It is simple to make and offers the unparalleled flavor of steak cooked on the bone without presenting the challenge of having to carve it at the table. I reserve this steak for special occasions, so with it I like to serve Wild Rice with Wild Mushrooms (see Index) and pour a first-quality Cabernet Sauvignon from California, such as a Shafer or Beringer–private reserve.

■ ■

1 rib steak from a standing rib roast
(about 1¾ pounds with bone) cut
2 inches thick
Salt and freshly ground black pepper
3½ tablespoons unsalted butter
⅓ cup minced shallots
2 tablespoons red wine vinegar
2 tablespoons chopped flat-leaf parsley
leaves
1 tablespoon steak sauce, such as A.1.
or Tabasco New Orleans-Style
1 teaspoon minced fresh rosemary
leaves

1. Season the steak generously on both sides with salt and pepper, patting the seasoning into the meat.

2. Heat a heavy skillet, preferably cast iron, over medium heat until hot. Add 1½ tablespoons of the butter. When melted, add the steak and cook until seared and well-crusted on one side, 10 minutes. Turn and cook 9 min-

utes more for rare and 10 minutes more for medium-rare. 11 to 12 minutes per side for medium. Transfer the steak from the pan to a cutting board and cover loosely with aluminum foil.

3. Pour the fat from the pan and wipe it with a paper towel. (Remember the pan is hot!) Return the pan to medium heat and add the remaining 2 tablespoons butter and the shallots. Stir until the shallots soften, about 2½ minutes. Add the vinegar and simmer for 3 minutes more. Add the parsley, steak sauce, and rosemary and simmer 1 minute longer. Keep the sauce warm.

4. Cut the steak from the bone, then cut the meat into ¼-inch-thick strips across the grain. Arrange meat on warm plates.

5. Pour the carving juices into the sauce and bring to a boil, stirring. Spoon sauce over the steak or pour into a sauceboat. Serve at once.

SERVES 2 TO 4

W.R.'S CHICAGO CUT

WITH GIBSONS ROASTING SALT

One of the most popular steak houses in Chicago is Gibsons, a raffish place that has no need to get back to basics because it never let go of them. The drinks are ample, the food is good, and the customers are conversationally inclined. When I suggested in print that it was too bad Chicago—unlike New York and Kansas City—did not have a steak to call its own, owners Steve Lombardo and Hugo Ralli quickly rectified the oversight and introduced a 20-ounce, bone-in rib steak they christened "W.R.'s Chicago Cut." Try it the way they prepare and serve it, seasoned only with a heretofore secret roasting salt and accompanied by Gibsons Hot Pepper Giardiniera. In the restaurant it's a single steak, but that's Chicago. At home, consider it enough for two.

■■■■■■■■■■■■■■■■■■■■■■■■■

1 rib steak with bone (1¼ to 1½
pounds), cut 1¼ inches thick
1 tablespoon vegetable oil, preferably
corn oil
½ teaspoon Gibsons Roasting Salt
(recipe follows)
Gibsons Hot Pepper Giardiniera
(page 201)

1. Preheat the oven to 450°F.

2. Allow the steak to come to room temperature. Pat the steak dry and lightly coat it with oil. Sprinkle ¼ teaspoon of the roasting salt on each side of the steak.

3. Heat a heavy ovenproof skillet over medium-high heat. Place the steak in the pan and cook it until seared and nicely browned on one side, about 2 minutes. Turn and sear the second side, 2 minutes more. Transfer the skillet to the oven and roast the steak for 10 minutes for medium-rare or 12 minutes for medium.

4. Transfer to a cutting board, cover loosely with aluminum foil, and let stand for 5 minutes. Carve the steak into ½-inch-thick slices. Serve with the giardiniera.

SERVES 2

83

GIBSONS ROASTING SALT

Do steak house chefs have secrets? Sure they do. One of chef Mike Clark's secrets at Gibsons is a seasoning mix he uses to start the flavor percolating in his steaks as soon as they hit the grill. At least it's been a secret, until now. I might as well disclose, too, the manner in which he uses it. He combines some of the salt with corn oil and keeps this flavored oil at hand to anoint each steak when its number is called. At home, with usually only a single steak to cook, I coat the steak lightly with oil then sprinkle about 1/4 teaspoon of the roasting salt on each side just before cooking. Use this seasoning on grilled vegetables and seafood as well as steak.

> ½ cup coarse (kosher) salt
> 1 tablespoon dried basil
> 1 tablespoon coarsely ground black
>   pepper
> 2 bay leaves, broken into pieces
> 2¼ teaspoons garlic powder
> 2¼ teaspoons onion powder
> 2¼ teaspoons dried thyme
> ⅛ teaspoon cayenne pepper

Combine the salt, basil, black pepper, bay leaves, garlic powder, onion powder, thyme, and cayenne in a food processor or blender. Blend for 30 seconds. Transfer to a clean jelly jar or two clean spice bottles, cover, and label. Store with your other spices.

MAKES ABOUT ½ CUP

SUCCULENCE AND SIMPLICITY

Steak is part of the same sanguine mythology as wine. It is the heart of meat, it is meat in its pure state; and whoever partakes of it assimilates a bull-like strength.... Like wine, steak is in France a basic element, nationalized even more than socialized. It figures in all the surroundings of alimentary life: flat, edged with yellow, like the sole of a shoe, in cheap restaurants; thick and juicy in the bistros which specialize in it; cubic, with the core all moist throughout beneath a light charred crust, in haute cuisine. It is part of all the rhythms, that of the comfortable bourgeois meal and that of the bachelor's bohemian snack. It is a food at once expeditious and dense, it effects the best possible ratio between economy and efficacy, between mythology and its multifarious ways of being consumed.... Steak is here adorned with a supplementary virtue of elegance, for among the apparent complexity of exotic cooking, it is a food which unites, one feels, succulence and simplicity.

—Roland Barthes, "Steak and Chips," (an essay in the collection *Mythologies*)

RIB-EYE

The rib-eye not only comes from the same impeccable uptown address as the rib steak, it comes without the rib steak's spare tire of fat. Trimmed by the butcher, it is truly the eye of the rib, a boneless cut. Cooked like a filet steak, panbroiled by preference, it emerges with a little more texture and a lot more flavor. As you can see from my Best Ever recipe, Rib-Eye Steak with Pinot Noir Beurre Rouge, this cut is very popular with French chefs and very receptive to sauces. Thanks to its depth of flavor, a rib-eye can keep company with some very zesty seasonings. A sizzling rib-eye takes well to mustard-beer sauce, cracked pepper and roasted onion sauce, or basil and green peppers. This versatile steak can also be served cold with caper sauce. When the exception to the rule is made and the rib-eye is cooked on the bone, try the recipe for W.R.'s Chicago Cut. Dressed in Latin-American flavor, Rib-eye Steak with an Island Accent forgoes the sauce and instead is complemented by the tropical flavors of plantains, black beans, and rice.

RIB-EYE

WITH PINOT NOIR BEURRE ROUGE

Steak, butter, and red wine make a delicious trio. In this presentation, the butter is made into beurre rouge, a pink version of the great fish sauce from Normandy. To fill the plate, serve something simple such as green beans and maybe some cottage fries. With the bottle already open, my choice of wine is self-evident.

3 rib-eye steaks (about 12 ounces each),
   cut ¾ inch thick
3 tablespoons vegetable oil
⅓ cup minced shallots
1 tablespoon red wine vinegar, or to
   taste
1 cup Pinot Noir wine
8 ounces (2 sticks) cold unsalted
   butter, cut into tablespoon-size
   pieces
Salt and freshly ground black pepper,
   to taste

1. Pat steaks dry, then coat them lightly with 2 tablespoons of the oil. Set aside.

2. Combine the shallots and 1 tablespoon vinegar in a small saucepan and bring to a boil over medium-high heat. Cook for 1 minute, then add the wine. Reduce the liquid to a syrupy glaze, 1 to 2 tablespoons. (Recipe may be done up to 1 hour ahead to this point.) Set aside.

3. Heat a large heavy skillet, preferably cast iron, over medium-high heat until hot. Add the remaining 1 tablespoon oil, then add the steaks. Cook until seared and well-crusted on one side, about 4 minutes. Turn and cook 3 minutes more for medium-rare or 4 minutes more for medium. Transfer the steaks to a cutting board and cover loosely with aluminum foil.

4. Reheat the glaze over medium-low heat. Add the butter, 2 pieces at a time, whisking constantly. Work on and off the heat so the butter liquefies without melting. When all the butter has been incorporated into the sauce, season it to taste with salt, pepper, and a little more vinegar. Keep the sauce warm but do not place over direct heat.

5. Cut the steaks into ½-inch slices and salt lightly. Pour ¼ cup of sauce onto each of 4 warm plates and top with slices of steak. Serve at once.

SERVES 4

PANBROILED RIB-EYE
WITH A MUSHROOM COMPOTE

This recipe offers further evidence why great steak cooks favor cast-iron cookware: it transmits heat so evenly and so well. The rib-eyes I used for this recipe were labeled "lean beef," but there was enough fat to keep the meat moist. Consider serving this dish with Fabulous Fried Zucchini (see Index), rice and a Merlot wine from California or Chile's Casa Lapostolle.

■ ■

6 ounces white button mushrooms

1 large red bell pepper, roasted, peeled, and seeded (page 88)

4 scallions, white and 2 inches of green, cut on a diagonal into ½-inch pieces

1 teaspoon mustard seeds, ground

1 teaspoon dried dill

½ teaspoon ground coriander

½ teaspoon coarse (kosher) salt

2 tablespoons olive or vegetable oil

2 rib-eye steaks (about 10 ounces each), cut ¾ inch thick

Salt and freshly ground black pepper, to taste

3 tablespoons plain yogurt

1. If desired, make the compote in the morning or even a day ahead. Cut the mushrooms into quarters, or sixths if large, and set aside. Cut the bell pepper into 2-inch square pieces and transfer to a food processor. Add the scallions. Purée the mixture to the consistency of a fine salsa, about 1 minute. Add the ground mustard seeds, dill, coriander, and coarse salt. Pulse just to incorporate the spices. You should have about ¾ cup sauce.

2. Place a medium-size skillet over medium heat. When warm, add 1 tablespoon of the oil and the mushrooms and sauté until they begin to glisten and give off juice, about 4 minutes. (For fun, toss the mushrooms into the air from time to time. It's safe. They are very obedient.) Turn off the heat, but leave the skillet on the stove. Add the pepper sauce.

3. Heat a cast-iron skillet over medium-high heat until very hot. Pat the steaks dry, then lightly coat with the remaining 1 tablespoon oil. Place in the pan and cook until seared and well-browned, about 4 minutes. Turn, season lightly with salt and pepper, and cook for 4 minutes more for medium-rare.

4. While the steak is cooking, reheat the mushroom mixture over medium heat until bubbling. Off the heat, stir in the yogurt, adjust the seasoning as desired, and spoon onto 2 warmed plates. Add a steak to each plate and serve.

SERVES 2 OR UP TO 4 IF STEAK IS SLICED

ROASTING PEPPERS

Roast peppers one at a time by placing the pepper over a flame on a gas burner, resting it directly on the burner, or place it under a preheated broiler. Turn often with tongs until the pepper is blackened all over. Put the peppers in a paper bag, close it, and let stand until the skin is loosened and the peppers are cool enough to handle, 10 minutes. Use the side of a knife to scrape away the blackened skin, holding the peppers under cold running water, if desired. Cut off the top of each pepper, slit open, and remove the seeds and veins. Use immediately or store, covered, in the refrigerator.

PANGRILLED RIB-EYE
WITH A SWEET-HOT MUSTARD-BEER SAUCE

This recipe and my Beer-Brewed Chuck Steak (see Index) illustrate how different cuts respond best to different methods of cooking. The tougher chuck steak is cooked in beer in the manner of a stew. The rib-eye, on the other hand, is marinated in beer, garlic, and parsley to gain flavor, not tenderness.

Tenderness is a rib-eye's middle name. This steak is then grilled quickly and served with a lively sauce made from sweet-hot mustard and a reduction of the marinade. It's a natural for a person with a craving for steak who is dining alone.

■ ■

1 rib-eye steak (about 12 ounces), cut 1 inch thick
2 tablespoons chopped garlic
2 tablespoons chopped fresh flat-leaf parsley leaves
1/2 teaspoon freshly ground black pepper
1 bottle (12 ounces) beer or ale, or more as needed
Vegetable oil, preferably corn
1/4 cup low-sodium chicken broth
Salt, to taste
2 teaspoons sweet-hot mustard, preferably Inglehoffer

1. Pat the steak dry. Combine the garlic, parsley, pepper, and the bottle of beer in a pan or bowl in which the steak will fit tightly. (I use an 8½-inch loaf pan.) Place the steak in the marinade and add additional beer, if needed, to completely cover the steak. Cover the container with plastic wrap and refrigerate for 4 to 8 hours.

2. Remove the steak from the marinade and pat dry. Coat lightly with 1 tablespoon oil.

3. Strain the marinade into a skillet and add the chicken broth. Bring the liquid to a boil over high heat and reduce to 1/3 cup, about 15 minutes. (Be alert. The carbonation still in the beer will cause it to boil up. Remove the pan from the heat and stir the liquid down before it boils over.)

4. When ready to cook, lightly oil a ridged grill pan or a cast-iron frying pan and heat it over medium-high heat until very hot. Place the steak in the pan and cook it until seared and nicely browned, about 4 minutes. Turn the steak, season the browned side with salt, and cook for 4 minutes more for medium-rare or 5 minutes more for medium.

5. Meanwhile, stir the mustard into the reduced broth and simmer, stirring often, until it thickens. Season with salt. Make a puddle of sauce on 1 or 2 warm serving plates. Serve the steak as it is or cut it into 1/2-inch-thick slices and place on top of the sauce.

SERVES 1 OR 2

TASTING STEAK

The haunting aroma of sizzling steak comes from a combination of the smell of melting fat and the breakdown of protein. This smell, in turn, colors what we taste. (Remember, the nose has veto power. If the aroma is off-putting enough, we won't put the food in our mouth.)

Inside the mouth, while the taste buds are sorting out the four sensations that are their specialty—sweet, sour, bitter, and salty—other members of the jury are at work, too. The teeth quickly detect if the steak is tender or tough. The tongue and sides of the mouth discover if it is juicy or not. Health considerations aside, it's not nearly as rewarding to do this with raw steak as cooked. What we consider meaty flavor develops with the application of heat.

Broil a steak and the moisture driven to the surface of the meat concentrates and changes the meat's color and flavor. Braise or poach meat and it will taste different than if that same cut had been roasted or broiled. Moist-heat flavors tend to be delicate, although the liquid, benefiting from flavor components leached from the meat, may be quite flavorful. Also, steaks from different cuts taste different, even if cooked in the same manner. Dining at home and in restaurants convinced me of that long ago.

But obvious areas of comparison had gone untested by me. I wanted to:

- Taste different grades of the same cut of steak.
- Taste different grades of the same cut cooked fresh and cooked directly from the freezer.

It didn't take much effort to convince the curious cooks at the kitchens of the National Cattlemen's Beef Association in Chicago to arrange just such a test. Marlys Bielunski, director of Test Kitchens and Editorial Services, and I agreed on our favorites and even agreed on the assets and defects of the steaks we tasted.

The big winner was ungraded brand-name steak. The loser was prime. Even in the one category where it was the favorite, the prime steak did not stand apart enough to justify its considerably higher price. The truth, it seems, is that whatever its credentials, steak is not absolutely predictable. It's a natural product subject to variation in taste and texture.

We tasted three flights of steaks. Each flight contained three steaks.

Flights 1 and 2: Prime, choice, and branded boneless top sirloin, fresh and frozen.

Flight 3: Prime, choice, and branded boneless rib-eye steak, fresh.

The branded meat was Maverick Ranch Gold Medal Brand Lean 'n Natural Beef. Also called lite beef, it is range raised and corn-fed. Promotional material says it contains "no detectable residues from chemicals associated with antibiotics, pesticides, and steroids." There's also a call to cook this meat for less time than graded steak.

The grade distinction among the fresh sirloins was readily apparent before cooking. The prime was liberally flecked with fat. There was less flecking in the choice steak. The branded lean steak was larger than the other two and darker in color.

Among the rib-eye steaks, the prime, purchased from a specialty butcher, "lacked prime visuals," meaning the marbling was less extensive than anticipated. There was no lack of fat, though. The steak was less well trimmed than the others and contained a clump of fat. The marbling of the choice and lean steaks was quite similar, with the choice also having less marbling than expected.

The steaks were broiled, 3 to 4 inches from the heat, to medium-rare. The results:

Fresh sirloin: All three had very similar color when cooked, with the amount of juice escaping very similar. The branded lean had an appealing beefy flavor, the choice was very acceptable, and the prime was somewhat disappointing. Probably not worth the difference in price to go for the higher grade.

Prime: Very even texture, not very juicy, pronounced sweet corn flavor.

Choice: Noticeably chewier, also juicier.

Lean: Very similar to the choice. It took longer to cook to medium-rare than the prime, probably because of the larger size.

Frozen sirloin: There were distinctly mixed results in this category, seemingly due more to the variables in beef than to freezing. If broiling steak (1-inch-thick or less) directly from the freezer, turn it twice during cooking.

Prime: Notably softer in texture, more pleasing than the fresh prime steak.

Choice: Grainier, drier than the fresh, not appealing.

Lean: Chewier than the other two, but very acceptable for both taste and texture. Best of this flight and maybe best overall so far.

Fresh rib-eye: The best-tasting cut of the day. Thickness was $1^1/_4$ inches for the lean and $^7/_8$ inch for the other two.

Prime: Quite firm to the tooth, only a rich fatty flavor at the end testified to its lofty grade.

Choice: An unappealing gray-brown, chewier than the prime but agreeably so because it had full flavor and was juicy.

Lean: Best color, probably because it was the thickest and therefore closest to the heat. The most juice, good flavor, and a pleasing aftertaste: The winner again.

RIB-EYE STEAK

WITH TANGY CAPER SAUCE

T he tart flavor of capers accented with tangy condiments will enliven a cooked and sliced steak served at room temperature. Serve with a potato salad or green bean salad or use the sauce as a dressing for a salad of steak and greens.

■ ■

1 rib-eye steak (about 10 ounces), cut 1 inch thick

1/4 cup large capers, drained and chopped

1 teaspoon Dijon mustard

2 teaspoons chopped onion

1/8 teaspoon freshly ground black pepper

1 tablespoon balsamic vinegar, or to taste

1/2 teaspoon Worcestershire sauce

1/2 teaspoon anchovy paste, or to taste

1/4 cup olive oil, preferably extra virgin

2 teaspoons chopped fresh flat-leaf parsley leaves

1. Preheat the broiler.

2. Bring the steak to room temperature and pat it dry. Broil until seared and nicely browned on one side, about 5 minutes. Turn and broil 3 minutes more for medium-rare or 4 minutes more for medium. Transfer the steak to a cutting board and allow it to cool to room temperature.

3. While the steak is cooling, combine the capers, mustard, onion, pepper, 1 tablespoon vinegar, Worcestershire, and 1/2 teaspoon anchovy paste in a small bowl. Stir well. Pouring slowly, whisk in the olive oil. Taste and adjust the seasoning with vinegar or anchovy paste, as desired. Whisk in the parsley. You should have about 1/2 cup sauce.

4. Just before serving, carve the steak into 1/4-inch-thick slices, making sure to cut away any fat. Arrange the steak slices on 2 or 3 plates. Spoon the sauce over the meat and serve.

SERVES 2 OR 3

RIB-EYE STEAK

WITH AN ISLAND ACCENT

During the two years that I lived in Puerto Rico, I came to love the magical combination of black beans and white rice as well as the tropical bananalike vegetable known as plantain. I felt presenting these island ingredients with tender rib-eye steak would make an enticing food marriage, and it does. Pour a Spanish red wine.

■ ■

9 tablespoons olive oil

1½ cups chopped onion

2 teaspoons chopped garlic

2 cups chopped tomatoes, fresh or canned

1 teaspoon cumin seeds, crushed

1½ teaspoons salt

¼ cup chopped fresh flat-leaf parsley leaves

½ cup chopped green bell pepper

2 cans (15 ounces each) black beans, rinsed and drained

½ teaspoon hot pepper sauce, preferably Tabasco

⅔ cup long-grain white rice

1⅓ cups boiling water

2 large, ripe plantains

2 tablespoons unsalted butter

2 rib-eye steaks (about 12 ounces each), cut ¾ inch thick

1. Heat 4 tablespoons of the oil in a large skillet over medium-low heat. Add 1 cup of the onions and 1 teaspoon of the garlic and cook until softened, about 5 minutes. Add the tomatoes, cumin, and 1 teaspoon of the salt. Cook, stirring occasionally, until thickened, about 15 minutes. Remove from the heat and stir in the parsley. Set aside.

2. Heat 2 tablespoons of the remaining oil in a small saucepan over medium-low heat. Add the bell pepper, the remaining ½ cup onions, and the remaining 1 teaspoon garlic. Cook, stirring often, until vegetables are soft, about 7 minutes. Add the black beans, cover, and cook 5 minutes more. Remove from heat, stir in the hot sauce, and set aside. (Recipe may be done ahead to this point. Refrigerate sauce and beans until time for final preparation.)

3. Prepare coals for grilling or preheat a gas grill or the broiler.

4. Heat 1 tablespoon of the remaining oil in a medium-size saucepan over low heat. Add the rice and cook, stirring, for 2 minutes. Add the boiling water and the remaining ½ teaspoon salt. Cover and cook until the liquid is absorbed, 15 to 20 minutes.

5. Rewarm the beans and stir them into the rice. Keep covered and warm. Reheat the tomato sauce over low heat.

6. Peel the plantains, cut each lengthwise into quarters, and cut each quarter into halves for 8 pieces. Heat the remaining 2 tablespoons oil with the butter in a large heavy skillet over medium-low heat. Add the plantains and cook until browned on all sides, about 8 minutes.

7. Grill or broil the steaks until seared and well-crusted on one side, 4 minutes. Turn and cook 3 minutes more for medium-rare or 4 minutes more for medium. Transfer the steaks to a cutting board and let them rest for 5 minutes.

8. Cut the steaks into ½-inch-thick slices and arrange equal amounts of meat on each plate. Add a scoop of rice and beans and 4 pieces of plantain for each serving. Spoon some tomato sauce over the steak slices and serve immediately.

SERVES 4

CRACKED-PEPPER
RIB-EYE STEAK
WITH ROASTED ONION SAUCE

This recipe features two great flavors: black pepper and onion. While the pepper is not as intense as in a True Steak au Poivre (page 15), it still provides a delightfully spicy perfume. As for the onions, instead of appearing in the familiar sautéed or deep-fried form, they are transformed into a sauce with a sweet accent, just right to calm the bite of the pepper.

■■■■■■■■■■■■■■■■■■■■■■■■■

1 medium sweet onion, cut into 8 wedges
1 teaspoon olive oil
Salt, to taste

⅔ cup beef broth
1 teaspoon soy sauce
4 teaspoons cracked black pepper
4 rib-eye steaks (about 10 ounces each), cut ¾ inch thick

1. Preheat the oven to 350°F.

2. Place the onion wedges in a baking dish. Drizzle with the oil and sprinkle with just a little salt. Stir to coat all the pieces evenly. Roast onions, uncovered, until browned and soft, about 1 hour. Remove and let stand until slightly cooled.

3. Put the onions in the blender. Add the broth and soy sauce and blend to a smooth purée. Transfer the sauce to a small saucepan or a microwavable dish, cover and set aside.

4. Preheat the broiler or prepare coals for grilling.

5. Press the cracked pepper onto both sides of each steak, using about 1 teaspoon of pepper for each steak. Broil or grill the steaks until seared and nicely browned on one side, about 4 minutes for medium-rare and 5 minutes for medium. Turn and cook 4 minutes more for both medium-rare and medium.

6. Reheat the onion sauce on the stove top or in a microwave oven while the steaks are cooking. Spoon the warmed sauce over each steak and serve.

SERVES 4

RIB-EYE
WITH BASIL AND GREEN PEPPERS

U sually cooking a steak beyond medium-rare means it will begin to dry out and toughen. Bad luck for those who prefer their meat thoroughly cooked. Yet by searing the meat, then cooking it covered on a bed of vegetables in a hot oven, I've been able to serve a cooked-through steak that is both moist and flavorful. For a vegetable accompaniment, sauté spinach in some of the basil-oil marinade. This recipe will yield a third portion if the steaks are sliced instead of served whole.

CARVING

There is one weapon (literally) that will effect the sensation of tenderness even after a steak is cooked: the carving knife. The knife itself and how sensibly it is used can make the difference between meat that melts in your mouth and a seeming lifetime sentence to chew. While more detailed information about carving appears with specific recipes, the essential knowledge that guides the carver is anatomical.

Muscle fibers run along a piece of meat, not across it, creating what is called the grain. What we want to do is chew with—in the direction of—the grain, which makes it easy for our teeth to sever the fibers.

All you need to carve the meat properly across the grain (and carving a steak presents nowhere near the challenge of carving a bone-in roast such as a leg of lamb) is a sharp knife, a fork, and a cutting board that will contain the juices that escape from the steak. (Play fair and be sure, if you are serving individual steaks instead of slicing them, that your guests have sharp steak knives.)

Uptown steaks are already cut across the grain by the butcher. Therefore, to carve a porterhouse or T-bone, start by cutting the bone away. Freeing it at the base of the T can be tricky. Leave some meat on the bone as a reward for the carver, then reassemble the steak and cut across both portions (and across the grain) to obtain matching slices of tenderloin and top-loin.

Incidentally, usually I do not favor slicing any of the uptown cuts into thin strips unless they are to become part of a sandwich or salad. For serving sliced steak as an entrée, I prefer to cut the meat across the grain into strips at least $1/2$ inch wide.

Also, while chefs in a hurry will tell you steaks and chops do not need to stand before carving, I disagree. In my experience, even a chop will benefit from a few minutes rest before facing the knife. What's the hurry? No steak you would want to eat is hot all the way through. If it were, it would be cooked extra-well.

*2 rib-eye steaks (about 10 ounces
each), cut ¾ inch thick*
½ cup shredded fresh basil leaves
5 tablespoons olive oil
*1 large green pepper, stemmed, seeded,
and cut into ¼-inch-thick strips*
⅓ cup thinly sliced onion
1 tablespoon finely chopped garlic
*2 tablespoons thinly sliced sun-dried
tomatoes, packed in oil*
¼ teaspoon curry powder
*Salt and freshly ground black pepper,
to taste*

1. Pat the steaks dry. Combine ¼ cup of the basil and 3 tablespoons of the oil in a medium dish or bowl. Add the steaks and turn to coat all surfaces. Set aside for 30 minutes to 1 hour, turning the steaks 2 or 3 times.

2. Preheat the oven to 425°F.

3. Combine the remaining 2 tablespoons oil, the pepper strips, onion, garlic, and tomatoes in a deep ovenproof sauté pan. Cook over medium-low heat, stirring often, until peppers begin to soften, about 10 minutes. Add the curry powder, salt, and pepper and stir.

4. Meanwhile, remove the steaks from the oil and pat dry. Coat the bottom of a large heavy skillet with the basil-oil. Heat over high heat until the oil is shimmering and nearly smoking. Add the steaks and sear them for 1 minute on each side. Season with salt and pepper.

5. Place the steaks on top of the vegetables in the sauté pan. Cover the pan and transfer it to the oven. Bake for 10 to 12 minutes.

6. Remove the pan from the oven, place the steaks on warm plates and spoon the vegetables and juices over them. Garnish with the remaining basil and serve at once.

SERVES 2

SIRLOIN

All agree the name sirloin came into usage when a king of England "jocularly knighted," as one historian put it, a baron of beef split in half along the backbone. But who was the king? Credit has been given to Henry VIII (seemingly the only gourmand ever to hold the throne of that gastronomically impoverished nation), Henry II and Charles II. More plausibly, sirloin is a translation of the French term *surlonge,* or top of the loin.

At the market, you'll find sirloin steaks with a round center bone and a long, flat center bone. The one with the flat bone is more tender than that with the round bone. But if you see a sirloin with a mid-sized pin bone, it should be more tender yet. There also may be boneless top sirloin, sometimes called butt steak. It is chewy but may have the best flavor of any loin steak.

I cook a sirloin by broiling, grilling, or panfrying. Since it's a moderately tender cut, it can be marinated or not, depending on your time and inclination. It's also large, so a couple of steaks, sliced will feed a crowd.

My Best Ever sirloin, Wine-Bathed Sirloin, is marinated in red wine, then broiled. Another recipe uses the ingredients of a Bloody Mary for the marinade, with enough left over to make a round of drinks. A third, a butt steak is cooked in a crust of salt. I also slice a sirloin tip roast and poach the slices for a beef salad.

WINE-BATHED SIRLOIN

There are occasions when you know from the make-up of the guest list, that you're going to spend more time talking than cooking when the company arrives. This is a recipe for that situation. Lengthy marination in a red wine-flavored dressing provides all the flavor the steak needs. Just cook and slice it. Serve the steak with two or three made-ahead salads, including Couscous Salad with Plum Tomatoes (page 190), and pour a moderately priced Merlot wine, such as Napa Ridge.

■■■■■■■■■■■■■■■■■■■■■■■■

2 bone-in sirloin steaks (1½ pounds each), cut 1 inch thick
⅔ cup minced onion
½ cup fresh minced flat-leaf parsley leaves
1 tablespoon crushed red pepper
1 cup dry red wine, preferably Merlot
½ cup olive oil
Salt and freshly ground black pepper, to taste

1. Pat the steaks dry and set aside. Combine the onion, parsley, crushed pepper, and wine in a small bowl. Whisk in the oil.

2. Divide the marinade between 2 large plastic storage bags. Place a steak in each bag and close tightly. Place the bags in a baking dish or pan and refrigerate for 4 to 6 hours, turning the bags occasionally.

3. Prepare coals for grilling or preheat the broiler.

4. Remove the steaks from the bags, pat dry, and let them come to room temperature. Grill or broil until browned and well-crusted on one side, about 4 minutes. Turn, season with salt and pepper, and cook for 3 minutes more for medium-rare or 4 minutes more for medium.

5. Transfer the steaks to a cutting board and let rest for 5 minutes. Carve into thin slices and serve at once.

SERVES 6

BLOODY MARY STEAK
AND SAUCE

Watching friends gathered on a patio sipping Bloody Marys while a sirloin cooked on the grill nearby, I found myself pondering a weighty subject: If they like their Bloody Marys so much, and the steak so much, is there a way to combine the two and, in that way, prolong the pleasurable flavors of both? My solution: I make a highly seasoned Bloody Mary mix and use it for a marinade, a sauce, and a round of drinks (see Note following).

■■■■■■■■■■■■■■■■■■■■■■■■

1 bone-in sirloin steak (about
  1¾ pounds), cut ¾ inch thick
⅓ cup Worcestershire sauce
¾ cup fresh lemon juice
2 teaspoons freshly ground black
  pepper
2 teaspoons salt
2 teaspoons celery salt
½ teaspoon hot pepper sauce,
  preferably Tabasco, or to taste
2 tablespoons vodka
2 tablespoons vegetable oil
¾ cup tomato juice
2 teaspoons tomato paste
1 tablespoon water
1 tablespoon cornstarch

1. Bring the sirloin to room temperature and pat it dry.

2. To make the Bloody Mary base, combine the Worcestershire, lemon juice, pepper, salt, celery salt, hot pepper sauce, and vodka in a small bowl; you should have about 1¼ cups. Stir well and combine ⅓ cup of the mixture and the oil in a large dish or bowl. Add the steak and turn to coat both sides. Marinate for 30 minutes at room temperature, turning once. (May be prepared up to 4 hours ahead. Cover and refrigerate until 30 minutes before cooking.)

3. Combine another ⅓ cup of the Bloody Mary base and the tomato juice in a nonaluminum saucepan. Stir in the tomato paste and bring to a simmer over medium heat. Simmer for 5 minutes, stirring often. Remove from the heat and set aside.

4. Ten minutes before serving, make a slurry by stirring the water into the cornstarch in a small bowl. Reheat the sauce to a boil, pour in the slurry, and stir until sauce thickens, 1 minute.

5. Preheat the broiler or prepare coals for grilling.

6. When ready to cook, remove the steak

101

from the marinade and pat dry. Broil or grill the steak until seared and nicely browned on one side, about 4 minutes. Turn and cook for 3 minutes more for medium-rare or 4 minutes more for medium.

7. Transfer the steak to a cutting board, let it rest for 5 minutes, then slice into 1-inch-thick strips. Spoon 2 tablespoons of the sauce onto each of 4 plates; pass the rest in a sauceboat.

SERVES 4

Note: For the drinks, combine the remaining Bloody Mary base with 2 cups additional tomato juice and additional vodka, to taste, in

---

TOMATO PASTE IN TUBES

For those of us who cook in small quantities, it is well worth seeking out tomato paste sold in tubes. The cost per ounce is higher than for canned tomato paste, but you can squeeze out as little as a teaspoon from the tube, screw the top back on, and put it away for another day.

---

a pitcher. Stir and pour over ice in each of four glasses. Garnish with celery or pickled okra.

GRILLED SIRLOIN
WITH GREEK OLIVE BUTTER

The flavors of charcoal, black olives, and ouzo evoke the lively tavernas of Greece. To add to the culinary ambiance at home, offer ouzo as a cocktail, start the meal with a Greek salad, and serve rice pilaf with the steak. Also look for a Greek red wine from Boutari or Boytris.

1 bone-in sirloin steak (about
    1½ pounds), cut 1 inch thick
2 tablespoons olive oil
2 tablespoons coarsely chopped
    imported black olives, preferably
    Kalamata

½ teaspoon dried oregano
1 teaspoon ouzo or other licorice-
    flavored liquor, such as
    Pernod
4 tablespoons (½ stick) unsalted
    butter, at room temperature,
    cut into 4 pieces
Salt, to taste

1. Prepare coals for grilling.

2. Pat the steak dry, coat lightly with the olive oil, and set aside.

3. Combine the olives, oregano, and ouzo in a small bowl and whisk together. Add the butter and continue to whisk until the mixture is homogeneous. Refrigerate for 10 to 15 minutes if the butter is very soft. (Composed butter may be made ahead and stored, covered, in the refrigerator. Return to room temperature before serving.)

4. Grill the steak until seared and nicely browned on one side, about 4 minutes. Turn, salt the meat, and cook for 4 minutes more for medium-rare or 5 minutes more for medium.

5. Transfer the steak to a cutting board, let it rest for 5 minutes, then cut it into 4 serving pieces. Slather 1 tablespoon of the composed butter on each piece and serve.

SERVES 4

JAPANESE-STYLE STEAK
WITH VEGETABLES

The Japanese have a talent for making steak especially appealing by flavoring it with marinades or sauces that contain counterbalancing amounts of sugar and salty soy sauce. In this recipe, fragrant sake is added to give a simple dish an exotic flair. Serve this dish with a Japanese or other Asian beer.

■ ■

*1 boneless sirloin steak (about
    1 pound), cut ¾ inch thick
8 scallions, white and some green
8 ounces napa cabbage
1 cup short-grain rice
4 ounces bean sprouts*

*1 tablespoon sugar
3 tablespoons soy sauce
2 tablespoons sake or dry sherry
1½ tablespoons vegetable oil*

1. Ask the butcher to cut the steak into very thin slices or partially freeze it at home and slice it yourself. Cut the slices crosswise so they

are no more than 2 inches long. Cut the scallions on the diagonal into 1½-inch pieces. Coarsely chop the cabbage. You should have about 2 cups. (The recipe may be prepared ahead to this point. Cover the meat and vegetables with plastic wrap and refrigerate.)

2. Cook the rice according to package directions. While the rice is cooking, place the meat and vegetables, including the bean sprouts, near the stove. Combine the sugar, soy sauce, and sake in a small bowl. Set aside near the stove.

3. Heat an electric frying pan, wok, or large skillet over medium heat. Add the oil, then about half the steak slices. Do not crowd the pan. Stir until the meat changes color, about 1 minute. Move the meat to the side of the pan and cook the remaining steak. Push it to the side. Add the scallions to the pan and stir until they begin to wilt, about 30 seconds. Push to another side, add the cabbage and bean sprouts, and stir until they begin to wilt, about 1 minute.

4. Sprinkle the sugar-soy mixture over the meat and vegetables, keeping them separate. Cook for 1 minute, stirring liquid into each ingredient.

5. Spoon the rice into 4 bowls or soup plates and top with equal portions of the meat and vegetables. Bring the liquid in the pan to a boil, reduce for 1 minute, and pour some over each portion. Serve at once.

SERVES 4

STEAK AND NOODLES
VIETNAMESE STYLE

The audience for Vietnamese food, often so complex and haunting, is growing in this country. Scanning the menu at a Vietnamese restaurant reveals the frequent mating, in soups and salads, of beef and noodles. In Vietnam, as elsewhere in Asia, noodles made from rice flour are popular. Available at Asian markets and health food stores, they come in various widths. For this recipe, flat noodles about the width of fettuccine noodles are best. You could, in a pinch, substitute regular wheat-flour pasta, but be warned—it won't taste very Asian. Even though the meat is beef, an off-dry white wine such as Riesling or Chenin Blanc works here.

½ cup chopped onions

1 stick (about 3 inches) cinnamon

4 tablespoons soy sauce

¼ teaspoon crushed red pepper flakes

3 cups low-sodium chicken broth

4 slices fresh ginger, each the size of a
    25-cent piece

2 cloves garlic, crushed with the side
    of a knife

1 boneless sirloin steak (about
    1 pound), cut ½ inch thick

1 teaspoon minced ginger

1 teaspoon minced garlic

1 teaspoon sugar

1 teaspoon fresh lemon juice

½ teaspoon Worcestershire sauce

¼ teaspoon dry mustard

¼ teaspoon freshly ground white
    pepper

3 tablespoons rice vinegar

2 tablespoons sesame oil

8 ounces banh pho (flat rice stick
    noodles)

2 tablespoons vegetable oil

2 ounces snow peas, cooked and
    chopped (about ¾ cup)

⅔ cup chopped scallions

½ cup rinsed and coarsely chopped
    water chestnuts (from a 4-ounce can)

1 medium carrot, peeled and shaved
    into strips with a vegetable peeler

1. Combine the onion, cinnamon stick, 2 tablespoons of the soy sauce, red pepper flakes, chicken broth, sliced ginger, and crushed garlic in a 10-inch sauté pan or other pan just large enough to hold the steak. Bring the liquid to a boil over high heat, lower the heat, and simmer until the onions are soft, about 10 minutes.

2. Pat the steak dry, place it in the broth, and poach it at a bare simmer, turning once, until cooked to medium, 8 minutes. Remove the pan from the heat and leave the steak in the broth until cool.

3. Meanwhile, combine the remaining 2 tablespoons soy sauce, minced ginger, minced garlic, sugar, lemon juice, Worcestershire, dry mustard, white pepper, vinegar, and sesame oil in a small bowl. Stir and set aside.

4. Transfer the steak to a cutting board; reserve the broth. Cut the steak across the grain into ¼-inch-thick slices. Cut the slices into 2-inch pieces.

5. Strain the broth, return it to the pan, and bring to a boil. Add the noodles to the broth and simmer for 2 minutes. Pour the noodles and broth into a colander set over a bowl. Save the broth for soup or another dish.

6. Transfer the noodles to a large bowl, add the vegetable oil, and toss. Add the steak, snow peas, scallions, water chestnuts, and carrot strips and toss to combine. Stir the reserved sauce, pour it over the salad, and toss again. Serve at room temperature.

SERVES 6

BUTT STEAK

BRAISED IN BARBECUE SAUCE

I f a little barbecue sauce added late is good for a steak, I reasoned, a lot added early should be better. And it is! This may be the easiest recipe in this book. If you want to make it more complicated, fashion a barbecue sauce to call your own (page 175).

■ ■

1 sirloin butt (boneless top sirloin)
    steak (about 12 ounces),
    cut 1¼ inches thick
1 cup commercial barbecue sauce,
    such as K.C. Masterpiece hickory
1 tablespoon vegetable oil
¼ cup water
Soft white bread, hamburger rolls, or
    steamed brown rice

1. Pat the steak dry and place it in an 8-inch square baking dish. Add the barbecue sauce, coating both sides generously, and cover the dish with plastic wrap. Refrigerate for 2 hours, or marinate at room temperature for 1 hour, turning once.

2. Preheat the oven to 350°F.

3. Lightly coat the bottom of a skillet with oil and heat the skillet over medium-high heat. Remove the steak from the dish, scraping sauce from the steak back into the dish. Pat the steak dry, place it in the skillet, and cook until brown, about 2 minutes. Turn and sear

the second side for 2 minutes. Meanwhile, add the water to the marinade and stir to mix well.

4. Return the steak to the baking dish, spooning sauce over the top and sides to encase it in the sauce. Bake until cooked to medium, 35 to 45 minutes, turning the steak once.

5. Transfer the steak to a cutting board. Stir the sauce and keep warm. Carve the steak into slices ¼ inch thick or thinner. Place on bread, inside rolls, or on top of the rice and cover with sauce. Serve at once.

SERVES 3 OR 4

CHARLIE'S
BUTT STEAK

E ven food purists have learned not to ignore back-of-the-box recipes. They may be self-serving for the manufacturers, but they also can be astonishingly tasty. I bit on one that appeared on a box of Morton's coarse (kosher) salt. It was for herbed beef in a salt crust and seemed to fill the gaps in a recipe from Charles H. Baker's *The Gentleman's Companion* that I'd long admired but never tried to make. A cup-and-a-half of salt later, Charlie's Butt Steak was encrusted in salt and in the oven. I recommend horseradish oil with this and mashed potatoes. The wine should be fruity and spicy, a Côtes du Rhône, Châteauneuf-du-Pape, or perhaps a Zinfandel from Sonoma County.

■ ■

⅓ cup olive oil
¼ cup grated onion
1 teaspoon garlic salt
1 teaspoon dried basil
½ teaspoon dried oregano
½ teaspoon dried thyme
¼ teaspoon freshly ground black pepper
1 sirloin butt (boneless top sirloin)
*   steak (about 12 ounces),*
*   cut 1¼ inches thick*
1½ cups coarse (kosher) salt
½ cup cold water
Infused Horseradish Oil
*   (recipe follows; optional)*

1. Pour the olive oil, onion, garlic salt, basil, oregano, thyme, and pepper into a Ziploc bag. Mix well. Pat the steak dry, place it in the bag, and massage the marinade over the meat. Close the bag tight, place it on a plate, and refrigerate for 6 to 8 hours, turning at least twice.

2. Preheat the broiler and set the broiler pan or rack about 3 inches from the heating unit.

3. Take the steak from the marinade. Pat it dry, but don't fuss too much over removing bits of onion or herbs. Set the steak in the middle of a baking sheet or other pan (a pizza pan, perhaps) that will fit under the broiler.

4. Pour 1 cup of the salt into a small bowl. Add about ¼ cup of the water, just enough to make a paste the texture of packable sand. Mound this paste over and around the steak. Place the steak under the broiler and cook until the top is firm, cracked, and starting to brown, about 10 minutes.

5. Meanwhile, combine the remaining ½ cup salt and 2 tablespoons or a bit more water to

make more paste. Remove the pan from the broiler. Turn the steak, push the salt that falls away back in place, and coat the second side with the new paste. Broil until brown in spots and cracked, about 10 minutes. Remove from the broiler.

6. Crack the salt casing, quickly rinse the steak under warm running water to remove any remaining salt, pat dry, and transfer to a cutting board. Carve into slices no more than $1/8$ inch thick and serve. Pass the horseradish oil in a cruet to drizzle on the steak, if desired.

SERVES 2

INFUSED HORSERADISH OIL

Beef and horseradish are a marvelous combination, and by infusing oil with the bite and flavor of horseradish you have a condiment that will enliven sliced steak, hot or cold, served by itself or in salads or sandwiches. Try it, too, on steamed new potatoes, green vegetables, or smoked fish.

3 ounces fresh horseradish root
$1/2$ cup olive oil
$1/2$ cup vegetable oil, preferably corn
1 tablespoon fresh lemon juice
$1/4$ teaspoon salt

1. Peel the horseradish root and cut it into small pieces. Turn on a food processor and drop the pieces through the feed tube, a few at a time, and process until evenly ground.

2. Combine the olive and vegetable oils, and with the machine running, pour through the feed tube in a steady stream. Add the lemon juice and salt. Pour the horseradish oil into a jar, cover tightly, and refrigerate for 8 hours or overnight.

3. Line a strainer with dampened cheesecloth. Place the strainer over a bowl and pour the oil into the strainer. Refrigerate the bowl and the strainer for about 4 hours to allow all the oil to drain into the bowl. Discard the contents of the strainer. Refrigerate the oil, tightly covered, for up to 2 weeks. Return to room temperature before using.

MAKES ABOUT $3/4$ CUP

SIRLOIN KEBABS
WITH YOGURT SAUCE

Mention the Mediterranean, meat, and yogurt and everyone thinks lamb. But the Greeks, with their superb olive oil and magnificent lemons, perfected many marinades and often use a quantity of onion along with the oil and lemon to tenderize beef. Serve this meat along with a yogurt sauce, Wild Rice with Wild Mushrooms (page 212), and one of the much-improved dry red wines from a progressive Greek producer such as Boutari. For a family meal, cook the marinade until the onions are soft. Spoon the mix onto pita bread along with some of the yogurt sauce and two or three pieces of the steak, cut into thinner pieces.

■ ■

1 large onion, cut into thin slices

¼ cup chopped fresh flat-leaf parsley leaves

3 sprigs of fresh thyme, coarsely chopped, or ½ teaspoon dried thyme leaves

½ teaspoon freshly ground black pepper

¼ cup julienned fresh basil leaves

¼ cup fresh lemon juice

¼ cup red wine

¼ cup olive oil

¼ cup vegetable oil

2 boneless sirloin steaks (about 1½ pounds each), cut 1 inch thick

2 lemons, each cut into 9 slices

18 bay leaves

36 whole fresh basil leaves

Salt, to taste

Yogurt Sauce (recipe follows)

1. Combine the onion, parsley, thyme, pepper, and julienned basil in a medium-size stainless steel or glass bowl. Combine the lemon juice, wine, olive oil, and vegetable oil in a small bowl. Stir well, pour over the onions and herbs, and stir until well mixed.

2. Cut the steaks into 1 x 1½ x 1½-inch pieces, cutting away fat and gristle. You should have about 30 pieces. Toss the steak pieces with the marinade, cover the bowl with plastic wrap, and refrigerate for 6 to 8 hours, turning the meat at least once.

3. When ready to cook, thread the meat onto 6 metal skewers. Start each skewer with a bay leaf, then alternate each piece of meat with either a lemon slice, basil leaf, or bay leaf, so that each piece has a flavoring agent on each side. Each skewer should have 3 bay leaves, 3 lemon slices, and 6 basil leaves spread evenly among the meat pieces. Set aside on a platter.

4. Prepare coals for grilling or preheat the broiler.

5. Cook the kebabs until one side is seared and nicely browned, about 4 minutes, then give each skewer a quarter turn every 2 minutes. Move skewers from the center to the edge of the grill or broiler pan as needed so the meat cooks evenly until it is medium-rare, about 10 minutes, or medium, about 11 minutes.

6. Remove the meat from the skewers, season with salt, and serve with the yogurt sauce.

SERVES 6 TO 8

YOGURT SAUCE

2 cups plain lowfat yogurt
2 tablespoons chopped fresh flat-leaf
parsley leaves
3 tablespoons shredded fresh basil
leaves
½ cup diced onion, preferably red
onion
1 teaspoon fresh lemon juice
Salt and freshly ground black pepper,
to taste

Combine the yogurt, parsley, basil, and onion in a small bowl. Whisk until well combined. Add the lemon juice and salt and pepper. Whisk well. Cover the bowl with plastic wrap and refrigerate until ready to serve.

MAKES ABOUT 2½ CUPS

BEEF SALAD
WITH THAI SEASONINGS

This is a mainstream dish, steak and cabbage, made intriguing by blending salt and sweet and tart flavorings in the manner of Thai cooks. Cut thin and poached, the beef emerges tender and flavorful with no added fat. Serve this as part of a buffet. Only the fish sauce requires a trip to a specialty food store or Asian market. Once purchased it keeps nearly forever and will inspire experiments with other Thai and Vietnamese dishes, such as Asian Beef Salad with Cucumbers (see Index). I use relatively mild jalapeños in this recipe, adding a few of the seeds when I want extra zing.

■ ■

1 sirloin tip roast (1 to 1¼ pounds)

2 tablespoons Thai fish sauce
    (nam pla; see Note)

3 tablespoons fresh lemon juice

1½ teaspoons sugar

½ cup beef or chicken broth

1 medium shallot, sliced thin and
    broken into rings

4 scallions, white and 3 inches of
    green, cut on the diagonal into
    ½-inch pieces

2 jalapeños, stemmed, seeded, and cut
    into fine dice

½ cup fresh mint leaves, torn into
    small pieces

2 tablespoons vegetable oil

1 small head bok choy or a
    combination of red radicchio and
    bean sprouts, coarsely chopped
    (about 4 cups)

1. Wrap the sirloin in plastic wrap and chill in the freezer until firm but not frozen, 2½ to 3 hours. Using an electric carving knife or a serrated knife, slice as thin as possible. Cut the slices into 2-inch strips. Set aside.

2. Combine the fish sauce, lemon juice, sugar and broth in a large skillet. Combine the shallot, scallions, jalapeños, and mint in a medium-size bowl. Place the bowl near the stove.

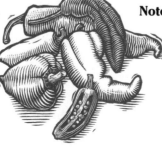

3. Bring the liquid in the skillet to a boil over medium heat. Add the beef strips without overcrowding the pan. Cook just until the beef loses its red color, turning the strips once, 1 to 1½ minutes. Use kitchen tongs to transfer the cooked beef to the bowl with the shallot mixture. Toss briefly. Add more beef strips to the skillet and repeat the process until all the meat is cooked.

4. Pour the cooking juices into a measuring cup and set aside. You should have ¼ to ⅓ cup. Return the skillet to the stove and raise the heat to medium-high. Add the oil, then the bok choy. Sauté, stirring often, only until it begins to soften, about 3 minutes.

5. Transfer the bok choy to the center of a serving platter. Arrange the beef strips around the bok choy. Pour the juices left in the bowl into the cooking juices. Taste and adjust seasoning. Pour over the cabbage and meat. Serve warm or at room temperature.

SERVES 4

Note: Thai fish sauce (nam pla) is available in Asian markets, specialty food stores, and some supermarkets.

TEXAS-STYLE CHILI

T his recipe is adapted from the one given to me by Anne Lindsay Greer, a Texas-based author and restaurant consultant. The ancho chilies, with hints of chocolate and tobacco, and the masa harina thickener give this stew an authentic border taste and texture. My beverages of choice are beer or sparkling wine.

∎∎∎∎∎∎∎∎∎∎∎∎∎∎∎∎∎∎∎∎∎∎∎∎∎

5 to 6 pounds boneless sirloin tip

1/4 cup vegetable oil, or more as
    needed

6 cloves garlic, minced

2 large onions, chopped

3 cups hot water, or more as
    needed

1 1/2 cups tomato sauce

1 bottle (12 ounces) beer or ale

12 ancho chilies

2 to 3 tablespoons ground cumin

1 tablespoon chopped fresh oregano
    leaves or 1 teaspoon dried oregano

1 1/2 tablespoons masa harina

3 tablespoons cider vinegar

1 teaspoon salt, or to taste

2 or 3 medium jalapeños, stemmed,
    seeded, and diced (optional)

2 ounces Longhorn Cheddar cheese,
    grated, for garnish (optional)

1 large sweet onion, diced,
    for garnish (optional)

2 1/2 cups cooked and seasoned
    (or canned, rinsed, and drained)
    pinto beans, for garnish (optional)

1. Trim the fat from the beef and cut it into 1/2-inch cubes. Heat the oil in a Dutch oven over medium-high heat until hot. Working in batches, brown the beef cubes on all sides, 4 to 5 minutes for each batch. Transfer the browned cubes to a colander to drain. Add additional oil, if needed.

2. When all the meat is browned, add the garlic and onions to the pot and sauté over medium heat until the onions soften, 4 to 5 minutes. Return the meat to the pot along with the hot water, tomato sauce, beer, ancho chilies, cumin, oregano, and masa harina. Lower the heat and simmer, covered, for 1 hour.

3. Uncover the pot and cook, stirring frequently, until the chilies have broken apart and the stew has thickened somewhat, 15 to 20 minutes. The chili should have enough liquid to make a rich broth. If necessary, add more hot water. Add the vinegar, salt, and jalapeños, to taste, if you'd like a hotter chili. Serve the chili and, if desired, pass the cheese, onions, beans, and remaining jalapeños.

SERVES 10 TO 12

CHUCK WAGON AND BOARDING HOUSE DINING IN THE WILD WEST

With men in uniform otherwise occupied, cattle herds proliferated during the Civil War. At war's end there were more cattle in Texas than any state in the Union. Between these cows and consumers east of the Mississippi there was land—lots of land (open range, luckily).

But people wanted steak and enough profit was to be had to make a good many entrepreneurs very hungry. Furthermore, the prospect of new stockyard facilities in Kansas and Missouri and Nebraska as the railroads stretched westward made the dream of driving the Longhorn cattle from grazing land to railhead feasible, if just barely. It meant moving as many as 2,000 head a thousand miles, which took about three months. (More than 200,000 head were driven north in the year immediately after the war ended, with the price per steer nearly doubling between the railhead and New York City.)

Getting them to the stockyards was the task of a caste of men who became, along with jazz musicians in the next century, America's great contribution to labor folklore. Called cowboys, they combined Mexican riding skills with new techniques of roping, branding, and herding. They were raucous and aggressive and mostly young men, who dressed like dandies when in town and shot off pistols to attract attention—the "brat pack" of the nineteenth century.

(continued)

113

On trail drives "the foreman was the stud. Next in rank was the cook," writes a former cowboy in *Home on the Range, A Culinary History of the American West* by Cathy Luchetti, an altogether wonderful collection of vignettes. "By tradition the cook was a single man, ornery, with a reputation for pettiness, peevishness, and temperamental displays of anger."

WHO DID WHAT

The cook cooked. He functioned from a "chuck box," and rode in a "chuck wagon" equipped with canned and dried supplies, a worktable, knives, hooks, cast-iron skillets, Dutch ovens, and logs for cooking. Others did chores for him, ranging from harnessing horses to the cook wagon and chopping wood to peeling potatoes. He did not collect or clean used plates and cups, which the cowboys had to scrape and drop into a communal "wreck pan." The cook dished up "chuck" for men whose "strong prejudices often included a hatred of mutton, raw greens, or rare meat." (Eating mutton was considered disloyal to their role as cowhands.)

The filet of the frontier was "mallet-softened" chicken-fried steak, served with freshly baked biscuits and beans and followed by canned peaches. Usually a beef was killed every third day and eaten fresh. The steers were tough from exercise, and so was their meat. One method of tenderizing was to roll the meat in a bedroll and hang it from a tree, cutting off steaks as they were needed. "Son of a bitch" stew contained the bone marrow of a mature cow plus peppers and potatoes.

Jerked beef, often served at ranches, was meat cut into strips and hung from ropes to dry while a smudge pot burned to keep flies away. The beef might be fried or boiled into a stew called a "jowler."

The cowboys' meat was cooked, like almost everything else, in cast-iron Dutch ovens. They liked their steaks fried in fat in the manner of this buffalo steak recipe from an unnamed chuck wagon cook: "Render some fat in a hot skillet. Add sirloin of buffalo steak and sear on both sides. Cook as beefsteak at a lower heat until done. Thicken juices with flour and cook gravy until thick. Thin with water or milk and bring to a boil with salt."

THE BOARDING HOUSE

Meanwhile, travelers who stopped at frontier-town hotels and town folk who lived in boarding houses endured a somewhat different regimen. In hotels and boarding houses, the guests ate in a "frenzied manner," often spending only a few minutes at the dining table. They also came to table early and promptly, in part due to the boarding house practice of putting all the food out at once. There was likely to be nothing left for a late-comer who hadn't been there at the moment of serving to claim his share. If all this haste weren't enough, Frances Trollope, the English traveler, complained about Westerners eating with their knives.

Beefsteak was served, but not in profusion. It had to compete with often more accessible and cheaper meat from game, ranging from venison, elk, and buffalo, to prairie dog. And every part of the animal got into the act. The "Texas meats" on a menu would turn out to be offal—sweetbreads, spleen, and the like, plus marrow.

In mining towns, those who struck it rich preferred fresh, unaged beef "off the hoof." In addition, in a preview of twentieth century Las Vegas, both the rich and would-be rich gorged on lavish free lunches in competing saloons. There was a craving for culture and "continental-style dining," which prompted a traveler to write, "Every broken-down barber, or disappointed dancing master . . . sets up as a cook."

A "willing arm and the ability to simply show up" could assure a man a job. Cooks who had "marginal" cooking skills, were considered unreasonably temperamental, and footloose. For women, at the same time, cooking in a boarding house was a respectable job.

LOGGING CAMPS

Logging camps were a world of their own. Loggers demanded, and got, better ingredients, a real cook, and a separate cookhouse.

From the earliest days in the then "new" West, meat enticed the hungry. Captain Frederick Marryat, a refugee from France exploring California in the 1830s, offers vivid testimony. His party sleeps, exhausted:

I found it was no easy matter to awake them. At last, I hit upon an expedient that did not fail; I stuck the ramrod of my gun into a smoking piece of meat, and held it so that the fumes should rise under their very noses. No fairy wand was ever more effective; in less than two minutes they all were chewing and swallowing their breakfast.

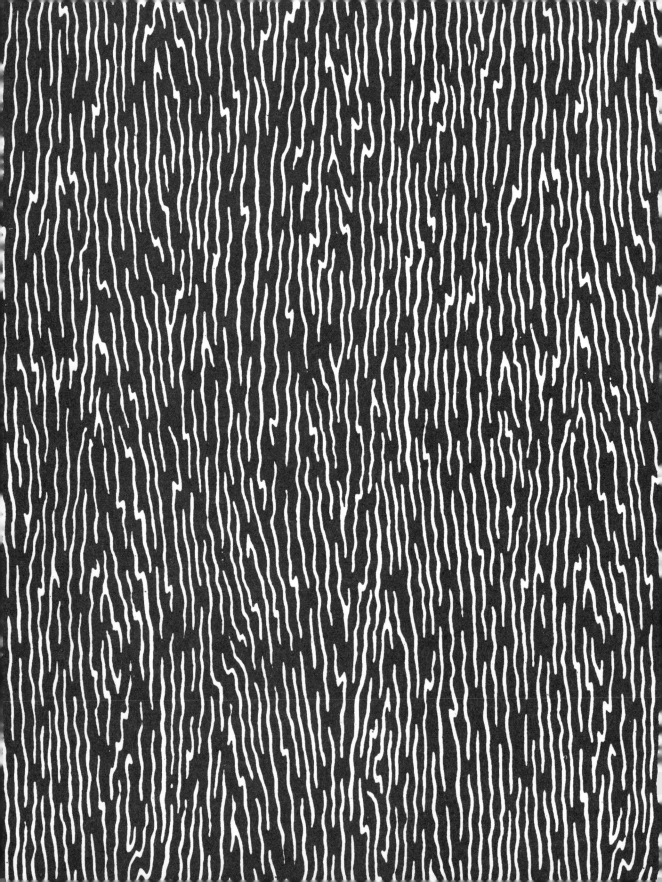

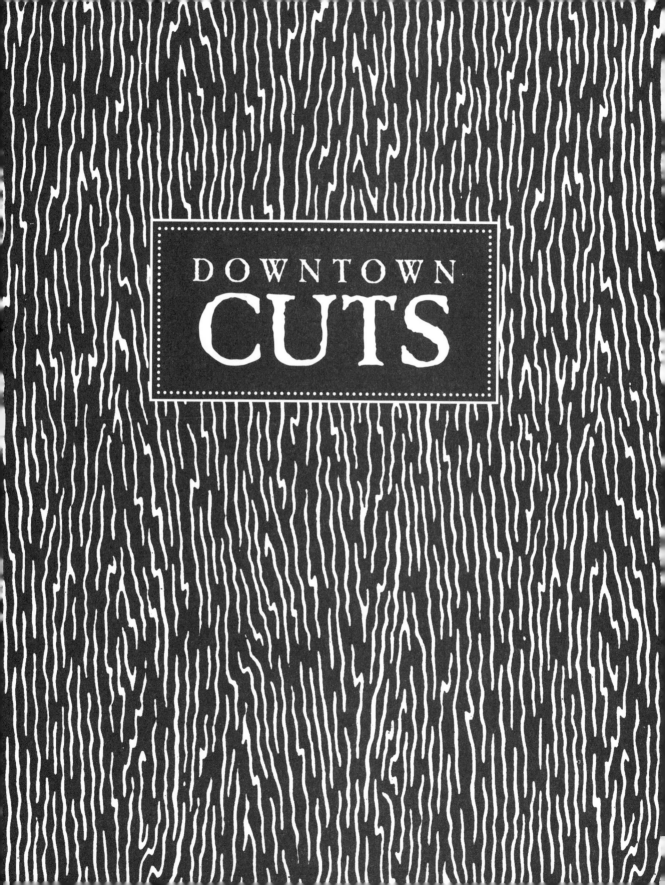

C huck is certainly best known as ground chuck, to me the most flavorful type of hamburger meat, but chuck deserves recognition as more than a character actor. It has the most complex bone and muscle of all the cuts, yielding more than half-a-dozen different steaks. The most important, from the top of the cut downward, are blade steak (bone-in), shoulder steak (boneless), arm steak (bone-in), and one called merely chuck steak (bone-in or boneless). Add to these seven-bone, under-blade, mock tender, and chuck eye and your refrigerator or freezer will be very full.

All these steaks have excellent flavor and good, if sometimes fibrous, texture. They can be cut thick or thin and broiled or roasted successfully, especially if marinated. But the Best Ever way to cook chuck steaks is to braise them.

Braising represents a three-pronged approach to cooking meat. First, the meat surfaces are seared in a pan. Then liquid—generally a small amount—is added to the pot or pan and brought to a boil. The heat is lowered, the pot or pan covered tightly, and the simmering liquid both poaches and steams the meat. This may be done on top of the stove or in a slow oven. Meat also may be braised and steamed in a pressure cooker.

With the temperature just below 212°F, braising is a less heat-intense method than roasting. Therefore the meat can cook for a long period of time and become tender without burning. Beware, however, of the liquid heating to a boil. Prolonged boiling can only render the meat dry and hard. Braising is the preferred way to cook a cut such as the deliciously tender chuck eye, often called a "beauty steak." Beauty steak is a coined term for the chuck eye steak, a prize part of the chuck. It's frowned on by the National Cattlemen's Beef Association, but the butcher who coined it did have an eye for beauty.

The Beauty Steak Braised with Mushrooms is my Best Ever recipe. After cooking it, take a tour of the chuck neighborhood by trying Homage to Pot Roast, made with boneless blade steak, and Baked Steak with Pan Gravy using an arm steak.

BRAISED BEAUTY STEAK
WITH MUSHROOMS

This is a method I devised for making lean beef both tender and tasty. Faced with a boneless chuck eye and not a lot of time to cook it on the day of serving, I decided to combine the traditional tenderizing methods of marinating and braising. (Braising means allowing the meat to barely swim in the cooking liquid, not drown in it; that technique is called poaching.) The marinated and seared meat emerges from its bath almost, but not quite, fork tender, a good match for the aromatic and meaty mushroom slices. For an extra taste fillip I sometimes use Consorzio mushroom oil (see Note) in place of plain oil. Serve with mashed potatoes, a green vegetable such as broccoli, and a glass of Pinot Noir.

■ ■

¼ cup vegetable oil
1 tablespoon fresh lemon juice
1 tablespoon bourbon
2 cloves garlic, coarsely chopped
½ teaspoon freshly ground black pepper
1 pound boneless chuck eye, cut about
*   1 inch thick*
2 portobello mushrooms (4 ounces each)
1 cup beef broth
2 tablespoons olive oil
Salt and freshly ground black pepper,
*   to taste*

1. Combine the vegetable oil, lemon juice, bourbon, garlic, and pepper in a nonreactive bowl or baking pan just large enough to hold the steak. Stir well, and add the steak. Cover with plastic wrap and refrigerate for 4 to 8 hours, turning the steak at least once.

2. About 30 minutes before cooking, remove the bowl from the refrigerator. Transfer the steak to a cutting board and pat dry.

3. Cut the stems from the mushrooms. Trim away the bottoms of the stems, then cut the rest of the stems into medium dice. You should have about ½ cup. Put the diced stems in a small saucepan, cover with the beef broth, and bring to a simmer. Cover the pan and keep warm over very low heat.

121

4. Heat a 10-inch heavy pan, preferably cast iron over medium-high heat. When hot, add 1 tablespoon of the olive oil. Add the steak and sear until nicely browned on one side, about 4 minutes. Turn the steak and sear the other side, about 4 minutes more. Pour in beef broth with the mushroom stems. Bring the liquid to a boil, lower the heat to a simmer, and cover the pan. Braise the steak for 8 minutes, turn, and braise for 7 minutes more. The steak will be cooked through but still very moist.

5. Meanwhile, cut the mushroom caps into large dice. Heat the remaining 1 tablespoon of olive oil in a sauté pan, add the diced mushroom caps, and sauté over medium heat until just softened, about 5 minutes. Lightly season with salt and pepper and keep warm.

6. Transfer the steak from the broth to a cutting board. Strain the braising liquid, then return it to the pan. Reduce the braising liquid to $3/4$ cup over high heat, 4 to 5 minutes.

7. Cut the steak into 1-inch-thick slices. Lightly salt and pepper the meat, if desired, and place on warm plates. Scatter diced mushroom caps over the meat and moisten with 2 or 3 tablespoons of the braising liquid. Pass remaining braising liquid in a sauceboat.

SERVES 3 OR 4

Note: Consorzio flavored oils are handsomely packaged products from California. These fragrant oils provide a new flavor dimension when used to coat steaks that will be grilled, broiled, or panfried. Flavors especially compatible with steak include roasted garlic, five-pepper, and porcini mushroom.

BEEFSTEAK CLUB RULES

While equipment has improved dramatically, the craft—dare I call it an art?—of steak cookery has changed very little over the years. Here are the cooking rules of an English organization called the "Beefsteak Club," circa 1734. There also was a Beefsteak Club in the colonies.

HOW TO COOK A BEEFSTEAK

Pound well your meat until the fibers break;
Be sure that next you have, to broil the steak,
Good coal in plenty; nor a moment leave,
But turn it over this way and then that.
The lean should be quite rare—not so the fat;
The platter now and then the juice receive.
Put on your butter—place it on your meat—
Salt, pepper; turn it over serve and eat.

JERK BEAUTY STEAK

The Caribbean flavoring mixture known as "jerk" can be painfully spicy. This is a gentler jerk, call it a tug or a nudge, but it's nonetheless tasty for that. Serve the steaks with rice, a sautéed green vegetable such as okra, and very cold beer.

■■■■■■■■■■■■■■■■■■■■■■■■■■

4 small green chilies, preferably
   finger chilies or serrano chilies
2 teaspoons ground allspice
½ teaspoon ground cinnamon
⅛ teaspoon freshly grated nutmeg
1½ teaspoons paprika
1 teaspoon salt
½ teaspoon freshly ground black
   pepper
4 scallions, white part and
   2 inches of green, cut into
   ½-inch-long pieces
2 tablespoons cider vinegar
1 tablespoon vegetable oil
2 to 4 boneless chuck eye beauty
   steaks (about 8 ounces each),
   cut ¾ inch thick

1. Cut off the stems and tips of the chilies, then cut them lengthwise in half. Remove seeds and veins and set aside. Cut the chilies into small pieces. You should have about 2 tablespoons.

2. Measure the allspice, cinnamon, nutmeg, paprika, salt, and pepper into a food processor. Add the chilies and scallions. Process for 20 seconds. Scrape down the sides of the bowl with a rubber spatula, add the vinegar and oil, and process for 20 seconds more, or until the mixture forms a paste. You should have about ⅓ cup. Taste the mixture and if desired, add ½ teaspoon or more of the reserved chili seeds and veins to increase the heat level.

3. Paint each steak on both sides with 2 tablespoons of the jerk mixture. (1½ tablespoons if preparing 4 steaks.) Place on a plate or platter, cover with plastic wrap, and refrigerate for 2 to 4 hours.

4. About 30 minutes before cooking, remove the steaks from the refrigerator and prepare coals for grilling or preheat the broiler.

5. Grill or broil the steaks until seared and well-crusted on one side, about 5 minutes. Turn and cook 4 minutes more for medium-rare or 5 minutes for medium. If desired, thin the remaining paste with water to a sauce consistency, heat, and pass at the table.

SERVES 2 TO 4

GRILLED BEAUTY STEAK

WITH DARK BEER SAUCE

New York chef Larry Forgione developed this steak sauce for an uptown cut of beef—tenderloin—to be served at his An American Place restaurant. I find this very flavorful marinade and resulting sauce to be just right for a less expensive downtown cut from the chuck. I think you will agree. Serve with noodles or rice and beer or a fruity Italian red wine such as Barbera.

■■■■■■■■■■■■■■■■■■■■■■■■

12 ounces dark beer

1½ cups beef broth

1 can (14½ ounces) diced tomatoes, drained

¼ cup chopped fresh flat-leaf parsley leaves

1 teaspoon chopped fresh thyme leaves or ½ teaspoon dried thyme

1 bay leaf

1 teaspoon Worcestershire sauce

5 drops of hot pepper sauce, preferably Tabasco

½ teaspoon freshly ground black pepper

½ teaspoon salt

4 chuck eye beauty steaks, (about 8 ounces each), cut ¾ inch thick

3 tablespoons vegetable oil

Salt and freshly ground black pepper, to taste

*4 tablespoons (½ stick) **unsalted** butter, at room temperature*

1. Combine the beer, broth, tomatoes, parsley, thyme, bay leaf, Worcestershire, pepper sauce, black pepper, and salt in a nonreactive dish large enough to hold the steaks in a single layer. Stir to mix. Place the steaks in the marinade, cover, and refrigerate for 3 to 6 hours, turning the meat once.

2. Prepare coals for grilling.

3. Remove the steaks from the marinade and pat dry. Pour the marinade into a medium saucepan, bring to a boil, and simmer and reduce the liquid to 2 cups, 15 to 20 minutes.

4. Rub the steaks with a little vegetable oil and salt and pepper. Grill the steaks until seared and well-crusted on one side, about 4 minutes. Turn and cook 4 minutes more for medium-rare or 5 minutes for medium. Remove from the grill to a cutting board.

5. To finish the sauce, remove the bay leaf from reduced marinade. Stir in the softened butter, 1 tablespoon at a time, over low heat, stirring constantly until the butter is completely incorporated into the sauce.

6. Cut each steak into slices, then spoon ¼ cup of the sauce onto each of 4 warm plates. Arrange slices of steak on top of the sauce and serve at once. Alternatively, serve the steaks uncut and spoon the sauce over them.

SERVES 4

BEER BREWED
CHUCK STEAK

Here's a hearty dish worth coming home to after a fall or winter's day spent out of doors. Serve it with a green salad or a hearty green vegetable such as Brussels sprouts, pour beer, and offer Mississippi Mud Pie (see Index) for dessert.

■ ■

*1 boneless chuck steak, (about
    2 pounds), cut 1¼ inches thick*
2 cloves garlic, cut in half
*6 sprigs fresh thyme or ½ teaspoon
    dried thyme*
6 sprigs fresh flat-leaf parsley
2 bay leaves
1 large baking potato
2 tablespoons unsalted butter
1 tablespoon vegetable oil
*Salt and freshly ground black pepper,
    to taste*
*1 large sweet onion, cut in half and
    thinly sliced*
Paprika
2 cups ale or dark beer
2 cups beef broth

1. Pat the meat dry with paper towels and set aside. Wrap the garlic, thyme, parsley, and bay leaves in cheesecloth, form into a bag, and tie tightly. Set aside. Peel the potato and cut it crosswise into ¼-inch-thick slices. Set aside in cold water until ready to use.

2. Heat the butter and oil in a large enameled cast-iron casserole or Dutch oven over medium heat. When the butter stops sizzling, add the meat. Brown well, about 3 minutes. Turn the meat, season with salt and pepper, and brown the second side about 3 minutes more. Remove the steak to a platter.

3. Add onion to the casserole and cook over medium heat, stirring often, until soft, 4 to 5 minutes. Add ½ teaspoon paprika and stir. Return the steak to the casserole. Pour the

beer and the broth over the steak. Add the cheesecloth bag. Bring to a simmer, cover, and simmer for 45 minutes, checking from time to time to be sure the liquid is not boiling.

4. Drain the potato slices and arrange on top of the steak in a single layer. Season with salt, pepper, and paprika. Cook, covered, for 20 to 30 minutes more, or until the potatoes are soft.

5. Remove the steak to a cutting board. Remove the cheesecloth bag and discard. Taste the broth and adjust seasoning.

6. Cut the steak crosswise into ½-inch-thick slices and divide among 3 or 4 plates. Cover generously with the potatoes, onions, and broth.

SERVES 3 OR 4

BAKED STEAK
WITH PAN GRAVY

This is an almost effortless way to cook steak. Just bake it in the oven at a moderate temperature with a little broth. This downtown cut emerges from the oven tender and juicy, while the well-flavored gravy should be introduced to some mashed potatoes on the plate. I always plan to have some meat left over to use in Superior Steak Hash (see Index), but it doesn't always work out that way.

■■■■■■■■■■■■■■■■■■■■■■■■■

1 boneless chuck steak, (about
  3¼ pounds), cut 1½ inches thick
2 tablespoons vegetable oil
Salt and freshly ground black pepper,
  to taste
½ cup beef broth
2 teaspoons cornstarch
1 tablespoon cold water

1. Preheat the oven to 325°F. Place a large, ovenproof skillet, preferably cast iron, over medium-high heat.

2. Pat the meat dry, and lightly coat it with oil on both sides. Place the meat in the hot pan and sear one side until nicely browned, 2 to 3 minutes. Turn, season with salt and pepper, and sear the second side, about 2 minutes. Turn again and season the second side.

3. Pour the broth into the pan and bring it to a boil. Transfer the pan to the oven and cook, uncovered, for 35 to 40 minutes for medium-rare or 40 to 45 minutes for medium.

4. Transfer the meat to a cutting board. Pour the broth into a small saucepan, and skim off

the fat that rises to the surface. Combine the cornstarch and water in a small dish. Bring the broth to a boil over medium heat, and stir in the cornstarch mixture. Whisk until the broth thickens slightly. Taste and season with salt and pepper if needed. Keep warm.

5. Slice the meat into long strips across the grain, arrange on warm plates, and moisten the meat generously with the gravy.

SERVES 6 TO 8

HOMAGE TO
POT ROAST

W hy talk? The proof is in the eating. My idea was simply to take some seasonings and ingredients associated with central Europe, braise them with the meat, and see what happened. According to my uptown-cut-oriented wife, what happened after the steak was cooked was an elysian fields version of pot roast. She warns, however, that to serve it without Magnificent Mashed Potatoes with Olive Oil and Herbs (see Index) is to risk a rare shot at finding bliss. A Petite Sirah from Parducci provided the fruit and body we wanted with this dish. Save the leftover cooking broth. It's nectar.

1 boneless blade steak, (about
    2 pounds), cut 1½ inches thick
Paprika, preferably sweet Hungarian
1 teaspoon caraway seeds
1 tablespoon coarsely chopped garlic
1 medium onion, thinly sliced
2 tablespoons red wine vinegar or
    distilled white vinegar
¼ cup plus 1 tablespoon corn oil

Salt, to taste
2 medium green bell peppers,
    stemmed, seeded, and coarsely
    chopped
1 can (13¾ ounces) beef broth
Freshly ground black pepper,
    to taste

1. About 8 hours before cooking, pat the steak dry. Combine 1 teaspoon of the paprika, the caraway seeds, and garlic in a mortar.

127

Pound into paste and rub over the steak. Place the steak in a Ziploc bag and add the onion slices. Stir the vinegar and $1/4$ cup oil together in a small bowl and pour into the bag. Squeeze the air out, seal, and massage so the meat is well covered. Refrigerate for 8 hours, turning at least twice.

2. Preheat the oven to 325°F.

3. Heat a large, heavy, ovenproof skillet, preferably cast iron, over medium-high heat, then coat the surface with the remaining 1 tablespoon oil. Remove all the onion slices from the bag, pat dry, and place in the skillet. Add the meat and sear until nicely browned on one side, about 2 minutes. Turn, season the browned side with salt, and sear the second side for 2 minutes. Turn, season with salt, then sear the sides of the steak.

4. Pour the marinade into the pan. Add the green peppers and the beef broth. Bring to a boil, cover the pan, and place in the bottom third of the oven.

5. Bake for 45 minutes. Remove the pan from the oven, turn the steak over, and baste it. Return to the oven and cook, covered, until tender, 45 minutes more. Transfer the steak to a cutting board and cover loosely with aluminum foil.

6. Pour the contents of the pan into a strainer set over a bowl. Purée the strained vegetables in a food processor or blender, adding salt, pepper, and paprika. You should have about 1 cup of purée.

7. Degrease the broth in the bowl. You should have 2 cups of broth. Stir $1/4$ cup of the broth into the purée. Pour the purée into one bowl and the remaining broth into a second bowl. Cover both bowls with plastic wrap and reheat in a microwave for 2 minutes.

8. Meanwhile, cut the steak across the grain into $1/8$-inch-thick slices. Arrange the slices on each of 4 warm plates. Top with 2 tablespoons of the purée, followed by $1/4$ cup of the broth.

SERVES 4

TENDERIZING

Meat may be made less tough by cutting (cube steak), grinding (hamburger), or mashing (pounded round steak) the connective tissue. It also can be tenderized by exposing it to acid marinades or plant enzymes.

Marinades are seasoned liquids, such as fruit or vegetable juices, wine, water, and/or oil, combined with herbs and seasonings that add flavor. To tenderize, the marinade must contain an acidic ingredient such as lemon juice, wine, vinegar, or yogurt and touch the steak for several hours. Do not over-marinate (more than 24 hours), or you risk overly soft, mushy meat. Dry marinades, also called rubs, add flavor but do not tenderize.

KNIFE-AND-FORK
BEEF STEW

While this stew preparation is somewhat involved and time-consuming, the result is classic and elegant and worthy of every minute spent. For a nostalgia night menu—and to spend more time with your guests than in the kitchen—buy smoked salmon or smoked trout for the first course. Pour the same Zinfandel used in the sauce and conclude with Hummers (see Index), the perfect after-dinner drink-dessert.

■■■■■■■■■■■■■■■■■■■■■■■

1 boneless chuck steak (about 2 pounds)
1 cup all-purpose flour
Salt and freshly ground black pepper,
  to taste
2 tablespoons unsalted butter
2 tablespoons vegetable oil
1 medium onion, finely chopped
2 medium carrots, finely chopped
1 rib celery, finely chopped
2 cups red wine, preferably Zinfandel
2 cups water
2 teaspoons instant beef bouillon or
  2 beef bouillon cubes
1½ tablespoons tomato paste
2 bay leaves
2 sprigs fresh thyme
2 sprigs fresh rosemary
4 sprigs fresh parsley
6 carrots, peeled
3 parsnips, peeled
2 large red potatoes, peeled
12 ounces white or red pearl onions,
  peeled

1. Cut the beef into 2- to 2½-inch chunks. Combine the flour and a generous amount of salt and pepper on a large plate. Dredge the beef chunks in the seasoned flour, shaking off excess. Set aside.

2. Heat the butter and oil in a large, enameled cast-iron casserole or Dutch oven over medium-high heat while dredging the meat a second time in the seasoned flour. Brown the meat on all sides, working in batches so as not to overcrowd the pan. As each piece of meat is browned, transfer it to a platter.

3. Pour off all but 2 tablespoons of the pan drippings. Add the chopped onion, carrots, and celery to the pan and reduce the heat to medium-low. Cook, stirring, until the vegetables soften slightly, about 5 minutes. Add the wine, raise the heat, and bring the wine to a boil. Boil the wine, stirring, for 2 minutes. Add the water and instant bouillon and return the meat to the pan. The liquid should come up halfway over the meat. Add more water, if necessary. Bring to a simmer and stir in the tomato

paste, bay leaves, thyme, rosemary, and parsley. Cover the pan and simmer gently over low heat, stirring occasionally, until the meat is very tender, about 2 hours.

4. Remove the meat to a platter. Discard the bay leaves and herb sprigs. Set a fine-mesh sieve over a medium-size **bowl and pour the** contents of the pan through the sieve, pushing to extract as much liquid as possible from the vegetables. Discard the vegetables and return the liquid to the pan. Skim off the fat that rises to the surface, then correct the seasoning. Return the beef to the pan. (The stew may be prepared to this point up to 2 days ahead. Refrigerate, covered, and reheat to finish.)

5. To finish the stew, cut the carrots, parsnips, and potatoes into 2-inch chunks. Steam or boil these vegetables and the pearl onions

STEWING

Stewing involves smaller pieces of meat and more liquid than braising. It's a time-consuming method because the meat is cooked well beyond the point at which it is done so its flavor will permeate the liquid. I like to use round and butt steaks as well as chuck to make stew. For example, try a round steak in the Knife-and-Fork Beef Stew.

until tender. Drain and add to the beef mixture. Reheat the stew, covered, over low heat for at least 15 minutes, or until the mixture is thoroughly hot.

SERVES 6

SUPERIOR
STEAK HASH

Since childhood, "hash" has been for me one of the most evocative menu words in the English language. I think the pleasure hash brings is a combination of its comfort food consistency and the voyage of discovery as you eat it. The standard definition is cooked meat—or poultry or even fish—cut into small pieces and recooked. But with what? The possibilities are virtually inexhaustible. Hash never needs to be made the same way twice. In this version,

I combined raw potatoes and seasoned broth with chuck steak and used celery as an aromatic. Why? Because it was there. That's the charm of hash. There is one constant, however: James Beard insisted that Heinz Chili Sauce (see Note) was the perfect condiment for beef hash, and it is.

■ ■

¾ cup chopped onion

⅓ cup diced celery

3 tablespoons vegetable oil

1 large baking potato, peeled and cut into ½-inch cubes

1 teaspoon paprika

1 tablespoon chopped celery leaves

1 tablespoon chopped fresh flat-leaf parsley leaves

1 pound cooked boneless chuck steak, cut into ½-inch cubes (about 3 cups)

1½ cups beef broth

½ teaspoon dried thyme

⅛ teaspoon cayenne pepper

¼ teaspoon freshly ground black pepper

½ teaspoon salt

1 teaspoon Worcestershire sauce

1. Combine the onion, celery, and oil in a large heavy skillet, preferably cast iron. Cook over

medium heat until the vegetables are soft, about 5 minutes. Add the potato and stir to coat the cubes with oil, about 1 minute. Add the paprika, celery leaves, and parsley and stir until they soften, 1 minute more.

2. Add the meat to the vegetables and stir to mix the ingredients well. Pour in the broth and bring to a simmer, about 3 minutes. Add the thyme, cayenne, black pepper, salt, and Worcestershire. Adjust the heat to maintain a steady simmer and cook, stirring occasionally, until the liquid has become syrupy and is almost gone, about 30 minutes. Serve warm.

SERVES 4

Note: Heinz Chili Sauce is a survivor from an era when the word chili didn't cause you to wince in anticipation of pain. There are peppers in this sauce—along with tomatoes, onion, and vinegar—but they are sweet peppers. It is a perfect companion to steak hash and hamburgers.

EQUIPMENT:
JUST THE BASICS

What the cook needs to perform (indoors) could result in an endless list, so I'll stick to some special items that relate to steak cookery and skip the all-purpose tools and "things" that fill my kitchen— and probably yours as well—to overflowing.

Knives: I use 3- and 4-inch paring knives, an 8-inch chef's knife and a 10-inch slicing knife often. A steak cook will also want to have a boning knife and cleaver within reach. A tool for sharpening (and knowing how to use it) is essential.

Keeping knives sharp means the knife is safer because it requires less pressure to do its job. It also will cut more quickly, more efficiently, and thinner. Don't hesitate to make the considerable invest-

ment necessary to obtain top-of-the-line knives, but be sure first that the knife feels comfortable in your hand.

Steak knives: Family and guests will be appreciative if there are first-rate steak knives at the table. The knives will pay for themselves by convincing folks that the occasional tough steak is really pretty easy to cut.

Chopping boards and a carving board: The surface is less important than the size. Buy them big, at least 18 x 12 inches for the carving board, which should have a trench to collect juices. I find I need at least two

chopping boards for any meal, except breakfast.

Tongs: I'm not sure if tongs is singular, but one (a pair) proves a singular tool when cooking at a hot stove. I think of the tongs as an extension of my hand, one that keeps me from burning it over a gas flame or under a broiler and that turns steaks in a gentle grasp without puncturing the meat. I have two sets (two pair?) so I can remain sane when one is in the dishwasher.

Pans: My standbys are 12- and 10-inch skillets with a nonstick surface. This allows me to use a minimum of oil. Nonstick pans, greatly improved in quality and endurance, also are very good for steaks that are cooked with a coating or after being marinated. A 10-inch cast-iron frying pan and a wok are tops for searing food and cooking it at high heat.

To season a new cast-iron frying pan or carbon-steel wok, rub lightly with oil inside and out and bake in a 300°F oven for 1 hour. The surface will become nonstick and resist rusting. From time to time, apply a light coating of oil after the pan has been cleaned and dried. Do not scour with steel wool.

Enameled cast-iron casserole: This pot goes from stovetop to oven (and sometimes refrigerator) while providing a perfect environment for moist-heat braises and stews featuring downtown steak cuts.

Ridged stovetop grill: This is a square pan with a handle and ridges across the cooking surface. The pan needs to be seasoned, but thereafter it is flawless in reproducing grill marks, grill taste, and grill smell for steaks and vegetables. As noted elsewhere, using it will create more smoke than your smoke alarm thinks is good for you.

Mortar and pestle: Don't misunderstand. I own and use a food processor. But the romance in the mortar and pestle is its links to the earliest kitchens and the practicality is in the way it reduces spices, herbs, and aromatics without destroying them.

Custard cups: I also find all manner of uses for a raft of 5- and 10-ounce clear custard cups. I pile them around my chopping board to fill when preparing Asian recipes—or any others that call for adding ingredients in quick succession.

ROUND/EYE ROUND/RUMP

This hind-leg cut provides steaks and roasts, bone-in or boneless. The steaks include the tip (also promoted as sirloin tip and often sold sliced for stir-fry); top round, which provides more tender steaks than bottom round; round or bottom round, which comes with a round bone; and eye round, which looks like tenderloin and has very little fat.

All these steaks, with the exception of the eye, are oval in shape and contain more connective tissue than the uptown cuts. The muscle fibers are firmer and the grain in the meat more pronounced. Rump steaks also come from this downtown neighborhood. So does the cube steak I used for Chicken-Fried Cube Steak with Pan Gravy (see Index).

These steaks benefit from marination, from being cut into cubes or slices before cooking, and from moist-heat cooking. They are receptive to strong flavorings, as you will discover when you prepare Nicole's Moroccan Steak Casserole or Siam Country Steak. The Best Ever recipe Italian Beef Sandwich, calls for thin strips of tip or top round poached in a seasoned broth.

The key to poaching successfully is patience. Usually the liquid is brought to a boil before the meat is added. From then on the cook must keep a watchful eye, and attentive ear, to be sure the liquid remains at a simmer. If subjected to a rolling boil, the meat surely will toughen and— in one of Mother Nature's practical jokes—emerge tasting very dry.

135

EYE ROUND STEAKS
WITH ONION-CREAM GRAVY

A lean cut of steak like eye round will always be more pleasing if accompanied with a liberal portion of sauce. In this recipe, the sauce is a combination of sweet onion and cream accented with mustard and cayenne. My wine choice is a red wine from the Medoc region of Bordeaux.

4 eye round steaks, (about 5 ounces each), cut ½ inch thick
2 tablespoons vegetable oil
2 tablespoons unsalted butter
1 medium sweet onion, preferably Vidalia, cut into large dice
1 sprig fresh oregano or ¼ teaspoon dried oregano
½ cup dry white wine
½ cup heavy (or whipping) cream
1 tablespoon balsamic vinegar
¼ teaspoon white pepper
Pinch of cayenne pepper, or more to taste
1½ teaspoons Dijon mustard
Salt, to taste (optional)
1 tablespoon minced fresh flat-leaf parsley leaves

1. Pat the steaks dry, then coat lightly with oil. Set aside.

2. Melt the butter in a medium-size saucepan over medium-low heat. Add the onion and cook until soft, about 4 minutes. Add the oregano and wine, raise the heat to medium, and simmer until the wine is nearly evaporated, 4 to 5 minutes.

3. Add the cream and bring to a boil. Simmer for 1 minute. Stir in the vinegar, white pepper, cayenne, and mustard. Remove the herb sprig, transfer the mixture to a food processor, and process for 30 seconds, or until blended. Pour the sauce into a small saucepan and season with salt and more cayenne, if desired. Set aside.

4. Heat a large heavy skillet over medium-high heat. When hot, add the steaks and cook until seared and crusted, about 2 minutes. Turn the steaks, season with salt, if desired, and cook 2 minutes more for medium-rare or 2½ minutes for medium. Transfer the steaks to a cutting board and let them rest while reheating the sauce.

5. Divide the sauce among 4 warm plates and top with whole steaks or cut them into ½-inch-thick slices. Garnish with the parsley.

SERVES 4

THE ITALIAN

BEEF SANDWICH

T he Italian beef sandwich is one of the culinary glories of Chicago, enticing to both blue-collar workers and celebrities alike with its simple, even primitive, charm. Shaved beef, a soft roll or miniature bread loaf, juice, and the marinated vegetable condiment known as giardiniera are all it takes to make great eating.

∎∎∎∎∎∎∎∎∎∎∎∎∎∎∎∎∎∎∎∎∎∎∎∎

3 cups beef broth
¾ teaspoon coarsely ground black
pepper
¾ teaspoon dried Italian herb
seasoning
1 large clove garlic, crushed with
the side of a knife and peel
removed
½ cup Gibsons Hot Pepper Giardiniera
(page 201) or bottled
Crushed red pepper flakes, to taste
(optional)
4 Italian buns or soft rolls, 6 to 7
inches long
1 pound tip or top round steak,
cut into thin strips

1. Combine the broth, black pepper, Italian seasoning, and garlic in a medium-size saucepan or a 12-inch sauté pan. Bring to a boil over medium heat, lower the heat, and simmer, covered, for 10 minutes. Strain the broth. (This may be done ahead. Store it in the refrigerator, tightly covered, until needed.)

2. Coarsely chop the giardiniera if the pieces are large. Stir in the red pepper flakes if a spicy sandwich is desired. Slice the buns lengthwise without cutting them completely in half. Set aside.

3. Using a meat pounder or the side of a cleaver or large knife, pound each strip of meat until very thin. Bring the broth back to a boil, then reduce the heat to a bare simmer and add the meat strips, a few at a time. Cook until they are brown and have cooked through, about 1 minute. Stir with tongs or chopsticks as needed to keep the slices apart. Do not let the broth return to a boil or else the meat will toughen. Remove the pan from the heat.

4. Drizzle 2 tablespoons of meat broth over the inside of each bun. Divide the beef strips among the 4 buns and moisten each portion with 2 more tablespoons of broth. Top with 2 tablespoons of giardiniera. Cut each bun in half crosswise and serve with plenty of paper napkins.

SERVES 4

ASIAN STEAK

WITH STIR-FRIED BEANS
AND SPROUTS

Asian cooks understand that while marinating less tender cuts of meat, such as round steak, helps to tenderize them, the technique used to cut the steak can be equally important. In this dish, cutting the broiled steak into thin slices across the grain helps achieve a more tender texture.

■■■■■■■■■■■■■■■■■■■■■■■■

2 medium to large cloves garlic,
* minced*
½ teaspoon salt
⅓ cup fresh lime juice
3 tablespoons soy sauce
1 tablespoon sugar
1 large jalapeño, stemmed and minced
* with the seeds*
⅓ cup chopped fresh cilantro leaves
2 eye round steaks, (6 to 8 ounces
* each), cut ¾ inch thick*
4 ounces green beans, cooked until
* crisp-tender*
3 scallions, white part only
1 tablespoon vegetable oil
1 cup fresh bean sprouts
1½ cups cooked long-grain white rice,
* hot*

1. Using a mortar and pestle or a chef's knife, mash the garlic. Add the salt and continue to mash until the mixture has a paste consistency. Stir the lime juice, soy sauce, and sugar together in a small bowl until the sugar is dis-

solved. Stir in the garlic paste, jalapeño, and cilantro.

2. Arrange the steaks in a shallow dish just large enough to hold them. Pour ⅓ cup of the marinade over the steaks, reserving the remaining marinade. Cover the dish with plastic wrap and set aside at room temperature for 1 to 2 hours, turning the steaks once.

3. Cut the green beans on the diagonal into 1-inch pieces. Cut the scallions into 1-inch-long julienne strips. Set aside.

4. Preheat the broiler.

5. Remove the steaks from the marinade and discard this marinade. Broil the steaks until seared and well browned on one side, about 4 minutes. Turn and broil 3 minutes more for medium-rare or 4 minutes for medium. Transfer the cooked meat to a cutting board and cover loosely with aluminum foil.

6. Heat a large skillet or wok over medium-high heat. When hot, add the oil, then the

scallions. Stir-fry until they begin to brown, about 45 seconds. Add the bean sprouts and continue to stir-fry for 30 seconds. Add the green beans and 2 tablespoons of the reserved marinade. Stir to mix and cover the skillet. Steam until the vegetables are softened, about 45 seconds.

7. Carve each steak across the grain into thin slices. Arrange a scoop of rice with the stir-fried vegetables on the serving plates. Top the vegetables with the slices of the beef. Drizzle any reserved marinade over the meat and rice.

SERVES 3 OR 4

EYE ROUND STEAKS

WITH PEANUT AND
AVOCADO SAUCES

Here is steak for a party, with sauces inspired by ingredients indigenous to Africa and the Caribbean. (For more than four guests, cook an eye round roast and carve it into thin slices.) Garnish each plate with rice and an assertive green vegetable like chard or beet greens. Pour a robust red wine such as Zinfandel or Merlot.

■ ■

4 eye round steaks, (about 6 ounces each), cut ¾ inch thick
1 teaspoon ground ginger
¾ teaspoon crushed red pepper flakes
½ teaspoon freshly ground black pepper
4½ tablespoons fresh lemon juice
5 tablespoons vegetable oil
1 small ripe avocado

1 scallion, white and some green, minced
Salt, to taste
Hot pepper sauce, preferably Tabasco
¼ cup smooth peanut butter
⅔ cup low-sodium chicken broth

1. About 4 to 8 hours before cooking the steaks, pat them dry and place them in a 1-quart plastic storage bag. Combine ½ teaspoon of the ginger, ½ teaspoon of the red

pepper flakes, $^{1}/_{4}$ teaspoon of the black pepper, 2 tablespoons of the lemon juice, and 4 tablespoons of the oil in a small jar. Cover and shake well, then pour this marinade over the steaks. Close the bag tightly, place on a plate, and refrigerate. Allow 30 minutes for the steaks to return to room temperature before cooking them.

2. Pit, peel, and dice the avocado. Transfer to a small bowl, add the remaining 1 tablespoon of oil, 1 tablespoon of the lemon juice, the scallion, the remaining $^{1}/_{2}$ teaspoon ginger, $^{1}/_{4}$ teaspoon black pepper, $^{1}/_{2}$ teaspoon salt, and $^{1}/_{4}$ teaspoon hot pepper sauce. Mash and stir to combine the ingredients, cover the surface with plastic wrap, and set aside. (If making the sauce more than 30 minutes before cooking the steak, refrigerate it.)

3. Spoon the peanut butter into a small saucepan. Add the broth, the remaining $1^{1}/_{2}$ tablespoons lemon juice, remaining $^{1}/_{4}$ teaspoon red pepper, and pinch of salt. Bring this mixture to a boil, stirring to combine the ingredients. Lower the heat and simmer until the sauce thickens, 1 to 2 minutes. Remove from the heat and set aside.

4. Preheat the broiler.

5. Remove the steaks from the marinade and pat dry. Place them under the broiler and cook until seared and nicely browned on one side, about 3 minutes. Turn and cook $2^{1}/_{2}$ minutes more for medium-rare or 3 minutes for medium. Meanwhile, reheat the peanut sauce and adjust the seasoning. Taste the avocado

sauce and adjust the seasoning.

6. Pour $^{1}/_{4}$ cup of peanut sauce onto a warm serving plate. Place a steak on the sauce and top with a generous dollop of the avocado sauce. Repeat with remaining steaks and sauces and serve at once.

SERVES 4

ADDING FLAVOR

One of the wonders of steak is that for all the taste and flavor it possesses, it also welcomes an extraordinary variety of seasonings, flavorings and sauces. Here are some from my repertoire:

Nicole's Moroccan Mix (page 149)
Pan Sauce (page 46)
Gibsons Roasting Salt (page 84)
Six-Shooter Spice Rub (page 37)
Infused Horseradish Oil
    (page 108)
Handmade Caper Mustard
    (page 168)
Mustard Butter (page 168)
Composed Butters
    (page 46)

TOP ROUND
WITH RED DEVIL TOMATILLO SAUCE

I trace the boom in popularity of Southwest recipes back to the moment when someone discovered you can prepare a combination of ingredients that once took hours of hand labor with a mortar and pestle in seconds using a food processor. The more widespread distribution of various chilies and tomatillos, such as are used in this red devil sauce, has helped, too. Pile some Celery Seed Coleslaw (see Index) on each plate.

■ ■

1 top round steak (1¼ pounds),
    cut 1¼ inches thick
1 tablespoon olive or vegetable oil
8 ounces tomatillos
8 ounces tomatoes, peeled, cored, and
    seeded (see page 142)
¼ cup chopped scallions
1 clove garlic, quartered
1 canned chipotle chili and 1 to 2
    teaspoons of the juice
¼ teaspoon sugar
¼ teaspoon salt
1 tablespoon sherry vinegar
1 tablespoon unsalted butter or
    vegetable oil

1. About 30 minutes before cooking, rub the steak all over with the olive oil. Set aside at room temperature.

2. Bring a saucepan of water to a boil. Peel and discard the husks from the tomatillos. Put them in the boiling water and cook until the color changes from bright to faded green, about 5 minutes. Transfer the tomatillos with a slotted spoon to a colander and cool under cold running water.

3. Cut the tomatoes into chunks. Put the tomatoes and tomatillos in a food processor. Add the scallions, garlic, chipotle, sugar, salt, and vinegar. Process until smooth, about 1 minute. Add chipotle juice, to taste. (Or mince the tomatoes, tomatillos, scallions, garlic, and chipotle by hand with a knife, transfer to a bowl, and stir in the sugar, salt, vinegar, and chipotle juice.)

4. Melt the butter in a small saucepan until it bubbles. Add the tomatillo mixture and cook over medium heat, stirring occasionally, until reduced by a third and somewhat thickened, 12 to 15 minutes. Let cool. (Sauce may be made ahead, covered, and stored in the refrigerator for up to 3 days.) Serve the sauce at room temperature.

5. Preheat the broiler or prepare coals for grilling.

6. Cook the steak until seared and well browned, about 7 minutes. Turn and cook 5 minutes more for medium-rare or 6 minutes for medium. Transfer the steak to a cutting board, cover loosely with aluminum foil, and let rest for at least 5 minutes. If serving at room temperature, allow the steak to cool completely before slicing.

7. Carve the meat on the bias against the grain into thin slices. Arrange slices on plates so they overlap slightly. Drizzle a line of sauce down the center of the meat or spoon a puddle on one side of the plate.

SERVES 4

PEELING TOMATOES

Anyone, like myself, who has virtually destroyed a tomato in trying to cut away its tightly clinging skin, will appreciate knowing this chef's trick. Bring water to a boil in a medium-size saucepan. Add the tomatoes and blanch for 20 to 30 seconds to loosen the skin. Transfer the tomatoes with a slotted spoon to a colander and cool under cold running water. Core and peel the tomatoes, cut crosswise in half, and remove the seeds. Cut it into chunks or dice as directed in the recipe.

SIAM

COUNTRY STEAK

My wife and I have a friend, a college student from Thailand named Jane, who grew up in a restaurant family and is studying design in hopes of creating restaurants one day. In the heat of summer, her air-conditioning failed, and we took her in. It was nothing special, but she insisted she owed us something and promised to return the next week to prepare a Thai meal. She did, making several delicious dishes, none of them more memorable than this rustic creation. (In answer to a question you soon will pose: Yes, the quantity of garlic is accurate and, no, you do not cook it.) Serve the steak with plenty of rice and cooling vegetables such as raw cucumber slices and chilled iceberg lettuce.

■ ■

2 boneless rump or butt steaks,
(about 10 ounces each), cut ½ inch
thick
1 teaspoon McCormick's Barbecue
Seasoning
1 tablespoon oyster sauce
1 tablespoon Thai fish sauce
(nam pla; see Note)
1 tablespoon fresh lime juice
2 large cloves garlic, cut into thin
slices
1 tablespoon thinly sliced chilies

1. Pat the steaks dry and place them in a shallow dish. Sprinkle the barbecue seasoning on the steaks and rub it into both sides of the meat. Drizzle the oyster sauce over the meat and rub it over the surface of both sides. Cover the dish and refrigerate for 24 hours.

2. Allow the steaks to come to room temperature while preparing coals for grilling or heating a ridged grill pan.

3. Combine the fish sauce and lime juice in a small dish. Set aside.

4. Grill the steaks until seared and nicely browned on one side, about 2 minutes for medium-rare or 2½ minutes for medium. Turn and cook 2 minutes more on the second side.

5. Transfer the steaks to a cutting board and let rest for 5 minutes, then carve them into thin slices. Arrange the slices on a platter. Drizzle the fish sauce-lime juice mixture over the meat, garnish with the garlic slices and sliced chilies, and serve just warm or at room temperature.

Note: Thai fish sauce *(nam pla)* is available in Asian markets, specialty food stores, and some supermarkets.

SERVES 4

ORANGE BEEF

Crispy orange beef is a Chinese culinary masterpiece, and like many masterpieces, it is deceptively simple. The traditional recipe has the meat cut into fine shreds, marinated, cooked, and cooked again until the pieces become caramelized. My version is simpler yet full of the flavor of orange. Serve the meat with rice steamed with orange peel or fried rice.

■■■■■■■■■■■■■■■■■■■■■■■■■■

1 tablespoon minced orange zest

½ cup fresh orange juice

2 tablespoons honey

1 tablespoon soy sauce

1 teaspoon minced fresh ginger

1 teaspoon minced garlic

1 teaspoon sesame oil

¼ teaspoon crushed red pepper flakes

1 top round steak (about 1¼ pounds), cut 1 inch thick

½ teaspoon salt

⅓ cup plus 2 teaspoons cornstarch

3 tablespoons vegetable oil

1. Combine the orange zest, juice, honey, soy sauce, ginger, garlic, sesame oil, and red pepper flakes in a shallow nonreactive dish or pan just large enough to hold the steak. Stir well and add the meat. Cover with plastic wrap and marinate for 1½ hours at room temperature or for up to 12 hours in the refrigerator, turning the meat once.

2. When ready to cook, combine the salt and ⅓ cup cornstarch in a shallow pan. Remove the steak from the marinade, pat dry, and dredge in the cornstarch mixture until coated on both sides. Set aside. Strain the marinade, reserving the liquid.

3. Heat the oil in a large skillet over medium-high heat until the oil shimmers. Add the steak and cook until seared and well browned on one side, about 5 minutes. Turn and cook 5 minutes more for medium-rare or 6 minutes for medium. Transfer the steak to a cutting board and let it rest for 5 minutes.

4. Pour the oil from the skillet and return to a burner. Stir 1 tablespoon of the marinade in a small bowl with the remaining 2 teaspoons cornstarch. Pour the remaining marinade into the skillet, add the cornstarch mixture, and whisk over medium heat until the mixture thickens, about 2 minutes.

5. Cut the steak on the bias across the grain into ¼-inch slices. Return the slices to the skillet and turn to coat with sauce. Serve at once.

SERVES 4 TO 6

BRAISED BEEF

WITH SWEET-AND-SOUR SAUCE

Sweet-and-sour sauce is not a specialty only of Asian chefs. The Italians, for instance, have been adding it to meat, game, and vegetable dishes for centuries. Here, the beef is braised in the marinade while the sweet-and-sour sauce is added as seasoning. Soft polenta is the ideal accompaniment.

■■■■■■■■■■■■■■■■■■■■■■■■

1 boneless beef bottom round or
   rump roast (about 2½ pounds)
2 medium onions, coarsely chopped
2 large carrots, coarsely chopped
2 large ribs celery, coarsely chopped
1½ cups dry red wine
¼ cup olive oil
2 teaspoons juniper berries, crushed
2 bay leaves
Salt and freshly ground black pepper,
   to taste
¼ cup sugar
¼ cup balsamic vinegar
2 large cloves garlic, chopped
Grated zest of 1 lemon
¼ cup golden raisins, plumped in
   warm water and drained
¼ cup chopped pitted prunes
¼ cup pine nuts

1. One day in advance or on the morning of serving, cut the meat into 2-inch chunks and place in a nonreactive dish. Add the onions, carrots, celery, and red wine. Cover and refrigerate overnight or at least 8 hours, turning the meat once.

2. Remove the meat from the marinade and pat dry. Heat the oil in a large heavy pot over medium-high heat until hot. Add the meat and brown on all sides, working in batches so as not to overcrowd the pan, 4 minutes per batch. Discard the pan grease. Return the meat to the pan and add the marinade and vegetables. Add the juniper berries and bay leaves. Bring the mixture to a simmer, reduce the heat to very low, cook, covered, at a bare simmer until the meat is tender, about 1½ hours.

3. Remove the meat and discard the bay leaves. Pass the vegetables and cooking juices through the fine holes of a food mill or purée in a food processor to make a sauce. Return the sauce and meat to the casserole. Season with salt and pepper.

4. Just before serving, combine the sugar, vinegar, garlic, and lemon zest in a medium-size skillet. Heat over medium heat until the sugar is melted, about 1 minute. Add the raisins, prunes, and pine nuts. Bring the mixture to a boil, pour it into the casserole and stir over low heat until the sauce is thoroughly hot. Serve immediately.

SERVES 6

HUNGARIAN
STEAK SOUP

Rightly or wrongly, central European cuisine has the reputation of being rich, heavy, and dull. This recipe is none of the above. A sprightly main-course soup, it has very little fat and no thickeners and offers a tongue-tingling array of pepper flavors, including the paprika so prized by Hungarian cooks. My preference is to make this soup in a pressure cooker, even when not pressured by lack of time. It will be equally tasty, however, made by the conventional method.

■ ■

*1½ pounds boneless round steak, cut
   ¾ inch thick*
*1 medium onion, preferably a sweet
   onion such as Vidalia*
1 medium green bell pepper
1 medium red bell pepper
2 tablespoons vegetable oil
*1 teaspoon sweet paprika, preferably
   Hungarian*
*½ teaspoon hot paprika, preferably
   Hungarian*
*¼ teaspoon freshly ground black
   pepper*
*½ teaspoon caraway seeds, briefly
   toasted (see Note)*
6 cups beef broth
2 bay leaves
1 tablespoon chopped garlic
2 teaspoons tomato paste
1 tablespoon salt
6 ounces wide egg noodles
Sour cream

1. Pat the meat dry. Trim away any excess fat and cut the meat into ¾-inch cubes.

2. Cut the onion in half and coarsely chop one half. Thinly slice the other half. Set aside. Core, seed, and cut the bell peppers in half. Cut one half of each pepper into chunks and the other half into ¼-inch strips. Set aside.

3. Heat oil in a pressure cooker or large heavy saucepan over medium-high heat until it shimmers, about 3 minutes. Add half the meat and brown on all sides, about 4 minutes. Transfer to a bowl with a slotted spoon. Add the remaining meat and repeat.

4. Add the chopped onion and bell pepper chunks to the pot. Stir frequently until the vegetables soften, 4 to 5 minutes. Add the

sweet and hot paprika, black pepper, and caraway seeds and stir for 1 minute. Pour in the beef broth. Add the bay leaves, garlic, and tomato paste. Return the meat and accumulated juices to the pot.

5. Cover and seal the pressure cooker, if using, and bring to full pressure over high heat. Regulate the heat and cook for 20 minutes. If using a saucepan, simmer, partially covered, for 1 to 1½ hours. Release pressure and uncover the cooker. The meat should be cooked through and tender. If not, re-cover the pot, bring back to full pressure, and cook for 5 minutes more.

6. Pour the soup through a colander into a bowl, leaving as much of the meat as possible in the pot. Pick out the meat cubes in the colander and return to the pot. Discard the bay leaves and vegetables in the colander as well as any remaining in the pot.

7. Add the onion slices and bell pepper strips to the pot and pour the broth back in over the vegetables and meat. Bring to a boil over high heat, reduce heat to low, and simmer, uncovered, until the vegetables are just tender, 7 to 8 minutes.

8. Meanwhile, bring water to a boil in a large saucepan. Add the salt and noodles and cook until the noodles are just tender. Drain the noodles.

9. Spoon ½ cup of noodles into each of 6 soup plates. Ladle the hot soup over the noodles and serve at once. Pass the sour cream at the table.

SERVES 6

Note: Toast the caraway seeds in a small skillet over medium-low heat, tossing often, until aromatic, about 5 minutes.

PEELING GARLIC AND SHALLOTS

Mash garlic by placing it under the flat side of the blade of a chef's knife and hitting the blade sharply with the side of your hand. The peel will pull away easily from the crushed clove. Peel shallots by taking off the first layer of the shallot with the skin. You lose some, but you'll save time because the skin by itself is very hard to pull away from the shallot.

NICOLE'S MOROCCAN
STEAK CASSEROLE

Nicole Bergere, who runs a specialty bakery in Chicago, has a gift for cooking up show-stoppers. Certainly a one-pot casserole meal made with rump steak and vegetables doesn't seem like gourmet fare. But when Nicole brings it to the table and opens the pot, everyone within smelling distance starts sniffing. Impolite, perhaps, but they just can't help themselves. The remarkably exotic aromas from her spice mix only begin the seduction, though. Tasting, you encounter contrasting textures of meat and vegetables with the graduated sweetness of meltingly soft sweet potato, pieces of baked banana, and pitted prunes. There's more to say, but, as usual when Nicole's casserole is served, my mouth is full. For an accompaniment consider serving beer. If wine is to be poured, seek out something simple but fruity, such as that old standby "hearty Burgundy" or a Zinfandel from California.

■ ■

1 rump steak, (about 1¼ pounds),
    1½ inches thick, cut into 3- to 4-inch
    chunks
3 tablespoons Nicole's Moroccan Mix
    (recipe follows)
4 tablespoons olive oil
1 medium onion, cut into ¼-inch slices
1 large sweet potato, peeled and cut
    into ¼-inch-thick slices
1 eggplant, peeled, quartered
    lengthwise and cut crosswise into
    ¼-inch-thick pieces
10 to 12 pitted prunes
4 medium cloves garlic, slivered
1 large baking potato, peeled and cut
    into ¼-inch-thick slices

2 medium carrots, peeled, quartered
    lengthwise and cut crosswise into
    ¼-inch-thick pieces
1 medium zucchini, quartered
    lengthwise and cut crosswise into
    ¼-inch-thick pieces
2 medium bananas, peeled and
    quartered lengthwise

1. Place the meat in a bowl. Add 1 tablespoon of the spice mix and toss with your hands until all the pieces are well coated. Set aside.

2. Preheat the oven to 350°F.

3. Heat 2 tablespoons of the oil in a large skillet over medium-high heat. Add the meat and brown the pieces on all sides. Transfer to a

cutting board and cut each piece in half horizontally.

4. Coat the bottom of a 3-quart Dutch oven or enameled cast-iron casserole with 1 tablespoon of oil. Arrange the onion slices on the bottom in a single layer. Sprinkle 1 teaspoon of the spice mix over the onions. Arrange the meat, cut side down, on top of the onions. Add the sweet potato slices, sprinkle with 1 teaspoon spice mix. Add half the eggplant pieces and 1 teaspoon spice mix. As you arrange the layers, fill in the gaps with prunes and slivers of garlic.

5. Spread the baking potato slices over the eggplant and sprinkle with 1 teaspoon spice mix. Add the remaining eggplant and the carrots in a single layer. Sprinkle with 1 teaspoon spice mix. Finally, make a layer of zucchini pieces and bananas, topped with the remaining 1 teaspoon spice mix. Drizzle the remaining 1 tablespoon olive oil over the top layer.

6. Cover the top layer with a sheet of aluminum foil and press down to make the layer even. Cover the casserole with a lid and bake for 45 minutes. Remove the casserole from the oven. Remove the lid and tilt the casserole. Using a bulb baster, remove juices from the bottom and drizzle them over the top. Replace the foil and the lid and bake for 30 minutes more.

7. Baste again, then bake for 15 minutes more. To check for doneness, push a long thin knife into the casserole in several places. It should pass through the layers easily. If not, re-cover the casserole and bake for 15 minutes more.

8. Remove the casserole from the oven and keep covered until ready to serve. Lift off the lid, allow the aromas to escape, then cut wedge-shaped portions from top to bottom. Spoon some cooking juice over each portion.

SERVES 5 OR 6

NICOLE'S MOROCCAN MIX

Use this nose-tingling seasoning for Nicole's Moroccan Steak Casserole or in small amounts to flavor meatballs, meatloaves, hamburgers, mayonnaise or soups.

2 tablespoons ground cumin
2 tablespoons coarse salt
1 tablespoon ground cinnamon
1 tablespoon freshly grated nutmeg
1 tablespoon paprika
2 teaspoons turmeric
2 teaspoons freshly ground black pepper

Combine the cumin, salt, cinnamon, nutmeg, paprika, turmeric, and the ground pepper in a small bowl and stir until thoroughly mixed. Transfer to a 1-cup jar with a tight-fitting lid or 2 empty spice bottles and label it. Store at room temperature.

MAKES ABOUT ⅔ CUP

THE STEAK IN HISTORY

For the sake of those eager to dine, here is 10,000 years of agricultural history telescoped so that it can be read in the time it takes to cook a minute steak.

The shift of early humans from hunters to farmers began during the Neolithic era as man began tending both plants and animals. It was Greece, or what became Greece, where the first oxen were domesticated. Some credit the Egyptians, who worshiped cattle as gods, with inventing the branding iron.

When their turn came to rule the world, several millennia later, the Romans put forth a candidate for the title "inventor" or "discoverer" of the pleasures of beef. He was Lucius Plaucus, a "Roman of rank," who was ordered by the emperor Trajan to perform the menial task of cooking the animal sacrifices to Jupiter. He tasted the burned meat and became the chief proponent of the original nouvelle cuisine. Pretty soon the Temple became the top restaurant in town.

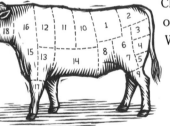

Eating meat as the centerpiece of a meal, however, didn't evolve in Europe until the late Middle Ages, and even then the practice of city folks buying portion-controlled pieces of beef was as unreal as cities without walls. There wasn't even a word for butcher until the Romans came up with *beccaio* in the thirteenth century.

Elsewhere, with population more dense, people ate easier-to-produce, high-er-yielding plants. The European diet before the Industrial Revolution included only 10 to 25 percent calories from meat.

The only important steak-related event in Europe before the invention of chateaubriand by Montmireil, chef to the nineteenth century French writer and diplomat François-René de Chateaubriand, was the occupation of Paris by Wellington's beef-eaters after Napoleon's defeat at Waterloo in 1815. The English soldiers met and were immediately conquered by something the Parisians called *bifteck*. The wily French served it with a vegetable the English feared, the potato. Cut up and boiled in fat until it changed color and got crispy, these *frites* fooled the English sentries every time.

Meanwhile, in the former British colonies, meat, in the form of wild game, was readily available. Before the Civil War, per capita meat consumption exceeded 175 pounds per person. (Today the figure for beef and pork combined is about 115 pounds.)

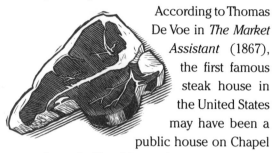

According to Thomas De Voe in *The Market Assistant* (1867), the first famous steak house in the United States may have been a public house on Chapel Street in New Haven, Connecticut, popular with travelers in the early nineteenth century. The host, a man named Butler, always prepared his famous "broiled beefsteak."

"You would find him, with his white cap and apron on, before a heap of live hickory coals, in front of the great wide old-fashioned chimney, having a long handle attached to a large double (hinged) gridiron and a fine steak fastened up in it, so that he could keep the steak turning, first on the one side then on the other, that not a drop of the fine gravy should drip off."

BRINGING THE CATTLE TO MARKET

Cattle, though, came before the steak houses. Columbus, Cortés, and Coronado all vied for the honor of becoming the Americas' first cattle baron. The longhorn literally ran wild in what would be Texas for centuries. But the continent's first cattle drive occurred far to the north—in Massachusetts, in 1655, when cows were marched eastward from Springfield to Boston.

Let's fast-forward through time and move west to Ohio and Illinois and eventually Iowa, where there was ample land to grow crops to feed cattle and create a beef industry on a scale never before conceived. Prior to the Civil War, the meat business was, according to John D. Hicks in *The American Nation,* a "local affair." A local butcher bought a cow from a local farmer, one of them slaughtered it, and it was cut up and on sale the next day. Problems included lack of choice and even lack of product. Railroads were used to transport live cattle to slaughterhouses in cities along the eastern seaboard, but loss of animals by death and the high cost of transport when only a portion of the carcass was usable sharply limited this practice.

The war, as wars always do, inspired advances in technology and a desire to develop the West in its aftermath. By 1873, a Chicago packer named Nelson Morris, who had made a small fortune selling cattle to the Union army during the war, was amassing a large one sending dressed western beef from

(continued)

Chicago to the East. In that pre-income tax year, his firm grossed $11 million.

Also taking a cut was Gustavus F. Swift, a cattle-buyer from the East who set up shop in Chicago in 1875 and funded the development of an improved refrigerator car that made it possible to transport meat safely in summer as well as winter. Philip Armour came to Chicago in the same year and also took advantage of the city's possibilities as a transportation hub. He used the new Union Stockyards to prepare beef and pork for shipment abroad as well as to domestic destinations.

With improved technology and surging immigration providing both labor and customers, and with eager railroad executives virtually underwriting processing and shipping facilities, the meat industry was in a position to expand rapidly. One avenue was to buy the descendants of the conquistadores' longhorn cattle cheaply in the Southwest and have drovers, soon celebrated as cowboys, drive them to railheads in the Midwest. Kansas City prospered. So did other processing centers along the Missouri River, including Sioux City and Omaha.

Even though hit by economic downturns, the industry had its way until Upton Sinclair's *The Jungle*, a polemic novel set in the slaughterhouses, published in 1906, caused people to turn away from red meat for a time. Depression struck the beef industry hard in the aftermath of World War I, and lower sales, in turn, led to sharply decreased demand for grain. The farmers had barely recovered when the Great Depression of the 1930s hit.

World War II and its aftermath was prime time for the beef industry, with the steak represented as the best fuel for strong bodies and the unofficial symbol of American prosperity.

Now, more than half a century later, health and diet concerns broadcast through the media and in books since the mid 1960s have led to both a shrinkage in the amount of fat in American meat (27 percent less in beef, according to the National Cattlemen's Beef Association) and less consumption. Beef sales declined from a high of 74.7 pounds per capita in 1985 to 61.5 in 1993.

Since then, however, the trend has been steadily upward, with 1996 consumption projected to reach 65.2 pounds and the increase of customer traffic at steak restaurants well ahead of other categories.

FLANK

Lean and boneless, flank steak is one of only two steaks cut from the underside of the animal, the other being skirt steak. It's a thin, oblong cut cursed with tough meat fibers and blessed with great flavor. A thin steak, it responds well to marinades and to brief high-heat cooking—as long as it is not cooked past medium. (To be sure, take the steak off the heat when it is still medium-rare. Better yet, learn to like it medium-rare so you can take it off while still rare.) It is essential for chewability to cut a flank steak into thin slices across the grain.

The Best Ever way to prepare flank steak is to grill it as in Grilled Flank Steak with Eggplant and Red Pepper. But this versatile steak often appears in Mexican-inspired recipes, like Three-Pepper Fajitas, and Asian recipes, such as Thai Red Beef Curry.

GRILLED FLANK STEAK

WITH EGGPLANT AND RED PEPPER

Why are cooks and those they feed so enamored of Mediterranean fare? Because of the wonderful colors and flavors of vegetables such as eggplant and bell pepper and seasonings such as lemon, anchovy, olive oil, and garlic. Combine them all in this recipe, then pretend you are in Provence. Serve a cold soup to start, a Côtes du Rhône red such as La Vieille Ferme with the steak, and a berry dessert. A simple meal? Yes. A feast? Yes again.

■■■■■■■■■■■■■■■■■■■■■■■■■

1½ tablespoons fresh lemon juice

3 anchovy fillets, minced

1 tablespoon minced fresh flat-leaf parsley leaves

1 teaspoon minced garlic

2 tablespoons virgin olive oil

Salt and freshly ground black pepper, to taste

1 flank steak (1 to 1¼ pounds)

1 medium eggplant, ends trimmed

1 medium red bell pepper, cored and seeded

Olive oil, garlic flavored if available

1. Combine the lemon juice, anchovies, parsley, and garlic in a small dish and stir to mix. Stir in the virgin olive oil. Season the sauce with salt and pepper.

2. Score both sides of the flank steak in a crisscross pattern, cutting about ⅛ inch deep. Place the meat in a shallow dish that it just fits in. Rub the steak all over with 2 table-spoons of the sauce. Cover and marinate at room temperature for 1 to 1½ hours.

3. Prepare coals for grilling or heat a ridged grill pan.

4. Cut the eggplant crosswise into ¼-inch slices. Cut the red pepper into 1-inch slices. Brush the vegetables with oil and grill until softened on both sides, 5 to 7 minutes. Cut the eggplant slices in half or quarters and the pepper slices in half, if desired. Place the warm vegetables into a dish and toss with the remaining sauce. Set aside at room temperature.

5. Cook the steak until seared and nicely browned on one side, about 4 minutes. Turn and cook 4 minutes more for medium-rare. Remove to a cutting board and let rest for 5 minutes.

6. Carve the steak on the bias across the grain into thin slices. Serve with the eggplant and peppers.

SERVES 4

FLANK STEAK
WITH SHALLOTS

Instead of a sauce, try your steak topped with shallots, the most flavorful member of the onion family. (Anything as difficult to peel as a shallot better taste good!) Serve with a hearty red wine such as Shiraz from Australia.

∎∎∎∎∎∎∎∎∎∎∎∎∎∎∎∎∎∎∎∎∎∎∎

12 medium shallots
2½ tablespoons olive oil
*1½ teaspoons mixed dried herbs, such
    as oregano, rosemary, and thyme*
*¼ teaspoon freshly ground black
    pepper*
½ cup dry vermouth or dry white wine
Salt
1 flank steak (about 1½ pounds)

1. Peel the shallots (see box, page 147, Peeling Garlic and Shallots) and  cut into thin slices. Heat 1½ tablespoons of the oil in a small saucepan over medium-low heat, add the shallots, and cook until they begin to soften, about 3 minutes. Add the herbs, pepper, and vermouth. Cover the pan and simmer for 5 minutes. Uncover the pan, turn up the heat, and boil the liquid until reduced by half, about 7 minutes. Remove from the heat, season with salt and additional pepper; set aside.

2. Prepare coals for grilling or preheat the broiler.

3. Pat the steak dry, then lightly coat it with the remaining 1 tablespoon oil. Grill or broil the steak until seared and nicely browned on one side, about 4 minutes. Turn and cook 4 minutes more for rare or 5 minutes more for medium-rare. Transfer the steak to a carving board and let rest for 5 minutes. Meanwhile, reheat the shallots.

4. Carve the steak on the bias across the grain into very thin slices. Season lightly with salt, if desired, and divide among warm plates. Spoon the shallots and their liquid over the meat and serve at once.

SERVES 4 TO 6

RED FLAG
FLANK STEAK

Raise the red flag when you serve this steak—or lower the spice intensity by removing most or all of the seeds from the jalapeño peppers. The meat is very tasty served hot from the grill or broiler and just as tasty served cold the next day in a sandwich or in a main course salad. Although beer is the most frequently suggested companion to spicy steak, a red wine such as Merlot or Syrah will taste fine, too. Don't pour a top-of-the-line wine, though. Its finesse and nuance will be lost.

■ ■

1 flank steak (1 to 1½ pounds)
¼ cup fresh lime juice
3 tablespoons vegetable oil,
 preferably peanut
1 tablespoon finely chopped
 jalapeño, with seeds to taste
1 tablespoon minced garlic
1 teaspoon chili powder
1 teaspoon coriander seeds,
 crushed
Salt, to taste
½ teaspoon freshly ground black
 pepper

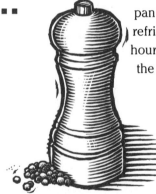

1. Pat the steak dry, and place in a shallow nonreactive pan or dish just large enough to hold it.

2. Combine the lime juice, oil, jalapeño, garlic, chili powder, coriander, ½ teaspoon salt, and pepper in a small bowl. Whisk the mixture together, then pour over the meat. Cover the pan with plastic wrap and refrigerate for at least 4 hours or overnight, turning the meat once.

3. About 30 minutes before cooking, prepare coals for grilling or preheat the broiler.

4. Remove the meat from the marinade and pat dry. Grill or broil until seared and nicely browned on one side, about 4 minutes. Turn and cook 3 minutes more for rare or 4 more minutes for medium-rare. Transfer the steak to a cutting board. Let rest for 5 minutes.

5. Carve the steak on the bias across the grain into thin slices. Arrange onto warm plates or a platter. If desired, sprinkle the slices lightly with salt before serving.

SERVES 6

THAI RED
BEEF CURRY

Preparing this recipe may require a visit to an Asian market to buy several key ingredients. While the dish will taste delicious when you cook it, long-term satisfaction will come from discovering the market and beginning to use it to expand your culinary repertoire. Serve this assertively spiced curry with rice and have plenty of beer on hand.

■■■■■■■■■■■■■■■■■■■■■■■■

2 cans (13 ounces each) unsweetened coconut milk (see Note)
1 cup heavy (or whipping) cream
2 to 3 tablespoons red curry paste (krung gaeng ped daeng; see Note)
1 flank steak (1½ pounds), cut into 2 x ½-inch strips
2 fresh kaffir lime leaves, shredded, (see Note) or ½ teaspoon finely grated lime zest
1 tablespoon shredded fresh basil leaves or 1 teaspoon dried basil
2 tablespoons chopped fresh cilantro leaves
2 fresh red chilies, seeded and sliced into strips
2 tablespoons Thai fish sauce (nam pla; see Note)
Salt, to taste

1. Simmer the coconut milk and cream in a wok or large skillet over low heat, stirring often, until the mixture thickens. Add the curry paste, increase the heat to medium and cook until the color and odor change noticeably, about 5 minutes.

2. Add the beef, lime leaves, basil, 1 tablespoon of the cilantro, chili strips, fish sauce, and salt. Bring the sauce to a boil, lower the heat to medium-low, and simmer, uncovered, until the meat is tender, about 10 minutes.

3. Pour the meat and sauce into a bowl, sprinkle with the remaining cilantro, and serve.

SERVES 6

Note: Canned coconut milk, red curry paste, and Thai fish sauce are available in Asian markets, specialty food shops, and some supermarkets; kaffir lime leaves are available in Asian markets.

THREE-PEPPER
FAJITAS

Restaurant chains have populated their menus with pseudo-fajitas, made with chicken, shellfish, and even vegetables. The original was made with beef, and steak fajitas still are the best. Confronted with inclement weather, I've cooked the beef in my oven broiler. Good but not great. The flavor that comes from charcoal grilling is the secret that makes fajitas so irresistible.

■■■■■■■■■■■■■■■■■■■■■■■■■

1 flank steak (1¼ to 1½ pounds)

1 scallion, white and 2 inches of green, coarsely chopped

2 large jalapeño or serrano chilies, seeded and coarsely chopped

1 cup fresh cilantro leaves

¼ cup plus 2 tablespoons vegetable oil

2 tablespoons fresh lime juice

Salt, to taste

1 teaspoon freshly ground black pepper

1 red bell pepper, seeded and cut into ¼-inch strips

1 green bell pepper, seeded and cut into ¼-inch strips

1 small onion, cut into thin strips

1 large avocado, pitted, peeled, and cut into thin slices

1 cup salsa, preferably homemade (see Note)

8 flour tortillas

1. Pat the steak dry and place it in a tight-fitting glass baking dish. Combine the scallion, jalapeños, cilantro, ¼ cup of the oil, the lime juice, 1 teaspoon salt, and pepper in a blender. Purée until well blended. Pour the mixture over the steak. Marinate at room temperature for 1½ to 2 hours, turning the steak at least once.

2. Prepare coals for grilling.

3. Heat the remaining 2 tablespoons oil in a large skillet or wok. When nearly smoking, add the bell peppers and onion. Stir-fry over high heat for 2 minutes, lower the heat to medium, and cook, covered, until the vegetables are soft, 3 to 4 minutes more.

4. Arrange the avocado slices and salsa in serving bowls and place them on a buffet or dining table.

5. Remove the steak from the marinade and pat it dry. Grill until seared and nicely browned on one side, about 4 minutes. Turn and cook 4 minutes more for medium-rare or 5 minutes more for medium. Transfer the steak to a cutting board. Let it rest for 5 minutes. Warm the tortillas on the grill.

6. Carve the meat across the grain into ¹/₄-inch-thick slices. Cut these slices lengthwise in thirds, salt the meat, and arrange the pieces next to the vegetables on a platter. Wrap the tortillas in a napkin and place on a plate. Place the platter and plate on the table and invite each diner to fill a tortilla with meat, vegetables, avocado, and salsa.

SERVES 6 TO 8

Note: Try my Tomato-Corn Salsa (page 216), with or without the corn.

A NOTE ON TEMPERATURE

Taking a steak directly from the freezer to the grill or broiler is satisfactory so long as you like meat rare or medium-rare in the center. In one experiment, it took three times as long to cook a 1-inch-thick frozen steak to rare than a room temperature steak (25 versus 8 minutes). A refrigerator-temperature steak took 13 minutes. Measure internal temperature in the thickest part of the meat (it cooks last) and avoid meat next to the bone (it cooks faster) or fat (it cooks slower).

FLANK STEAK
SANDWICHES WITH RED PEPPER–DILL KETCHUP

These sandwiches are a nice centerpiece—and conversation piece—at a casual lunch. Arrange them on a platter and offer a selection of chips in bowls. The sandwiches are spread with homemade bell pepper ketchup, mild, pleasant, and much less sweet than commercial tomato ketchup. There will be some ketchup left over. Use it as a condiment or turn it into a sauce for pasta by stirring in pasta cooking water, a tablespoon at a time, until it is thinned to the proper consistency.

STEAK AND DIET

S teak is back, in a big way. Sales have increased steadily through the 1990s and Americans have been choosing steak house restaurants for special meals in record numbers.

The diet police frown. They have lavished vast amounts of time and energy on pointing up the nutritional downside of consuming red meat. In so doing they have made steak a forbidden fruit. The vision of a thick, prime, crust-on-the-outside, rosy-red-on-the-inside steak-house cut slathered with butter and garnished with garlands of fried onion rings dances in many heads, including mine.

But scientists are not distracted by the sizzles when cutting into a steak in the laboratory. They focus on protein and fat, vitamins and minerals, calories and cholesterol, and sodium too. What they find is an impressive amount of most of these. Well past the middle of this century the industry needed to do no more than boost red meat as the prime source of protein, which Americans translated into energy and vigor. In the current era, with athletes using "carbohydrate loading" for energy, protein is less honored than it was. So beef's cheerleaders now let us know that in addition to protein, steak is a "significant source" of B vitamins, iron, zinc, niacin, and even phosphorus. Antagonists,

meanwhile continue to target beef's fat, cholesterol, and calorie content.

Genetic engineering and closer trimming have given us steak with less fat than a decade ago. But the public, tired of inconclusive and contradictory studies, seems to be sympathetic when the president of the National Cattlemen's Beef Association says, "The Catch 22 in all of this is that we can produce very lean meat but you wouldn't want to eat it." Americans are reassured, too, when an overwhelming majority of nutritionists testify that steak, eaten in moderation, is healthy.

There's no question, though, that everything in moderation is a creed that's difficult to follow in a steak house.

But what I reaffirmed in developing and testing the recipes for this book is that a steak dinner doesn't have to be a larger-than-life feast to be enjoyable and satisfying. At home, it can be a family meal, part of a varied diet, with the meat served in portions that fit easily within the dietary guidelines.

While I offer menu and side-dish suggestions, for the most part I leave it to you to add the vegetables, carve down the portions, or cut away the dessert altogether. Use common sense and sculpt your steak dinner into something compatible with the diets of those who will eat it.

1 flank steak (about 1¼ pounds)

2 red bell peppers, roasted, peeled, and seeded (see page 88)

½ cup minced scallions, white only

1 teaspoon paprika, hot or sweet, preferably Hungarian

¼ teaspoon freshly ground black pepper

¼ teaspoon white pepper

¼ teaspoon sugar

2 tablespoons fresh lemon juice or red wine vinegar

½ cup olive oil

⅓ cup chopped fresh dill

Salt, to taste

2 tablespoons vegetable oil

8 slices of crusty white bread or 4 French or kaiser rolls

1. Pat the steak dry and set aside to come to room temperature. Preheat the broiler.

2. Cut the bell peppers into chunks and place them in a food processor or blender. Add the scallions, paprika, black pepper, white pepper, sugar, and lemon juice. Process until the mixture forms a smooth purée. With the machine running, add the olive oil in a thin stream. Pour the ketchup into a small bowl and stir in the dill. Add the salt. Adjust the flavor with additional pepper or sugar, if desired. (The ketchup may be made ahead. Cover tightly and store in the refrigerator for up to 4 days.)

3. Coat the steak lightly with vegetable oil. Place it under the broiler and cook until seared and nicely browned on one side, about 4 minutes. Turn and cook 3 minutes more for medium-rare or 4 minutes more for medium. Let the steak cool on a cutting board. (The steak may be cooked ahead and refrigerated.)

4. Coat each slice of bread with 1 tablespoon of the ketchup, or coat the inside of each roll with 2 tablespoons. Carve the steak on the bias across the grain into thin slices. Lightly salt the meat, then stack it on the bread or in the rolls. Close the sandwiches or rolls, cut in half, and serve.

SERVES 4

SKIRT

Think of this sweet and juicy steak from the very downtown plate cut as the flank steak's less inhibited cousin. Shaped like a belt and more flexible than the flank, it can be stuffed and rolled more easily as well as cooked flat. Nonetheless, either cut can substitute for the other in most recipes.

Long a virtual secret reserved to ethnic diners, the skirt steak was thrust into the spotlight when the fajita enjoyed its fifteen minutes of mass popularity. (Prepared well, as in Three-Pepper Fajitas made with freshly-grilled flank or skirt steak, fajitas are still delicious.)

For the Best Ever skirt steak, try Broiled Skirt Steak with an Asian Accent. You'll enjoy this worldly cut, too, when barbecued in the Korean style, served with a Caribbean Sauce or curried with a yogurt relish.

SPICY SKIRT STEAK

T his pleasantly spiced, juicy steak is a treat anytime. But when I serve it with scrambled eggs and home-fried potatoes, it becomes the linchpin for a lively Sunday brunch. This is the original expandable brunch when you think of steak as an accordion. I have served a skirt steak to as few as four and as many as ten. If unexpected guests show up, I just slice the meat thinner. It is not a spontaneous occasion, however. I parboil a quarter of a pound of potatoes per person the day before and marinate the steak overnight. I also make sure I have at least two eggs per person on hand and Champagne or a chilled light red wine such as Beaujolais.

■ ■

1 or 2 skirt steaks (1 to 1½ pounds total)
2 sprigs of fresh thyme
1 tablespoon dry sherry
1 tablespoon sherry vinegar
1 tablespoon fresh lemon juice
½ teaspoon ground cumin
½ teaspoon chili powder
1 canned chipotle chili pepper plus
    1 teaspoon of the juice
¼ cup dry white wine
¼ cup vegetable oil
Salt, to taste

1. Pat the steak or steaks dry, cut in half crosswise, and place in a nonreactive dish or gallon-size Ziploc plastic bag.

2. Combine the thyme, sherry, vinegar, lemon juice, cumin, chili powder, chipotle pepper and juice, wine, and oil in a blender or food processor and blend to purée. Pour over the steak and cover the pan or seal the bag. Refrigerate for 8 hours or overnight.

3. Remove the steak from the refrigerator and allow it to come to room temperature. Preheat the broiler or prepare coals for grilling.

4. Broil or grill the steak until seared and nicely browned on one side, about 3 minutes. Turn and cook for 2½ minutes more for medium-rare or 3 minutes for medium. Transfer the steak to a cutting board, cover loosely with aluminum foil, and let rest for 5 minutes.

5. Cut the meat on the bias across the grain into ¼-inch-thick slices. The meat will look rarer than it is. Sprinkle with salt before serving.

SERVES 4 TO 6

Note: To cut cooked skirt steak or flank steak across the grain, angle the knife slightly horizontally to cut at a slant instead of vertically.

BROILED SKIRT STEAK

WITH AN ASIAN ACCENT

Here is one of the most basic, and tastiest, ways to prepare this easy-to-cook cut. Serve it with carry-out coleslaw or fried rice and you will have reduced cooking time to close to zero.

■ ■

1 skirt steak (about 1 pound)
¼ cup soy sauce
¼ cup rice wine or dry white wine
¼ cup chopped scallions, white only
2 tablespoons rice wine vinegar
2 teaspoons minced fresh ginger

1. Arrange the skirt steak in a shallow dish just large enough to hold it, cutting it in half if necessary. Combine the soy sauce, wine, scallions, vinegar, and ginger in a small bowl and stir well. Pour this marinade over the meat. Cover the dish and refrigerate for 2 to 3 hours, turning the meat once.

2. Preheat the broiler or prepare coals for grilling.

3. Drain the meat and pat it dry. Broil or grill until seared and nicely browned on one side, about 3 minutes. Turn and cook the meat for 2 minutes more. Because of the uneven shape of the steak, it will be cooked from rare to medium-well. Transfer to a cutting board and let rest for 5 minutes.

4. Cut across the grain on the bias into thin slices and serve.

SERVES 3 OR 4

GRILLED SKIRT STEAK
WITH FRESH TOMATO SAUCE

I n the Heartland, we save this combination for August when the local tomatoes are achingly ripe and there's fresh corn in every farmstand and market. I keep the steak marinade simple so it won't intrude on the subtle fresh flavor of the sauce. A hint: Make the tomato sauce at the last minute so that it won't become soggy with excess juices.

■■■■■■■■■■■■■■■■■■■■■■■■■

1 skirt steak (1 to 1¼ pounds)
¼ cup plus 1 tablespoon fresh
    lemon juice
3 tablespoons finely chopped fresh
    basil
Salt and freshly ground black pepper,
    to taste
1 cup vegetable oil
1 medium tomato, seeded and diced
1 small red bell pepper, roasted,
    peeled, seeded and diced
    (see page 88)
¼ cup diced sweet onion
¼ cup olive oil, preferably extra
    virgin

1. Pat the steak dry and place it in a shallow dish or bowl. Combine ¼ cup of the lemon juice, 2 tablespoons of the basil, ½ teaspoon salt, and ½ teaspoon black pepper in a small bowl. Stir in the vegetable oil. Pour this marinade over the steak, coating all sides. Cover the dish and marinate the steak in the refrigerator for 2 to 4 hours, turning once.

2. Prepare coals for grilling or preheat the broiler.

3. Combine the tomato, bell pepper, and onion in a bowl. Add the remaining 1 tablespoon basil and season liberally with salt and pepper. Stir in the olive oil and remaining 1 tablespoon lemon juice. Taste and adjust seasoning as desired.

4. Remove the steak from the marinade and pat it dry. Broil or grill until seared and nicely browned on one side, about 3 minutes. Turn and cook for 2 minutes more. Because of the uneven shape of the steak, it will be cooked from rare to medium-well. Transfer the steak to a cutting board and let rest for 5 minutes.

5. Cut on the bias across the grain into thin slices. Serve with the tomato sauce.

SERVES 4

CURRIED SKIRT STEAK

WITH YOGURT RELISH

This meat and relish preparation is nearly effortless, perfect for casual summer entertaining or a backyard family meal. Choose either of these two particularly good accompaniments to complete the menu: Okra with Onions and Toasted Cumin or Hot Bulgur Salad (see Index).

■■■■■■■■■■■■■■■■■■■■■■■■■

1 skirt steak or flank steak
  (1 to 1¼ pounds)
1 tablespoon curry powder
3 tablespoons vegetable oil
1 cup plain lowfat yogurt, drained
  of excess liquid
½ cup peeled and chopped English
  (seedless) cucumber
¼ cup minced scallions,
  white only
1 tablespoon chopped fresh
  cilantro leaves
¼ teaspoon white pepper
Salt, to taste
⅛ teaspoon cayenne pepper

1. Cut the steak in half for easier handling. Pat dry and arrange flat in a shallow pan. Mix the curry powder and oil together in a small dish. Brush this mixture on all sides of the meat, coating well. Cover with plastic wrap and set aside to marinate at room temperature for 1 hour or in the refrigerator for at least 2 hours.

2. Combine the yogurt with the cucumber,

scallions, cilantro, white pepper, ½ teaspoon salt, and cayenne in a medium-size bowl. Stir to mix the ingredients thoroughly. (The relish may be made ahead and kept refrigerated until 30 minutes before serving.)

3. If the meat has been refrigerated, remove it from the refrigerator 30 minutes before cooking. Prepare coals for grilling or preheat the broiler.

4. Grill or broil the meat until seared and nicely browned on one side, about 3 minutes. Turn and cook for 3 minutes more for rare or 4 minutes more for medium. Sprinkle the meat lightly with salt after turning to cook the second side. When cooked, transfer it to a cutting board. Let rest for 5 minutes. Cut the meat on the bias into ¼-inch-thick slices, and arrange on warmed plates. Spoon the yogurt relish alongside the meat.

SERVES 3 OR 4

MUSTARD

Mustard has a sublime affinity for beef in general and steak in particular. For proof, try these mustard creations with a steak. Mustard Butter is simplicity itself. On top of a hot broiled or panbroiled steak, this composed butter gradually melts, flavoring the meat and juices.

Handmade Caper Mustard is very well suited to grilled or broiled flank or skirt steak or as a spread on bread for a steak sandwich.

MUSTARD BUTTER

2 tablespoons Dijon mustard
1 tablespoon chopped fresh flat-leaf
  parsley leaves
1 tablespoon minced shallots
8 tablespoons (1 stick) unsalted butter,
  softened
½ teaspoon salt
¼ teaspoon white pepper

1. Combine the mustard, parsley, and shallots in a small bowl. Blend thoroughly with a small whisk. Cut the butter (it should be soft but not melted) into several pieces and add them to the bowl. Whisk vigorously until well blended. Season with salt and pepper.

2. Spread a sheet of plastic wrap on the table. Using a rubber spatula, transfer the butter to the plastic wrap. Push and shape the butter into a log the diameter of a 25-cent piece. Roll up in the plastic wrap and refrigerate or freeze.

3. Allow the butter to come to a temperature at which it is easy to cut. Cut ¼-inch-thick slices and place them on top of a hot steak. Freeze or refrigerate remaining butter for a future meal.

SERVES 8

HANDMADE CAPER MUSTARD

3 tablespoons mustard seeds
⅓ cup dry mustard
½ cup hot water
½ cup white wine vinegar, preferably
  tarragon flavored
½ cup dry white wine
1 large sprig fresh tarragon
1 teaspoon coarse salt
1 teaspoon granulated sugar
2 tablespoons capers, the smaller
  the better, rinsed and drained

1. Combine the mustard seeds, dry mustard, water, and vinegar in a small bowl. Cover and set aside for at least 3 hours.

2. Pour the wine into a nonreactive saucepan. Add the tarragon sprig, bring to a boil, and strain over the mustard seed mixture. Stir in the salt, sugar, and capers. Purée in a food processor or blender until smooth.

3. Return to the saucepan and cook over very low heat, stirring often, for 10 minutes. Transfer the mustard to a bowl and let it cool. Refrigerate, covered, for at least 24 hours before using.

MAKES ABOUT 1 CUP

DAVID SCHY'S

DAVID SCHY'S
SKIRT STEAK
WITH CARIBBEAN SAUCE

I n an era of free-form cooking when the disparate elements employed in the name of fusion cuisine often refuse to fuse, David Schy, chef-owner of Chicago's popular Hubbard Street Grill, has emerged as a master at shaping complex flavor combinations into coherent finished dishes. His skirt steak recipe can become the centerpiece of a party menu that might include fish, soup or salad, rice and black beans, a rum-flavored tropical fruit dessert, and Red Stripe beer from Jamaica. When your guests learn what's on the menu and ask to bring friends, simply double the recipe.

3 tablespoons soy sauce

½ cup Worcestershire sauce

¼ cup pineapple juice

2 tablespoons fresh lime juice

1 tablespoon red wine vinegar

1 tablespoon dry red wine

1½ teaspoons dried oregano

¾ teaspoon dried basil

¾ teaspoon granulated garlic

¾ teaspoon ground ginger

¾ teaspoon ground allspice

¾ teaspoon Chinese five-spice powder

½ teaspoon crushed red pepper flakes

Freshly ground black pepper

¼ teaspoon salt

½ cup commercial barbecue sauce, such as K.C. Masterpiece hickory

½ cup Ketchapeño (see Note)

2 tablespoons honey

2 or 3 skirt steaks (about 3 pounds total)

1 tablespoon minced garlic

¼ cup olive oil

1. Make the sauce 1 or 2 days ahead. Combine the soy sauce, Worcestershire, pineapple juice, 1 tablespoon of the lime juice, the vinegar, wine, oregano, basil, granulated garlic, ginger, allspice, five-spice powder, red pepper flakes, ¾ teaspoon black pepper, and salt in a large saucepan. Stir in the barbecue sauce, Ketchapeño, and honey. Bring the mixture to a boil, lower the heat, and simmer, uncovered, for 30 minutes, stirring frequently, to blend the flavors. Allow sauce to cool. Refrigerate, covered, until ready to grill the meat.

2. Cut the steaks crosswise into 12 pieces. Arrange them in a nonreactive pan or baking dish. Combine the minced garlic, remaining

tablespoon lime juice, $1/4$ teaspoon black pepper, and olive oil in a small bowl. Stir well and coat the steaks. Cover and marinate the steaks in the refrigerator for 4 to 6 hours.

3. Prepare coals for grilling or preheat the broiler.

4. Reheat the sauce to boiling. Lower the heat and simmer while cooking the steak. Grill or broil the steaks, in batches if necessary, until seared and nicely browned on one side, about 3 minutes. Turn and cook for 2 minutes more for medium-rare or 3 minutes for medium. Transfer the steaks to a cutting board and let rest for 5 minutes.

5. Cut the steaks on the bias across the grain into thin slices. Serve on a platter, accompanied by the warm sauce.

SERVES 6 TO 8

Note: Ketchapeño is a tomato-based condiment Chef Schy developed. It is marketed in major cities. If unavailable, substitute $1/2$ cup ketchup mixed with 1 teaspoon hot pepper sauce.

BARBECUED SKIRT STEAK
KOREAN STYLE

The Koreans are masters at marinating and seasoning beef. They also enjoy grilling to such an extent they have created special tables with dome-shaped metal grills in their restaurants so seated guests can cook their own meat. Lacking such a table, an oven broiler will cook the meat adequately. But I prefer to use a ridged grill pan. (Victor is the brand name of mine, and Victor's right at home in a house where a number of inanimate objects have human names.) The marinade's sweet-salty tug-of-war and its heavy accent of sesame makes the meat irresistible. The marinade works equally well with short ribs. Serve with bottled kim-chee ("mild" on the label provides cabbage that is hot enough for me) and rice.

■■■■■■■■■■■■■■■■■■■■■■■■

1 skirt steak (about 1¼ pounds)
    trimmed of fat, well chilled
1 tablespoon sesame seeds
½ cup minced scallions
1 tablespoon minced garlic
½ teaspoon freshly ground black
    pepper
1½ tablespoons sugar
¼ cup soy sauce
1 tablespoon dry sherry or white wine
1 tablespoon sesame oil
1 tablespoon vegetable oil

1. Cut the steak on the bias into ³/₈-inch-thick slices. You should have 27 to 30 pieces. Place the slices in a single layer in a shallow pan or platter. Set aside. Toast the sesame seeds in a small skillet over medium-low heat, tossing often, until golden and aromatic, about 5 minutes. Grind the seeds in a mortar with a pestle or in a spice grinder.

2. Combine the ground seeds with the scallions, garlic, pepper, sugar, soy sauce, sherry, and sesame oil in a small bowl. Stir until the sugar has dissolved and the ingredients are well mixed. Pour this marinade evenly over the steak. Marinate for 1 hour, turning the meat once.

3. Coat a ridged grill pan with the vegetable oil or line an oven broiler pan with aluminum foil and heat. When very hot, add 9 pieces of beef directly from the marinade to the grill pan in rows of 3. Cook until seared and nicely browned, 1½ minutes. Turn the meat, and cook 1 minute more for rare or 1½ minutes more for medium-rare. Transfer the cooked meat to a plate and keep warm. Repeat until all the slices are cooked. If using a broiler, cook the meat in 2 batches, allowing the same amount of time as in the grill pan. Serve at once.

SERVES 4

JEAN JOHO'S

HERBED SKIRT STEAK

C hef Joho, who made his reputation as an innovator high above Chicago in his elegant fortieth floor aerie, Everest, came down to earth in 1995 to establish the casual and constantly bustling Brasserie Jo. While the chef uses his right hand to combine truffles and filet at Everest, his left is creating tastes just as special at Brasserie Jo. In one dish he presents fragrant herbs and humble skirt steak in a beautiful pinwheel pattern. For this dish I've simplified the presentation. Serve this steak brasserie style, with home-fried potatoes and a garnish of watercress. Drink Beaujolais or Côtes du Rhône.

■ ■

3 tablespoons chopped fresh
*   rosemary leaves*
3 tablespoons chopped fresh thyme
*   leaves*
1/2 cup plus 2 tablespoons chopped
*   fresh flat-leaf parsley leaves*
1 skirt steak (about 1 1/4 pounds)
8 tablespoons (1 stick) unsalted
*   butter, at room temperature*
1 1/2 teaspoons fresh lemon juice
Dash of Worcestershire sauce
Salt and freshly ground black pepper,
*   to taste*
1/2 tablespoon oil, preferably
*   grape seed*
1/3 cup beef broth

1. Combine the rosemary, thyme, and ½ cup of the parsley in a small bowl. Mix well.

2. Cut the skirt steak crosswise into four equal pieces. Place one piece of steak on a sheet of plastic wrap. Cover with one-quarter of the mixed herbs. Top with a second piece of meat to make a sandwich and sprinkle another one-quarter of the herb mixture on top. Fold the plastic wrap over the meat and herbs to make a tight package. Repeat the process with remaining meat and herbs to make a second sandwich. Wrap it tightly and

refrigerate for 6 to 8 hours or overnight.

3. Place the butter in a small bowl. Add the remaining 2 tablespoons parsley, the lemon juice, and the Worcestershire and beat with a whisk to combine the ingredients. Season with salt and pepper. Cover and refrigerate until ready to cook the meat.

4. Remove the meat from the refrigerator, unwrap it, and discard the plastic wrap. Remove the flavored butter from the refrigerator as well. Season the layered steaks with salt and pepper.

5. Heat the oil in a skillet large enough to hold both sandwiches in a single layer. When hot, add the steaks, herb-free side down. Sear the steaks for 1 minute, then pour in the broth, reduce the heat to low, and cover the pan. Simmer the steaks until each layer is rare to medium-rare, 10 to 12 minutes.

6. Transfer the meat to a cutting board and let rest 2 minutes. Slice each sandwich crosswise into eight equal pieces. Portion onto warm plates, top each portion with a dollop of parsley butter, and serve.

SERVES 4 TO 6

CROSSTOWN CUTS

Inevitably, the steak-lover is tempted to cook other cuts of beef. The most popular alternative, by far, is ground beef. I've spent endless summers forming hamburgers, seeking the perfect thickness, original seasoning combinations, and compatible toppings. I think you will enjoy one I call the Herb-Burger. (No, it's not named for a person.)

Another cut that appeared often at the dinner table during my boyhood was cube steak. I thought I'd never make it taste special until I prepared it as chicken-fried steak. Beef ribs, too, are a challenge to cook; or they were until I learned to prepare them in a smoker.

SMOKED BEEF RIBS

WITH BILL'S RUB

I n my experience, beef ribs usually emerge from a conventional barbecue tough and fatty and are far less agreeable to eat than pork ribs. So I applied the virtues that tame many creatures, gentleness and patience, seasoned the ribs with a lively herb-and-spice rub, and cooked them in an outdoor smoker. After several hours of smoking (largely unsupervised), the ribs emerged tender, aromatic, and almost fat free. In a word: realgood. Meaty beef short ribs respond beautifully to the same treatment. If they are your preference, note that they'll smoke in less time. Serve these ribs dry or with plenty of your favorite barbecue sauce on the side.

■■■■■■■■■■■■■■■■■■■■■■■■■

4 slabs beef back ribs (3 to 3½ pounds each) or 10 beef short ribs (8 to 12 ounces each)

Bill's Rub
2 tablespoons black peppercorns
1 tablespoon white peppercorns
1 tablespoon cumin seeds
1 tablespoon chili powder
2 teaspoons cayenne pepper
2 teaspoons dried oregano
1½ teaspoons granulated garlic
1 teaspoon dry mustard
1 teaspoon celery salt

1. Bring the ribs to room temperature, pat them dry and set aside.

2. Coarsely grind the black and white peppercorns and the cumin seeds in a mortar with a pestle, or in a spice grinder, or a pepper mill. Combine with the chile powder, cayenne, oregano, garlic, mustard, and celery salt in a small bowl. Stir well.

3. Prepare the smoker following the manufacturer's directions.

4. Coat each slab of ribs with about 2 tablespoons of the rub, pressing the mixture into the meat, or allow 1 tablespoon of the rub per short rib. Cook until the ribs are between golden and dark brown and the meat has begun to pull away from the bone, about 5½ hours for back ribs and 5 hours for short ribs, turning the ribs once or twice.

5. To serve, cut the slabs into individual ribs and offer 2 or 3 to each person or serve each person 1 short rib.

SERVES 10 OR MORE

MAKING BARBECUE SAUCE

There is cooking that is work and cooking that's fun. For me, making pastry falls into the work category, while making barbecue sauce is pure fun, an indoor sport that provides me with something tasty to call my own.

It's fun because if I start with a commercial sauce, most of the problems I create can be fixed with a little tinkering. Playing chef, I add a spoonful of this and pinch of that. My object is to doctor it until something distinctly different and pleasing emerges.

The sauce I choose as my base almost certainly will have sprung from one of three roots: tomato, vinegar, or molasses. My objective is to look beyond that base and decide in which of five well-defined flavor areas I want my sauce to be parked and then choose ingredients to get me there. The flavor areas are:

Sour or tart: Lemon juice, lime juice, tamarind, plain and flavored vinegars.

Sweet: Brown sugar, honey, hoisin sauce, corn syrup.

Salty: Coarse salt, celery salt.

Spicy: More or less in descending order of popularity—coarsely ground black pepper, cayenne pepper, paprika, chili powder, garlic powder, cumin (ground and seeds), anise or fennel seeds, onion powder, ground ginger, white pepper, coriander seeds, ground cinnamon, ground clove, ground allspice, grated nutmeg, dried basil, dried oregano.

Tomatoey: Ketchup, tomato paste, tomato juice, chili sauce.

A combination of flavors from two or more of these categories is fine. The game, and this should be a game, is to experiment. Use a liquid, even if it's only water, to thin the sauce if it becomes too thick. Add some sugar if you've been too heavy-handed with the cayenne.

Don't rush things, either. Your palate needs time to recover between tastes. Give the sauce plenty of time to simmer (as much as two hours, stirring every five minutes, for a from-scratch sauce). In fact, try to make the sauce at least a day ahead so the flavors really come together and develop.

Other advice I've learned to heed is to work with small quantities to limit the expense of failure and to limit the number of ingredients as well. If something doesn't have a negative effect, leave it in, but you will reach a point of diminishing returns where whatever is added has virtually no effect on the smell or taste of the sauce.

Instead of offering a recipe—and immediately quenching the fire of creativity—I send you into the kitchen with this inspirational message: Trust your taste buds!

CHICKEN-FRIED
CUBE STEAK
WITH PAN GRAVY

Few meats or meat preparations have received a worse rap over the years than the chewy cube steak or the greasy, tough chicken-fried steak served in the South and Southwest. Chicken-fried steak usually is made from top round, pounded extensively in an attempt to tenderize it, and then fried in the same fashion as chicken. Since the cube steak already has been tenderized by machine (those tracks on the steak show where tendons have been cut), I thought it would be the ideal cut to turn into a quicker and easier chicken-fried steak. And so it is. Serve with mashed potatoes or rice.

2 cube steaks (about 6 ounces each)
1/4 cup plus 2 tablespoons all-purpose
   flour
Salt, to taste
Freshly ground black pepper, to taste
Paprika, to taste
1 cup vegetable oil
2 tablespoons diced tomato
1 tablespoon diced onion
1 1/4 cups milk, or more if needed

1. Pat the steaks dry and set aside. Combine 1/4 cup flour, 1/2 teaspoon salt, 1/2 teaspoon pepper, and 1/2 teaspoon paprika on a plate and stir with a fork until well mixed. Coat the steaks with the flour mixture and pound lightly on both sides with a rolling pin or the side of a cleaver to help the meat absorb the flour. All the flour should be used.

2. Heat the oil in a skillet until very hot (375°F). Add the steaks and cook until seared and well-crusted on one side, about 2 1/2 minutes. Turn the steaks with tongs and cook 2 minutes more for medium. Transfer the steaks to a plate lined with paper towels and keep warm.

3. Pour off all but 2 tablespoons of the cooking oil. Return the pan to a burner, add the remaining 2 tablespoons flour, and whisk over medium-low heat for 1 minute. Add the tomato and onion. Add the milk and whisk until a thick gravy forms. Continue to cook for 1 minute more, adding more milk if the gravy is too thick. Season with salt, pepper, and paprika.

4. Spoon 1/3 cup of gravy onto each of 2 warm plates. Slice each steak and place on top of the gravy. Pass the remaining gravy at the table.

SERVES 2

THE HERB-BURGER

No food, except perhaps the comfort food custard, is more likely to bring out the child in us than the hamburger. Certainly no child could be more stubborn and unyielding than some of my otherwise easygoing friends when it comes to the size, shape, type of bread or roll, and condiments involved in the perfect hamburger. I insist upon hamburgers that are unadorned with cheese, fitted into a toasted bun (which does a much better job of keeping the juices captive than sandwich bread), and garnished with nothing more than onion—raw, cooked, or both—and ketchup. The burger that follows is simple, noble, and as fancy as I want a hamburger to be. Placing several shards of ice in the center was a trick used by James Beard to keep the center moist. I've been making my hamburgers very successfully with ground round steak in an 85 to 15 percent lean-fat ratio. For added flavor, use homemade Red Pepper–Dill Ketchup (see page 159).

■■■■■■■■■■■■■■■■■■■■■■■■■

5 ounces ground chuck or round
1 tablespoon finely chopped onion
1 teaspoon dried herbs such as basil,
*   oregano, or herbes de Provence*
Freshly ground black pepper, to taste
1 ice cube, cracked into shards (optional)
Vegetable oil or unsalted butter
Salt, to taste
1 hamburger bun
1 slice (¹/₄-inch thick) sweet onion, raw
*   or sautéed (optional)*
Ketchup

1. Spread the meat with your fingers to make a thin layer. Sprinkle the chopped onion, herbs, and ¹/₄ teaspoon pepper over the surface. Place 4 or 5 ice shards, if using, in the center and, working the meat as little as possible, form a patty 1 inch thick.

2. Heat a heavy frying pan, preferably cast-iron, over medium-high heat. When hot, add a glaze of oil and the hamburger. Cook until the meat is crusty brown on one side, 4 minutes. Turn, season the cooked side with salt, and cook until brown throughout but still tender and juicy, 5 minutes more.

3. Meanwhile, open the bun, spread a little oil or butter over the inside surfaces and toast it.

4. If desired, place the onion slice on the bun. Top with the burger. Season with salt and pepper and anoint with ketchup. Eat!

SERVES 1

WHAT TO DRINK

BEFORE AND AFTER YOUR STEAK

For guidance in stocking your home bar, the best place to look is the bar of a fine steak house. The martini has had no need to make a comeback in steak houses, so a first-class gin—my choice is Bombay—is de rigueur. I buy dry vermouth by the half-bottle and keep it in the refrigerator, otherwise, like an open bottle of wine, it will oxidize.

Cocktails are still popular among beefeaters, with brand-name vodkas being poured on the rocks and in a wide variety of mixed drinks. The other liquors I keep on hand are blended Scotch, bourbon, and tequila. I'm inordinately fond of a slightly bitter-tasting Italian cocktail called "negroni," made of equal parts of gin, sweet vermouth, and Campari, so I stock those ingredients and occasionally drink the Campari with sparkling water.

Non-alcohol wines and beers continue to improve in quality and I always have both available as well as traditional wine to be poured by the glass. If possible, I will convince a guest to choose fruit juice over a soft drink.

Bartenders tell me there has been a downturn in demand for rich after-dinner drinks. Perhaps that's due to the improvement in restaurant dessert selections. In their place, in my home as well as in restaurants, guests seem delighted at the opportunity to taste, and perhaps compare, single-malt Scotch, Cognac, port, and even cigars.

Here's a starter set of recipes I use. With the exception of the Caribbean blush, they are strong enough that you will not need to make a second batch. The daiquiri comes from Ed Moose of Moose's restaurant in San Francisco. The margarita is from Maida Heatter.

In sum, pour a taste of the good life.

MY MARTINI

¾ cup gin, preferably regular Bombay
2 tablespoons dry vermouth, preferably
  Boissiere
8 ice cubes
4 small pimiento-stuffed olives, skewered on
  2 toothpicks

1. Combine the gin and vermouth in a cocktail shaker. Add the ice cubes and shake vigorously (to a waltz rhythm, according to William Powell in one of the *Thin Man* films) until your hand tells you to put down the cold shaker.

2. Place the olive skewers in 2 martini glasses and pour the cocktail over them. Add any remaining shards of ice, if desired.

Note: My wife has a taste for anchovy-stuffed olives. Their saltiness is intriguing, but ask your guest's permission before popping one into the glass.

MAKES 2 COCKTAILS

QUEEN MAIDA'S MARGARITA

3 tablespoons fresh lemon juice
⅓ cup Cointreau
⅔ cup top-quality tequila
Ice cubes
Salt (optional)

1. Pour the lemon juice, Cointreau, and tequila into a blender. Add 8 ice cubes or enough to bring the level to 2 cups. Blend until only a few shards of ice are left.

2. Salt the rims of 2 outsized wine or brandy glasses, if desired. Divide the margarita between the glasses and add extra ice cubes.

MAKES 2 COCKTAILS

CARIBBEAN BLUSH

⅔ cup dry white wine, chilled
¼ cup pink grapefruit juice cocktail, chilled
1 tablespoon grenadine syrup
1 or 2 ice cubes (optional)

Mix the wine, grapefruit juice cocktail, and the grenadine in a wine glass. Add the ice cubes, if desired.

MAKES 2 COCKTAILS

WHISKEY SOUR MADE SIMPLE

2 tablespoons superfine sugar
3 tablespoons fresh lemon juice
¾ cup top-quality bourbon
8 ice cubes
1 thin slice orange, cut in half (optional)

1. Pour the sugar and lemon juice into a cocktail shaker and swirl until the sugar dissolves. Add the bourbon and ice cubes and shake vigorously (to a fox-trot rhythm) until your hand tells you to put down the cold shaker.

2. Pour into 2 rocks glasses, adding the remaining shards of ice. Garnish each glass with an orange slice half, if desired.

MAKES 2 COCKTAILS

HEMINGWAY'S DAIQUIRI

⅓ cup light rum, preferably Bacardi
3 tablespoons fresh lime juice
1 tablespoon maraschino liqueur
1 tablespoon fresh grapefruit juice
4 ice cubes

1. Pour the rum, lime juice, maraschino liqueur, and grapefruit juice into a cocktail shaker. Add the ice cubes and shake vigorously.

2. Serve straight up or on the rocks.

MAKES 2 COCKTAILS

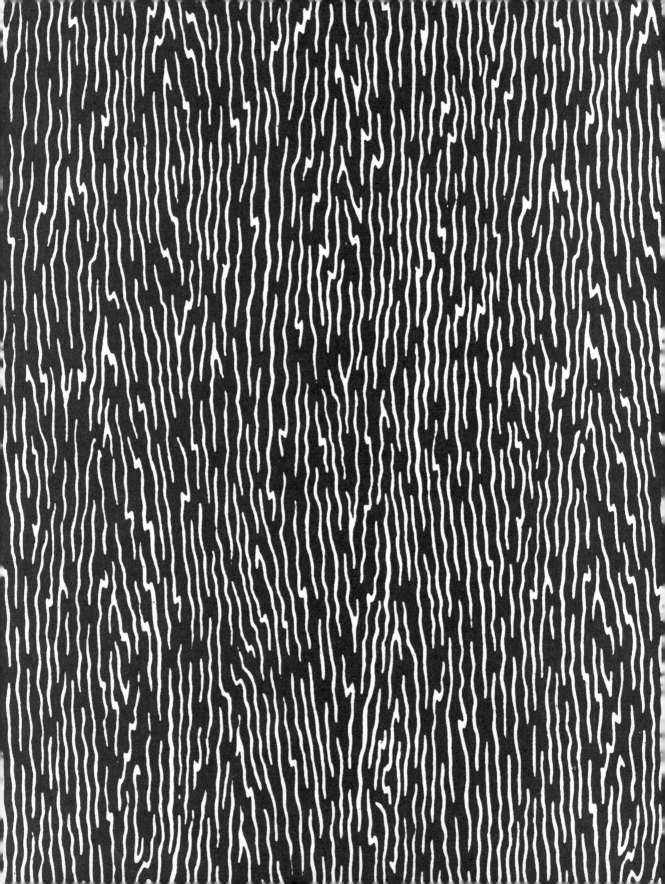

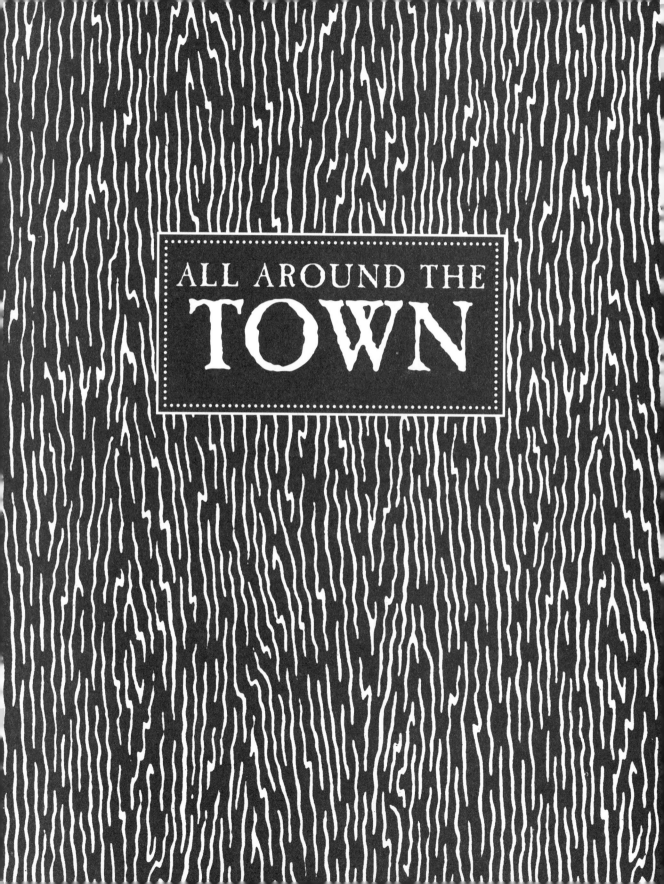

ALL AROUND THE
TOWN

BEFORE THE STEAK

Generally speaking, there's not much culinary foreplay when steak is the main course of a meal. Shrimp cocktail (usually jumbo) or a salad (also outsized) is considered sufficient for already whetted appetites. But in my own kitchen at home I need not be as single-minded as the steak house cook. I like to serve guests a first course, but one that is more stimulating than filling—soup, salad, or a vegetable dish when eating indoors, a preliminary nibble such as a dip or pâté while my guests watch their steaks cook on an outdoor grill. My outdoor dining suggestions also include Mango Guacamole, White Gazpacho, and Italian Eggplant and Pesto Dip. When dining indoors, give special consideration to my Fabulous Fried Zucchini and the Pancetta and Winter Vegetable Salad.

PRE-GAME

BEER AND CHEESE SPREAD

A time-honored way to ward off hunger before or during a sports event on TV or while waiting for the grill to heat up is to put out a spread or dip with crackers or chips. This cheese spread is a hit with beer drinkers, but I don't always put it away when the meal begins. I find it makes a terrific topping for hamburgers or flank or skirt steak.

■■■■■■■■■■■■■■■■■■■■■■■■■■

8 ounces sharp Cheddar cheese,
 cut into small pieces
2 ounces blue cheese, cut into small
 pieces
3 ounces cream cheese, cut into small
 pieces
1 teaspoon caraway seeds
1 teaspoon paprika
½ cup ale

Combine the Cheddar, blue, and cream cheeses in a food processor. Add the caraway seeds, paprika, and ale. Process until the mixture is smooth. Transfer the spread to a serving bowl, cover and refrigerate until needed. Serve at room temperature.

MAKES ABOUT 2 CUPS

ITALIAN

EGGPLANT AND PESTO DIP

O ven-roasted eggplant has the perfect texture for a dip and combines beautifully with basil- and oil-rich pesto sauce. When I'm pressed for time in preparing for company, a common occurrence, I cut a corner by picking up a jar of bottled pesto at the market. Pita chips or lavash crackers make fine shovels for moving this dip from bowl to mouth.

■ ■

1 medium eggplant
3 tablespoons pesto sauce, homemade or bottled
½ teaspoon salt, or to taste
2 teaspoons fresh lemon juice

1. Preheat the oven to 400°F.

2. Place the eggplant in a pie pan and bake until very soft, about 45 minutes.

3. Remove the eggplant from the oven and let cool. Peel away the skin, cut the eggplant open and discard the seeds. Finely chop the pulp by hand or in a food processor.

4. Transfer the pulp to a bowl, add the pesto, salt, and lemon juice and whisk until thoroughly blended. Taste and adjust seasoning. If not using immediately, cover with plastic wrap and refrigerate. Serve at room temperature.

MAKES ABOUT 1¼ CUPS

MANGO
GUACAMOLE

A wonderfully pleasing appetizer (or topping for a salad or a plate of steamed vegetables), this guacamole was created for a Super Bowl menu by Jody Denton while he was executive chef of the Eccentric in Chicago. Served with chips or raw vegetables, it's sure to calm down those clamoring for you to put the steaks on the grill right now.

■ ■

6 ripe avocados, pitted, peeled, and diced
1 ripe mango, peeled, sliced, and diced
2 cloves garlic, minced
1 jalapeño, seeded and minced
2 ripe tomatoes, seeded and diced
2 tablespoons chopped fresh cilantro leaves
Juice of 2 limes
Salt, to taste

Combine the avocados, mango, garlic, jalapeño, tomatoes, and cilantro in a big bowl. Add the lime juice and salt. Mix, taste, and adjust seasoning as desired. If not serving immediately, cover the surface of the guacamole with plastic wrap.

SERVES 10 TO 12

LUSH

CHICKEN LIVER PATE

Among the more celebrated marriages of food and spirits, single malt Scotch with smoked salmon for instance, one that's never gone on the rocks is the pairing of chicken liver pâté with the dry martini. Try it during the prelude to a steak feast at home. This is not the super-rich chopped chicken liver of New York City steak houses. It's smoother and slimmer, but with a lively kick of horseradish. Serve the pâté with French bread or crackers.

■■■■■■■■■■■■■■■■■■■■■■■■■

1 tablespoon vegetable oil
1 shallot or 2 scallions, white only,
  minced
8 ounces chicken livers
¼ teaspoon dried thyme
Salt and freshly ground black pepper,
  to taste
Freshly grated nutmeg, to taste
2 tablespoons Madeira or brandy
2 tablespoons unsalted butter, softened
2 teaspoons Worcestershire sauce
2 teaspoons prepared horseradish

1. Combine the oil and shallot in a medium-size skillet and cook over medium heat until the shallot softens, about 1 minute. Add the chicken livers and thyme and cook, turning the livers often, until they are medium-rare, 3 to 4 minutes.

2. Transfer the contents of the pan to a food processor or food mill set over a bowl. Return the pan to the stove over a turned-off burner. Add the salt, pepper, and nutmeg to the liver mixture and purée. Pour the Madeira into the skillet and bring it to a boil. Remove the skillet from the heat. Carefully ignite the Madeira with a long kitchen match and gently shake the pan until the flame dies out (make sure your hair is tied back and your sleeves are rolled up before you do this). Scrape the bottom of the pan with a wooden spoon to deglaze it.

3. Pour the deglazing liquid into the purée. Add the butter, Worcestershire, and horseradish and blend well. Scrape the pâté into a bowl or ceramic crock and refrigerate until firm, at least 2 hours.

MAKES ABOUT ¾ CUP

WHITE
GAZPACHO

"Refreshing" is the one-word description that fits this unusual gazpacho, which makes use of the tomato only as a garnish. Since it's both light and a stimulant to the appetite, I find it an ideal starter for summer steak meals. The obvious wine companion is sherry, but the soup is fine on its own.

■ ■

*1 large cucumber, peeled, cut
    lengthwise in half, seeded, and
    chopped*
1 clove garlic, chopped
1½ cups low-sodium chicken broth
1 cup sour cream
½ cup plain yogurt
*1½ tablespoons vinegar, preferably
    sherry vinegar*
1 teaspoon salt
1 teaspoon white pepper
*1 medium tomato, peeled and
    chopped (page 142)*
*¼ cup chopped scallions,
    white only*
*¼ cup chopped fresh flat-leaf
    parsley leaves*
*⅓ cup sliced almonds, toasted
    (see Note)*
4 teaspoons olive oil (optional)

1. Combine the cucumber, garlic, and ¼ cup of the chicken broth in a blender and purée. Pour the remaining 1¼ cup broth into the blender and blend briefly.

2. Spoon the sour cream and yogurt into a bowl and whisk until blended. Pouring slowly, whisk in the cucumber purée. Stir in the vinegar, salt, and pepper. Cover the bowl with plastic wrap and refrigerate for at least 1 hour or up to 8 hours. Chill bowls for the gazpacho.

3. When ready to serve, place the tomato, scallions, parsley, and almonds in small bowls and arrange them on a tray that can be passed at the table. Stir the gazpacho and ladle it into the chilled bowls. Invite guests to add their own garnishes, finishing with an optional teaspoon of olive oil.

SERVES 4

Note: Toast the almonds in a small skillet over medium-low heat, tossing often, until lightly golden and aromatic, about 5 minutes.

SHELLFISH & MUSHROOM
APPETIZER

Here's an ideal warm-up dish to eat before tackling a juicy steak. Two steak house favorites, shellfish and mushrooms, are tied together by an Italian-inspired herb and garlic dressing. It's a satisfying yet stimulating dish, well suited to an Italian white wine such as Pinot Grigio.

■ ■

8 ounces large raw shrimp, unpeeled
8 ounces bay scallops (see Note)
8 ounces white button mushrooms
2 cloves garlic, minced
¼ cup fresh lemon juice
½ teaspoon minced fresh oregano or
   marjoram leaves
½ teaspoon minced fresh thyme leaves
Freshly ground black pepper
½ cup olive oil, preferably extra virgin
Salt
4 to 6 soft lettuce leaves, such as Boston
2 tablespoons chopped fresh flat-leaf
   parsley leaves

1. Bring 4 cups water to a boil in a medium saucepan over medium heat. Add the shrimp and simmer until just firm, about 3 minutes. Remove with a slotted spoon. Add the scallops and cook until just firm, 2 minutes. Drain.

2. Peel and devein the shrimp; cut into chunks. Place in a medium-size bowl with the scallops.

3. Wipe the mushrooms with damp paper towels. Cut off and discard the base of the stems. Thinly slice the mushrooms and place them in a separate bowl.

4. In a third bowl, combine the garlic, lemon juice, oregano, thyme, and 3 or 4 grinds of the pepper. Slowly whisk in the olive oil. Pour half of this mixture over the seafood and half over the mushrooms. Stir well.

5. Cover the 2 bowls with plastic wrap and let stand at room temperature for 2 hours or in the refrigerator for up to 8 hours, stirring both 2 or 3 times. Remove bowls from the refrigerator half an hour before serving.

6. Just before serving, combine the seafood and mushrooms and season to taste with salt. Place a lettuce leaf on each of 4 to 6 appetizer plates, top with the seafood and mushroom mixture, and garnish with parsley.

SERVES 4 TO 6

Note: If scallops are not available, use 8 ounces cleaned squid, both tentacles and bodies. Cut the bodies into rings. Simmer for 30 seconds.

FABULOUS
FRIED ZUCCHINI

This unusual shallow-fry preparation carries the threat of sputtering cooking oil but offers the reward of crisp, beautifully golden zucchini slices that have absorbed virtually no oil. This is equally true if you fry eggplant slices—a true miracle. I use a long-handled Chinese strainer to transfer the slices to and from the oil.

■ ■

2 medium zucchini
⅓ cup all-purpose flour
½ teaspoon freshly ground black pepper
Salt, to taste
½ teaspoon paprika
2 cups vegetable oil

1. Wash and dry the zucchini and trim the ends. Slice them on the bias into ¼-inch-thick slices. Place the slices on paper towels and pat them dry.

2. Combine the flour, pepper, ½ teaspoon salt, and paprika in a medium-size bowl. Dredge the zucchini in the flour mixture and set aside. Fill a bowl with ice and water.

3. Heat the oil to 400°F in a large deep skillet. It should shimmer, but not smoke.

4. Dip the zucchini a few at a time, into the ice water then transfer them immediately to the hot oil. Be careful of sputtering oil; it's best to stand back when doing this. Cook until the zucchini pieces are golden brown but still soft, 4 to 5 minutes. Remove with a slotted spoon as ready and drain on paper towels. Salt while hot and serve immediately or hold briefly in a warm oven.

SERVES 4

COUSCOUS SALAD
WITH PLUM TOMATOES

Light and mildly flavored, couscous soaks up a variety of flavors and sauces equally well. I serve it before or with grilled or broiled steaks that have been seasoned or marinated with spices from the Middle East. Instant couscous is readily available in supermarkets.

2 cups vegetable broth
1 cup instant couscous
¼ cup olive oil, preferably extra virgin
4 to 5 medium plum tomatoes
1 cup (firmly packed) fresh mint leaves
1 tablespoon fresh lemon juice
1 tablespoon balsamic vinegar
Salt and freshly ground white pepper, to taste

1. Bring the broth to a boil in a medium-size saucepan. Stir in the couscous, cover, and remove the pan from the heat. Let stand until all the liquid is absorbed, about 15 minutes. Fluff the couscous with a fork, transfer to a large bowl, and set aside to cool. When cooled, stir in the oil.

2. Core, seed, and chop the tomatoes. Chop the mint leaves. Add both to the couscous. Stir in the lemon juice, vinegar, salt, and pepper. Serve the salad at room temperature

SERVES 6

FENNEL
AND PARMESAN SALAD

Sometimes the perfect introduction to a steak entrée is a crisp, first course with lots of flavor to stimulate the appetite. This salad fills the bill. With only a modest amount of lemon juice in the dressing, it will be reasonably hospitable to a dry white wine such as Sauvignon Blanc.

1 medium fennel bulb

8 anchovy fillets

2 ounces Parmesan cheese

1 tablespoon fresh lemon juice

1/4 cup olive oil, preferably extra virgin

Freshly ground black pepper, to taste

4 cups bite-size pieces romaine lettuce

1/2 red bell pepper, cored, seeded, and
    cut into julienne strips

1. Cut away the top, base, and tough outer parts of the fennel. Cut the bulb into very thin slices. Set aside.

2. Rinse the anchovies, pat dry, and cut each one into thirds. Cut the Parmesan into thin chips. Set aside.

3. When ready to serve, pour the lemon juice into a small bowl, and pouring slowly, beat in the oil. Add a generous grinding of pepper. With anchovy and Parmesan, both salty, there should be no need for salt.

4. Divide the romaine among 4 salad plates. Spread the fennel over the lettuce in a single layer, then add the pepper strips, anchovy pieces, and Parmesan chips as though garnishing a pizza. Spoon the dressing over the salad and serve.

SERVES 4

SALAD A LA JOE

Much of the color and character of the best steak houses is provided by the waiters. One of the legendary servers is Joe Pacini, who for years has patroled the front room tables facing the bar at Gene & Georgetti's, a Chicago institution. In addition to delivering platters of steaks and chops, he makes a salad that defies even his most sincere attempts to reduce it to an exact formula. So here, as described by the creator, is Salad à la Joe.

You slice tomatoes, 2 or 3 or 4, then a half an onion, a half a [green bell] pepper, 4 or 5 mushrooms, a red pimiento from a jar. You take 2 pieces of broccoli, steamed fresh, and slice them up. You tear up enough lettuce to fill your bowl. You take 5 or 6 peperoncini from a jar.

In the salad bowl, you put a touch of [minced] fresh garlic and some oregano and salt, if you like. You put in some vinegar and stir. You still stir and pour in olive oil. Now add the lettuce and everything else and turn it until everything is covered with sauce. I do all this in the kitchen then I grind black pepper at the table. Serves 4

TAPAWINGO'S
FENNEL AND CABBAGE SALAD
WITH GOAT CHEESE

Tapawingo, located in tiny Ellsworth, Michigan, near Grand Traverse Bay, is the sort of country restaurant that's hard to find even in France. Chef Harlan ("Pete") Peterson's devotion to local ingredients is inspiring, but the scope of his extraordinary cooking allows for some inspiration from abroad as well. This salad, with its soft and crunchy ingredients and tangy cheese, is an ideal starter before a steak entrée.

3 tablespoons cider vinegar
1 tablespoon Dijon mustard
*6 ounces goat cheese, preferably blue
    veined*
Freshly ground black pepper, to taste
Salt (optional)
2/3 cup olive oil
2/3 cup oil, such as grape seed
1 head romaine lettuce
1 head frisée or chicory
1 medium fennel bulb
1/2 small red cabbage
12 thin slices French bread
2 tablespoons chopped fresh chives

1. Combine the vinegar, mustard, half the goat cheese, and pepper in a blender or food processor. (Add salt only if not using blue-veined cheese). Blend until smooth. With the motor running, add the olive and grape seed oils in a thin stream. Taste and adjust the seasoning. Refrigerate the dressing.

2. Clean, trim, and tear the lettuces into bite-size pieces. Cut the stalks, base, and outer pieces from the fennel and the outer leaves and base from the cabbage. Cut the fennel and cabbage into julienne strips. Crumble the remaining cheese and set aside. (The recipe may be done ahead to this point. Bag and refrigerate the lettuces, vegetables, and cheese separately.)

3. When ready to serve, return the dressing and cheese to room temperature and toast the bread. Toss the lettuce and vegetables with as much dressing as needed in a large bowl. Spoon the salad onto serving plates and garnish with crumbled cheese and chives. Pass the toast at the table.

SERVES 6

WINTER VEGETABLE SALAD

WITH PANCETTA

D on't ask me why, but steak lovers crave bacon. In steak houses they have it wrapped around filet mignon, wrapped around scallops, on top of hamburgers, and scattered over spinach in a salad. Here's a salad garnished with bacon, or, in this case, an easy-to-crisp Italian bacon called pancetta. It's an ideal first course to serve at home before a festive steak entrée because it needs only last-minute tossing.

■ ■

2 medium beets
8 ounces Jerusalem artichokes, celery
    root, or potatoes (see Note)
1/4 cup finely chopped pancetta or
    mildly smoked bacon
1 medium napa cabbage
1/4 cup coarsely chopped scallions,
    white and 2 inches of green
1 1/2 teaspoons Dijon mustard
4 tablespoons olive oil, preferably
    extra virgin
1 tablespoon fresh lemon juice
1 tablespoon red wine vinegar
Salt and freshly ground black pepper,
    to taste

1. Preheat the oven to 400°F.

2. Cut the stems and leafy green tops from the beets but do not peel them. Wrap each beet in aluminum foil and bake until tender when pierced with a paring knife, about 50 minutes. Remove the beets from the oven and unwrap them. When the beets are cool, peel and cut them into 1/2-inch cubes. Set aside.

3. Bring water to a boil in a small saucepan over medium-high heat. Add the Jerusalem artichokes and cook at a boil, partially covered, until crisp-tender, about 15 minutes. Drain. When cool, peel and cut them into 1/2-inch cubes. Reserve.

4. While the vegetables are cooking, fry the chopped pancetta in a small skillet over medium-low heat, stirring often, until crisp, 7 to 8 minutes. Transfer to a paper towel to drain. Set aside the drippings. You should have about 2 tablespoons.

5. Slice off 1½ inches of the cabbage stem and remove the outer leaves. Cut the remaining cabbage crosswise into ½-inch sections and break them apart with your hands.

6. When ready to serve, combine the beets, Jerusalem artichokes, cabbage, and scallions in a salad bowl. In a small saucepan, combine the mustard, reserved pancetta drippings, the olive oil, lemon juice, and vinegar. Bring to a boil

over medium heat, whisking constantly. Pour the sauce over the salad and toss thoroughly so the red of the beet colors the other ingredients. Season with salt and pepper as desired, remembering the pancetta is salty. Divide the salad among 4 plates. Scatter pancetta over each and serve.

SERVES 4

Note: If using celery root or potatoes, peel and cut them into ½-inch cubes. Boil until they are tender, about 10 minutes. Plunge into cold water to stop the cooking, drain, and set aside.

WITH THE STEAK

A great steak can stand on its own, but the best steak houses take pride in their side dishes and work hard to make them memorable. So should you. How to begin is as easy as saying "meat and potatoes." Find or create a potato preparation to call your own. Steak fries, potato hash, and creamed potatoes flavored with rosemary are mainstays in my repertory. Baked beans and coleslaw, onion rings, and spinach also are time- and tradition-honored steak companions. For a change of pace, or because it's a relatively formal meal, I sometimes prepare a side dish of okra or Italian-style greens. In addition to the greens, the Italian way with vegetables is reflected in Old Country Rice and Beans, and Tuscan Beans and Potatoes. Meaty mushrooms, either wild or tame, are a delightful garnish for steak, or can be served in combination with wild rice or in a mushroom strudel.

Tomato lovers will want to pair my Broiled Strip Steak with Italian Tomato Sauce with Spaghettini with Golden Valencia Tomatoes for a party of flavors.

COWBOY BEANS

The problems beans can cause to the digestion are part of the folklore of the Old West, but urban cooks will be just as troubled if they add salt to the water at the beginning of the cooking cycle. The beans just won't become tender. Follow the directions and these beans are a cinch to make, easy to digest, and palate-pleasing to boot. My favorite bean for this recipe is the sweet and mealy Anasazi from the Southwest. If you can't find it, pinto will do very well.

■■■■■■■■■■■■■■■■■■■■■■■■

1 cup dried beans, preferably Anasazi
2 tablespoons vegetable oil
½ cup diced red onion
½ cup diced green bell pepper
1 tablespoon Six-Shooter Spice Rub
* (page 37)*
Half a 14½-ounce can diced tomatoes,
* drained*
1 teaspoon salt
Pinch sugar

1. Place the beans in a medium-size bowl and fill with cold water to cover by 3 inches. Let soak at room temperature for 6 to 8 hours.

2. Drain the beans and transfer to a Dutch oven or medium-size saucepan. Add 4 cups cold water, cover the pan, and bring to a boil. Reduce the heat to low and cook at a bare simmer until beans are tender, about 1½ hours. Remove from the heat but leave the cover on.

3. Heat the oil with the onion and green pep-per in a medium-size skillet over medium-low heat until the vegetables are almost soft, about 4 minutes. Add the spice rub and stir for 1 minute. Add the tomatoes and simmer, stir-ring occasionally, until the tomatoes melt, about 2½ minutes. Add the salt and sugar. Drain the beans, reserving ½ cup of the cook-ing liquid. Stir the beans into the vegetables in the skillet. Taste, adjust the seasoning, and add the reserved bean water.

4. Rewarm for 5 minutes over medium-low heat before serving.

SERVES 4

NANCY BAROCCI'S
TUSCAN BEANS
AND POTATOES

Nancy Barocci, founder of a trio of food shops and restaurants called Convito Italiano, usually cooks with an Italian accent when she entertains at home. One evening, despite the presence of a beautifully cooked strip roast, the vegetable side dish refused to play a supporting role. Everyone wanted seconds and I came away with the recipe as well. Serve the beans and potatoes with any grilled or broiled steak. It also makes a good pillow on which to arrange sliced steak.

■■■■■■■■■■■■■■■■■■■■■■■■

1 pound new potatoes, peeled and cut into ½-inch cubes

5 tablespoons olive oil, preferably Italian extra virgin

2 tablespoons unsalted butter

2 medium cloves garlic, minced

2 ounces pancetta, finely diced

¾ cup chopped shallots

¾ cup chopped red onion

2 cups cooked or canned white beans, such as Italian cannellini

½ cup beef broth

6 fresh sage leaves, chopped

Salt and freshly ground black pepper, to taste

1. Pat the potato cubes dry with paper towels. Line a baking pan with paper towels.

2. Heat 2 tablespoons of the oil, the butter, and garlic in a large heavy skillet, preferably cast iron, over medium-low heat until the garlic just begins to turn golden, about 2 minutes. Pat the potatoes dry again and add them to the skillet. Sauté until the potatoes are golden brown on all sides and cooked through, about 20 minutes, stirring and shaking the pan from time to time to turn them. Transfer the potatoes and any garlic that clings to them to the prepared baking pan and set aside.

3. Pour off any grease and wipe the skillet clean. Add the remaining 3 tablespoons of oil and place the skillet over medium-high heat. Sauté the pancetta until crisp, stirring often. Add the shallots and onion and reduce the heat to medium-low. Cook until the shallots and onions are very soft but not browned, 10

to 15 minutes. (The recipe may be prepared to this point several hours in advance.)

4. Add the beans (rinsed and drained if canned), broth, sage, salt, pepper, and potato cubes to the skillet and cook over medium heat until hot, stirring to evenly distribute the ingredients. Serve hot.

SERVES 5 OR 6

HOT BULGUR SALAD

B ulgur is available in at least three different grinds. For this salad, use medium grind. This salad is a good companion to steaks that have been marinated.

■ ■

2 cups vegetable broth
1 cup medium bulgur
1 small tomato
1 teaspoon minced jalapeño
1 teaspoon fresh lemon juice
1/4 cup chopped fresh cilantro leaves
1/2 teaspoon salt
*1/4 teaspoon freshly ground black
    pepper*

1. Bring the broth to a simmer in a medium-size saucepan over medium heat. Stir in the bulgur, reduce the heat to low, and cover the pan. Cook until the bulgur is tender and the liquid is absorbed, about 15 minutes (see Note).

2. While the bulgur is cooking, core the tomato. Cut it in half and squeeze out the seeds.

Cut the tomato into cubes and set aside.

3. When the bulgur tests tender, remove the pan from the heat. Stir in the tomato, jalapeño, lemon juice, cilantro, salt, and pepper. Cover the pan and set aside until ready to serve. Stir the salad to fluff up the bulgur before spooning onto serving plates. This salad is best served warm or at room temperature.

SERVES 4

Note: You may also simply pour boiling liquid over the grains in a bowl, cover the bowl, and let steep until all the liquid has been absorbed.

CELERY SEED
COLESLAW

Searching for the perfect coleslaw is a natural adjunct to searching for the perfect ribs, perfect fried chicken, or perfect grilled steak. For me the path to perfection is built on a bed of finely chopped cabbage. Come along, and if you feel compelled to sprinkle a little sugar en route, I'll understand.

■ ■

½ small onion, finely chopped
2 tablespoons vegetable oil
2 tablespoons tarragon vinegar
½ teaspoon celery seeds
Salt and freshly ground black pepper,
*   to taste*
½ head green cabbage, cored and outer
*   leaves removed, finely chopped*
⅓ cup mayonnaise
¼ cup chopped fresh flat-leaf parsley
*   leaves*

1. Mix the onion, oil, vinegar, celery seeds, and a small amount of salt and pepper in a medium-size bowl. Add the cabbage and toss until well mixed. Cover the bowl with plastic wrap and refrigerate for 2 to 4 hours.

2. Remove the bowl from the refrigerator at least 1 hour before serving. Add the mayonnaise and the parsley and mix well. Adjust the seasoning to taste with salt and pepper and serve lightly chilled or at room temperature.

SERVES 6 TO 8

ENGLISH
APPLE-STILTON COLESLAW

I love to serve this crisp and crunchy slaw with steak grilled over apple wood. Its role in my menu playbook is not that confined, however. It also makes a good companion to almost any steak sandwich.

■ ■

½ small head green cabbage, outer
*   leaves removed*
1 firm, tart apple
½ cup chopped onion
2 tablespoons Stilton cheese, softened
½ teaspoon ground allspice
Salt
¼ teaspoon dry mustard
2 tablespoons cider vinegar
½ teaspoon Worcestershire sauce
¼ cup vegetable oil

1. Cut the cabbage in quarters. Remove and discard the core. Shave the cabbage crosswise into thin strips, and chop coarsely. You should have about 4 cups. Wash but do not peel the apple. Cut it in half, remove and discard the core, then cut the apple into ½-inch cubes. Combine the cabbage, apple, and onion in a bowl.

2. Place the Stilton in a small bowl. Add the allspice, ½ teaspoon salt, and mustard. Using a whisk or fork, stir in the vinegar and Worcestershire. Whisk in the oil.

3. Pour the dressing over the cabbage mixture and toss well. Cover the surface tightly with plastic wrap, refrigerate, and let mellow for about 1 hour. Add salt to taste, toss the slaw again, and serve.

SERVES 4

GREAT GARLIC BREAD

This decadent recipe is for those who seriously love garlic. Think of the spread as escargot butter without the snails! It's perfect served along with plain grilled steak.

■ ■

1 small head of garlic, unpeeled
4 tablespoons (½ stick) unsalted
*   butter, at room temperature*
½ teaspoon minced garlic
¼ teaspoon lemon pepper seasoning
Salt, to taste
1 medium French baguette

1. Preheat the oven to 350°F.

2. Wrap the garlic completely in a piece of aluminum foil and bake until very soft, 30 minutes. Let cool. Push the pulp out of each clove into a small bowl. (If preparing the bread now, raise the oven temperature to 400°F.)

3. Add the butter to the garlic pulp, stirring

until blended. Stir in the minced garlic, lemon pepper, and salt. Cover and set aside if not using right away.

4. Cut the bread on the diagonal into 1-inch-thick slices without cutting all the way through to the bottom. Generously brush each cut side of bread with the garlic butter. Spread any remaining butter over the top of the loaf. Wrap the loaf in aluminum foil, folding the corners down and securely tucking them under the loaf.

5. If not already preheated, preheat the oven to 400°F.

6. Bake the wrapped bread until it is heated through and the butter has melted into each slice, about 10 minutes. If you like soft bread, serve it right out of the oven this way. For a crustier loaf, unwrap the foil and return bread to the oven until the top is browned and crusty, 3 to 5 minutes.

SERVES 6

GIBSONS HOT PEPPER
GIARDINIERA

Call it an Italian salsa. Call it anything, for that matter—and you may be tempted to do so if you bite into a mouthful thinking it is a bland vegetable relish. At Gibsons, the Chicago steak house that makes the giardiniera, it is served as a condiment for grilled steak. But at home, you might also want to spoon some on top of an Italian beef or sausage sandwich or salad.

■ ■

1 medium red bell pepper, cored, seeded, and diced

1 medium green bell pepper, cored, seeded, and diced

2 inner ribs celery, diced

1 cup sport peppers (jarred hot Italian peppers), cut into ¼-inch pieces

1 cup peperoncini, cut into ¼-inch pieces

2 jalapeños cored, seeded, and cut into pieces

2 tablespoons olive oil

2 tablespoons distilled white vinegar

1. Combine both bell peppers, celery, sport peppers, peperoncini, and the jalapeños in a bowl. Toss with the oil and vinegar until well mixed.

2. Transfer the giardiniera to a 1-quart jar, cover, and store in the refrigerator until needed. It will stay crisp for 3 to 4 days.

MAKES ABOUT 1 QUART

ITALIAN-STYLE GREENS

Sautéed escarole is a standard side dish in many Italian steak houses. This slightly bitter leafy green is a delicious counterpoint to the rich taste of steak, but I like to combine it with romaine to produce a more intriguing texture and more subtle taste. In the steak house tradition, you may want to serve these greens with a broiled strip steak or porterhouse.

∎∎∎∎∎∎∎∎∎∎∎∎∎∎∎∎∎∎∎∎∎∎∎∎

1 head escarole
½ head romaine lettuce
2 tablespoons olive oil
4 cloves garlic, slivered
¼ teaspoon sugar
⅛ to ¼ teaspoon crushed red pepper
  flakes
1 tablespoon red wine vinegar or
  balsamic vinegar
2 tablespoons pine nuts, toasted
  (optional; see Note)
Salt and freshly ground black pepper,
  to taste

1. Core the greens, discarding any browned or bruised leaves, and wash thoroughly. Drain and dry. Cut or tear the greens into large pieces.

2. Heat the oil in a large skillet over medium heat. Add the garlic and cook until lightly golden. Sprinkle the sugar and red pepper flakes into the pan, shaking the pan briefly to disperse. Add the greens. Stir and turn until all the leaves begin to wilt. Cover the pan and cook until the greens are tender, 5 minutes.

3. Sprinkle the vinegar over the greens and stir. Add the pine nuts, if using, and correct the seasoning to taste with salt and pepper. Serve hot.

SERVES 4

Note: Toast the pine nuts in a small skillet over medium-low heat, tossing often, until lightly golden and aromatic, about 5 minutes.

ALLEN STERNWEILER'S
MUSHROOM STRUDEL

Created by one of Chicago's most talented young chefs, this savory strudel is a great asset to anyone cooking a dinner party solo. It can be prepared ahead, takes only 15 minutes to cook, and can be served by itself as a first course or to accompany a filet steak or sliced tenderloin.

■ ■

2 tablespoons unsalted butter
¼ cup olive oil, preferably extra virgin
1 large shallot, minced
2 cloves garlic, minced
1 to 1½ pounds assorted wild mushrooms, such as shiitakes, oysters, and morels, sliced
Salt and white pepper, to taste
8 tablespoons mixed minced fresh thyme, tarragon, flat-leaf parsley, and chives
1 large egg stirred with 1 large egg yolk
3 sheets frozen phyllo dough, thawed
¼ cup melted unsalted butter

1. Melt the 2 tablespoons butter with the olive oil in a medium-size sauté pan over medium-low heat. Add the shallot and garlic and cook until softened, 2 to 3 minutes. Add the mushrooms and raise the heat to medium. Season with salt and pepper and cook, stirring occasionally, until tender, about 5 minutes. Stir in 6 tablespoons of the herbs, remove from the heat, and let cool. Transfer the mushrooms with a slotted spoon to a medium-size bowl and combine with the egg and egg yolk.

2. Preheat the oven to 400°F. Grease a baking sheet.

3. Spread out a phyllo sheet on a work surface. Working quickly, paint it with the melted butter and sprinkle on some of the remaining 2 tablespoons herbs. Repeat with the second and third sheets, placing one sheet on top of the other as you finish. Use up all the herbs and as much melted butter as needed. Spread the mushroom mixture evenly over three fourths of the top sheet, leaving a 1-inch border around the other 3 edges. Starting with the short end, roll the phyllo up tightly around the

filling, jelly-roll style. Tuck the sides underneath, with the seam side down. (The strudel may be prepared to this point up to 1 day in advance. Wrap tightly in plastic wrap and refrigerate.)

4. Transfer the strudel to the prepared baking sheet and bake until golden brown all over,

12 to 15 minutes. Remove the strudel from the oven and let it rest for 3 to 5 minutes before slicing. To serve, cut off the ends, then slice into eight 1-inch-wide medallions.

SERVES 4 AS AN APPETIZER OR 8 WITH A STEAK MAIN COURSE

OKRA
WITH ONIONS AND TOASTED CUMIN

Most people who say they dislike okra are referring to the unpleasant texture that results from stewing it for a long time. Instead, try sautéing okra in a little oil over medium-high heat until it is tender but still retains a slight crunch. It's delicious.

■ ■

*1 pound okra, washed, ends
    trimmed, and drained*
1 teaspoon cumin seeds
3 tablespoons vegetable oil
*1 medium sweet onion, thinly
    sliced*
1 teaspoon salt
*½ teaspoon freshly ground black
    pepper*

1. Cut each okra in half on the diagonal. Set aside.

2. Place the cumin seeds in a large skillet, preferably nonstick, over medium-low heat.

Toast, tossing often, until browned and aromatic, 1 to 2 minutes.

3. Add 2 tablespoons of the oil to the skillet. Add the onion slices and cook, stirring occasionally, until softened and slightly browned, 7 to 10 minutes.

4. Increase the heat to medium. Add the remaining 1 tablespoon oil and the okra. Cook the okra, stirring occasionally, for 5 minutes. Add the salt and pepper and continue to cook until the okra is tender but still retains a slight crunch, about 5 minutes more. The onions will be toasty brown by this time. Serve hot.

SERVES 4

OUTRAGEOUS
ONION RINGS

"Outrageous" because they taste so good and are consumed so fast. A couple of tricks: first, use popcorn salt (a commercial product available in supermarkets). It's great on any fried food because it is finely ground and sticks to surfaces. Second, cut the rings thick because a thick ring retains the sweet taste of onion. Serve with the steak or before it.

■ ■

1 very large sweet onion
1½ cups all-purpose flour
1 teaspoon salt
¼ teaspoon freshly ground black pepper
⅛ teaspoon cayenne pepper
1½ cups buttermilk
Vegetable oil for frying
Popcorn salt, to taste

1. Peel the onion, removing the tough outer layer of onion with the skin. Cut crosswise into slices about ½-inch thick. Separate the slices into individual rings. Do not discard the onion centers.

2. Combine the flour, salt, black pepper, and cayenne in a shallow bowl. Stir to mix. Pour the buttermilk into another bowl.

3. Dredge the onion rings, a few at a time, in the flour mixture, shaking off the excess flour and set them onto a baking sheet. One or two at a time, immerse the onion rings into the buttermilk. Remove and dredge again in the flour mixture, shaking off the excess flour. Transfer to the baking sheet. Repeat the process with all the remaining onion rings.

4. Pour the oil to a depth of ½ to 1 inch in a cast-iron skillet and heat over medium-high heat. When the temperature reaches 375°F on a frying thermometer, add the onion rings, a few at a time, without overcrowding the pan. Cook, turning once, until deep golden brown on both sides, about 3 minutes. Remove the onion rings from the oil and drain on a plain brown paper bag. While the onion rings are still hot, add salt, to taste. Make sure the oil returns to 375°F before frying additional rings.

5. When all the onion rings have been fried and have drained, serve at once or place them on an ovenproof platter and keep warm in a 200°F oven until ready to serve.

SERVES 4

MAGNIFICENT
MASHED POTATOES
WITH OLIVE OIL AND HERBS

I won't play the tease. A look at the recipe and you'll realize these potatoes gained their "magnificent" rating in the company of my Homage to Pot Roast. You're going to love them as well with Charlie's Butt Steak and Eye-Round Steaks with Onion-Cream Gravy (see Index). And, I promise, even though oil and water are not supposed to mix, they make the purée more delicious than would butter and cream.

■■■■■■■■■■■■■■■■■■■■■■■■■

2 pounds baking or yellow Finn
  potatoes, peeled and cut into
  quarters
Salt
½ cup olive oil, preferably extra
  virgin
Freshly ground pepper, preferably
  white
1 tablespoon chopped fresh herb,
  such as basil, oregano,
  rosemary, or thyme

1. Bring a large saucepan of water to a boil. Add the potatoes and 1 tablespoon of salt. Simmer, partially covered, until soft, 20 minutes. Remove the pan from the heat and leave the potatoes in the hot water for up to 15 minutes to keep them warm.

2. Spoon out ½ cup of the warm cooking water and pour into a bowl. Add the olive oil. Drain the potatoes and either put them through a ricer placed over the bowl or transfer them to the bowl and use a potato masher to reduce them to a pillowy-soft purée. Season with salt, pepper, and your herb of choice. Beat with a wooden spoon until well combined and fluffy.

3. Serve at once or keep warm in the top of a double boiler over simmering water.

SERVES 4 TO 6

MORE THAN
MASHED POTATOES

Many cooks consider potatoes mashed with some milk, butter, salt, and pepper, perfection, so they ask, "Why play with perfection?" Try this recipe and you'll know why. I like to pair these potatoes with grilled steak served without a sauce.

---

1 can (14½ ounces) low-sodium
   chicken broth
2 white button mushrooms, quartered
   (optional)
2 cloves garlic, peeled and halved
1 leek, white only, diced
1 small celery root, peeled and cut into
   1-inch pieces
2 medium parsnips, peeled and cut
   into 2-inch pieces
Salt and freshly ground black pepper,
   to taste
2 pounds potatoes, preferably yellow
   Finn, peeled and cut into quarters
White pepper, to taste
¼ cup olive oil
¾ cup chopped fresh basil leaves
½ cup crème fraîche or heavy
   (or whipping) cream (optional)
Accumulated steak juices, if any

1. Combine the broth, mushrooms, if using, and garlic in a medium saucepan. Bring to a boil, cover, and reduce heat to low. Simmer for 5 minutes.

2. Add the leek and celery root. Cook, uncovered, for 10 minutes. Add the parsnips and simmer until all the vegetables are soft, 10 minutes more. Let cool. Transfer the vegetables and broth to a food processor and purée. Season with salt and black pepper. (The recipe may be done ahead to this point. Place the purée in a container and refrigerate.)

3. About 30 minutes before serving, bring water to a boil in a large pan. Add 1 tablespoon salt and the potatoes. Cook, partially covered, until soft, 20 minutes. Meanwhile, place salt and white pepper, olive oil, basil, and crème fraîche, if using, in a large, warm bowl.

4. Reheat the vegetable purée. Drain the potatoes, reserving ½ cup potato water. Transfer the potatoes to a bowl, and mash with a potato masher. Stir in the vegetable purée, any steak juices, if using and as much reserved potato water as needed to keep the mixture loose. Taste and correct for seasoning. Serve at once.

SERVES 6

207

HERBED
POTATO HASH

Meat and potatoes is the classic American food pairing. As a result, people who know and love steak also tend to be potato connoisseurs. Therefore, every successful steak house pays careful attention to the selection and preparation of its potato "sides." Ruth's Chris, for example, has nine different potato offerings on its menu. I came to know this dish at the Pump Room in Chicago, where a variation of it is served with a sizzling hot platter of sliced strip steak.

■ ■

Salt
3 large baking potatoes, scrubbed
¼ cup olive oil
¼ cup diced red bell pepper
¼ cup diced green bell pepper
¼ cup diced yellow bell pepper
½ cup diced onion
Freshly ground black pepper, to taste
Chopped fresh flat-leaf parsley leaves,
*   for garnish*
Snipped fresh chives, for garnish

1. Bring a large saucepan of water to a boil. Add salt and the potatoes, lower the heat, and simmer, partially covered, until tender but still slightly firm when poked with a sharp knife, about 25 minutes. Drain the potatoes, let them cool, then peel and cube them.

2. Heat the oil in a large nonstick skillet over medium heat. Add the potatoes and cook, stirring occasionally, until golden brown on all sides, about 8 minutes. Add all three bell peppers and the onion and continue to cook, stirring often, until the vegetables are tender, 5 minutes more.

3. Season with salt and pepper, garnish with parsley and chives, and serve.

SERVES 4 TO 6

PAN-FRIED POTATOES,
RED PEPPERS, AND MUSHROOMS

P arboiling diced potato before panfrying is a useful shortcut. This beef-friendly combination can be ready in the time it takes to prepare and cook your steak.

■ ■

½ tablespoon salt

*1 large baking potato, peeled and cut
    into ½-inch dice*

1 tablespoon vegetable oil

1 tablespoon unsalted butter

*½ medium red bell pepper, cored,
    seeded, and diced*

*2 ounces shiitake mushrooms, stems
    removed and caps cut into julienne
    strips*

1 medium clove garlic, minced

*1 teaspoon paprika, preferably
    Hungarian*

*Freshly ground black pepper and salt,
    to taste*

*1 tablespoon chopped fresh flat-leaf
    parsley leaves (optional)*

1. Bring 2 cups water to a boil in a small saucepan. Add the salt and potatoes and simmer, partially covered, until the potato is tender, 5 to 7 minutes. Drain and set aside.

2. Heat the oil and butter in a heavy medium-size skillet over medium heat. When the butter is bubbling, add the red pepper and sauté, stir-ring 2 to 3 times, until they start to soften, 2 minutes.

3. Add the mushrooms, garlic, and potato. Turn the heat to medium-low and cook, stir-ring occasionally, for 5 minutes. Season with the paprika, pepper, and salt. Continue cook-ing and stirring until the potato pieces begin to crust, 3 to 5 minutes more. If desired, stir in chopped parsley just before serving.

SERVES 2

PARSLEY

T here's a rift in the parsley family. The short leaf, curly stuff found in every supermarket not too far from the iceberg lettuce is so bland and boring it puts your taste buds to sleep. But an Italian cousin, known as Italian flat-leaf or merely flat-leaf parsley, has flair and flavor. Don't hesitate to pay a higher price for the latter. You can use the stems as well as the leaves in mari-nades, soups, or sauces.

STEAK FRIES
WITHOUT THE FRYER

Large wedges of seasoned potatoes are a simple and delicious partner to almost any steak. The recipe name refers to the deep-fried potatoes served in many steak restaurants. At home, I prefer to bake the wedges until crisp on the outside and creamy within.

■■■■■■■■■■■■■■■■■■■■■■■■■

2 tablespoons vegetable oil
½ teaspoon paprika, preferably Hungarian
¼ teaspoon ground cumin
¼ teaspoon salt
¼ teaspoon cracked black pepper
2 large baking potatoes, scrubbed

1. Preheat the oven to 400°F.

2. Combine the oil, paprika, cumin, salt, and pepper in a medium-size bowl. Stir to mix.

3. Cut the potatoes into quarters lengthwise, then cut each quarter crosswise in half to form wedges. Transfer the cut potatoes to the bowl of seasonings. Mix well to coat the potatoes evenly and thoroughly. Space the seasoned potatoes out on an ungreased baking pan without overcrowding. Bake until well browned and fork-tender, about 30 minutes. Serve right away.

SERVES 4

POTATO POT PIE
WITH ROSEMARY CREAM

Susan Weaver, executive chef at the Four Seasons Hotel in New York City, created this dish to go with strip steak at the hotel's 5757 restaurant. Fragrant and meltingly soft, it provides a wonderful textural counterpoint to the meaty steak. Try the same combination at a home dinner party. Although Chef Weaver makes the pies in individual servings, I take an easier path and make this single large pie.

■ ■

*1½ pounds waxy potatoes, such as
    new potatoes*
2 cups heavy (or whipping) cream
*¼ cup finely chopped fresh rosemary
    leaves*
1 tablespoon finely chopped garlic
Freshly ground pepper, to taste
Salt, to taste
1 large egg
1 tablespoon cold water
*1 package (17¼ ounces; 2 sheets)
    frozen puff pastry sheets, thawed*

1. Peel and slice the potatoes into ⅛-inch-thick rounds. Combine the potatoes, cream, rosemary, garlic, and pepper in a large sauté pan. Bring to a boil over medium-high heat, reduce the heat, and simmer, uncovered, stirring occasionally, until the potatoes are tender, about 20 minutes. Season with salt and let cool in the pan.

2. Preheat the oven to 400°F.

3. Stir the egg with the water in a small bowl. Set aside.

4. Roll out each puff pastry sheet on a lightly floured surface. Line a 1½ quart gratin pan with 1 pastry sheet. Press the dough well along the pan sides. Fill the pan evenly with the potato mixture. Brush the dough edges of the pastry with the egg wash. Cover the pie filling with the second sheet of pastry and press to seal the rim. Trim away any excess pastry and crimp the edges. Cut a small hole in the middle of the pie to vent steam. (Recipe may be prepared ahead to this point. Refrigerate the pie until ready to bake.)

5. Brush the pastry top with egg wash and place the pie on a baking sheet. Bake until golden brown and cooked through, about 25 minutes. Serve hot.

SERVES 8

WILD RICE
WITH WILD MUSHROOMS

Here's an easy-to-make, elegant side dish that will dress up a downtown cut of steak such as Grilled Flank Steak with Eggplant and Red Pepper or Grilled Skirt Steak with Fresh Tomato Sauce.

1 teaspoon minced garlic

2 tablespoons olive oil

1 pound mixed wild mushrooms, such as shiitakes, oysters, and portobellos, stems trimmed and coarsely chopped

2 teaspoons fresh lemon juice

¼ teaspoon salt

Freshly ground black pepper, to taste

2 tablespoons chopped fresh flat-leaf parsley leaves

1 cup wild and white rice blend, such as Uncle Ben's

1. Heat the garlic with the oil in a medium-size skillet over medium-low heat until the garlic begins to turn golden, 2½ to 3 minutes. Add the mushrooms, raise the heat to medium-high, and sauté, turning occasionally, until the mushrooms soften and begin to give up their juices, about 5 minutes. Add the lemon juice, salt, and pepper and cook for 2 minutes more. Remove from the heat and stir in the parsley. (Recipe may be done ahead to this point.)

2. Prepare the rice following the package directions. Do not use the seasoning packet, if included.

3. Reheat the mushroom mixture and stir into the hot rice. Serve hot.

SERVES 6

OLD COUNTRY
RICE AND BEANS

Never underestimate the ability of Italian-inspired recipes to charm you into making them again and again. I serve this dish on its own or as a side dish with grilled T-bone, The Famous Fiorentina (see Index).

∎∎∎∎∎∎∎∎∎∎∎∎∎∎∎∎∎∎∎∎∎∎∎∎

1 cup dried white beans
3 tablespoons olive oil
1 medium onion, chopped
2 cloves garlic, chopped
1 inner rib celery, minced
¼ cup chopped fresh flat-leaf parsley
*   leaves*
1 tablespoon minced fresh oregano
*   leaves or 1 teaspoon dried*
*   oregano*
1 can (14½ ounces) plum tomatoes,
*   drained and coarsely chopped*
Salt and freshly ground black pepper,
*   to taste*
1 cup rice, preferably Arborio
6 tablespoons olive oil or red wine
*   (optional)*

1. **Place** the beans in a medium-size bowl and fill with cold water to cover the beans by 3 inches. Let soak at room temperature for 6 to 8 hours.

2. **Drain** the beans in a colander, then transfer them to a medium-size saucepan. Add 4 cups of cold water, cover the pan, and bring to a boil. Do not add salt. Reduce heat to low and cook at a bare simmer until the beans are tender, about 1½ hours. Remove the beans from the heat but leave the cover on.

3. While the beans are cooking, heat the oil in a medium-size skillet over medium-low heat. Add the onion, garlic, celery, parsley, and oregano, and cook until the vegetables are almost soft, about 4 minutes. Add the tomatoes, salt, and pepper and simmer for 10 minutes. Set aside.

4. Meanwhile, cook the rice following the package directions. When the rice is ready, drain the beans, combine them with the vegetables, and reheat if necessary. Add the cooked rice to the bean mixture and serve hot. If desired, add a tablespoon of olive oil or red wine to each portion at the table.

SERVES 6

STEAK HOUSE
SPINACH

One of the most popular side dishes at classic steak houses is spinach. A few steak houses, notably Sparks in Manhattan, simply steam the spinach and serve the pristine leaves. Others prepare creamed chopped spinach using béchamel sauce. My approach is a middle route that preserves the fresh taste and lightens the sauce. For maximum pleasure, use fresh instead of frozen spinach.

■■■■■■■■■■■■■■■■■■■■■■■■■■

2 bunches or bags fresh spinach
(about 20 ounces) or 2 packages
(10 ounces each) frozen leaf
spinach, thawed and drained
½ cup chopped onion
¼ teaspoon freshly grated nutmeg
⅛ teaspoon ground cinnamon
Salt
½ cup low-sodium chicken broth
½ cup heavy (or whipping) cream

1. If using fresh spinach, wash and remove any large stems. Place in a large nonreactive saucepan and cook covered, over medium heat, in the water still clinging to the leaves, until wilted, about 4 minutes. Turn the spinach once with kitchen tongs during wilting. If using frozen spinach, prepare it following the package directions. Transfer spinach to a bowl filled with cold water to stop the cooking. Drain.

2. Combine the onion, nutmeg, cinnamon, ⅛ teaspoon salt, broth, and cream in a small saucepan. Boil, uncovered, over medium heat until reduced to ³/₄ cup, about 15 minutes.

3. Squeeze the spinach between your hands to remove excess liquid. Coarsely chop the spinach and add it to the sauce. Season with salt. Set aside. (The recipe may be done ahead to this point. Cover and refrigerate the spinach mixture until ready to serve.)

4. Reheat the creamy spinach in a medium-size saucepan or skillet over medium heat, stirring often, until it is bubbling hot, about 4 minutes.

SERVES 4 TO 6

SPINACH

SPOON BREAD SOUFFLE

Quite rustic and less delicate than a traditional soufflé, this dish has considerable flavor but is still mild enough not to intrude upon the meat or the sauce you have chosen for it. Don't worry if it falls during serving; the texture and taste will be fine.

■ ■

2 bunches or bags fresh spinach
   (about 20 ounces) or 2 packages
   (10 ounces each) frozen leaf
   spinach, thawed and drained
3 tablespoons freshly grated Parmesan
   cheese
2 cups milk
½ cup white cornmeal
8 tablespoons (1 stick) unsalted butter,
   cut into chunks, at room
   temperature
4 large eggs, separated, at room
   temperature
1 teaspoon baking powder
1 teaspoon salt
¼ teaspoon freshly grated nutmeg
¼ teaspoon white pepper

1. If using the fresh spinach, wash and remove any large stems. Place in a large nonreactive saucepan and cook, covered, over medium heat, in the water still clinging to the leaves, until wilted, about 4 minutes. Turn the spinach once with kitchen tongs during wilting. If using frozen spinach, prepare it following the pack-age instructions. Transfer the spinach to a bowl filled with cold water to stop the cooking. Drain, squeeze excess water from the spinach, and coarsely chop it. Set aside 1½ cups.

2. Preheat the oven to 350°F.

3. Butter a 2-quart soufflé mold and sprinkle the bottom and sides with 1½ tablespoons of the Parmesan. Set aside away from the heat.

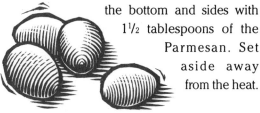

4. Heat the milk and cornmeal in a medium-size saucepan over medium heat. Cook, stirring constantly, until the mixture is the consistency of a thick cream sauce and begins to bubble, about 5 minutes. Lower the heat slightly and continue to stir for 1 minute more. Remove the pan from the heat. Stir in the butter until melted. Stir in the egg yolks, baking powder, salt, nutmeg, and pepper. Stir in the 1½ cups of chopped spinach, mix to blend, and set aside.

5. Beat the egg whites to stiff peaks. If neces-

sary, reheat the spinach mixture over medium heat until warm. Using a rubber spatula, fold the whites gently but thoroughly into the spinach mixture. Pour into the soufflé mold. Sprinkle the top with the remaining 1½ tablespoons of Parmesan.

6. Bake the soufflé until the top is puffed and golden brown, 35 to 40 minutes. Present the soufflé in the dining room, if you wish, then spoon onto warm plates.

SERVES 6

TOMATO-CORN SALSA

FOR GRILLED STEAK

As you might suspect, corn and beef have a great affinity. So do corn and tomatoes. Not so coincidentally, corn, tomatoes, and steak all have an affinity for the grill. Which means, while you can serve this succulent salsa year round, I recommend you make it for the first time when summer vegetables are at their peak. That way, you'll never forget it, though you may forget what else you served that night. There will be no need for a sauce or vegetable to accompany the steak.

■■■■■■■■■■■■■■■■■■■■■■■■

2 cups fresh corn kernels, from 2 or 3 ears of corn, or frozen kernels
2 large ripe tomatoes, cut into ¼-inch dice
⅓ cup peeled and diced jicama
⅓ cup diced onion
¼ cup coarsely chopped fresh cilantro leaves
⅓ cup fresh lime juice
1 teaspoon ground cumin
1 jalapeño, halved, seeded, and minced
1 clove garlic, minced
¾ teaspoon salt

1. Bring water to a boil in a small saucepan over medium heat. Add the corn and simmer for 2 minutes. Drain, rinse under cold water to stop the cooking, and drain again. Pat dry with paper towels.

2. Combine the corn, tomatoes, jicama, onion, cilantro, lime juice, cumin, jalapeño, garlic, and salt. Stir well, cover with plastic wrap, and put aside at room temperature for 1 to 2 hours.

SERVES 4 TO 6

STUFFED TOMATOES

Why a stuffed tomato recipe? Because on more than one occasion I've envisioned a magnificent steak, or magnificent slices of steak, on a plate and said to myself, "Help! What can I put on this plate that will justify its presence because it is pretty and very tasty?" Here's my answer, a recipe from Chicago chef Lee Keating.

6 medium firm-ripe tomatoes, washed and patted dry
⅓ cup soft bread crumbs
¼ cup milk
2 or 3 sprigs basil, flat-leaf parsley, or cilantro, finely chopped
1 medium clove garlic, finely chopped
2 large egg yolks, lightly beaten
¼ cup freshly grated Parmesan cheese
Salt and freshly ground black pepper, to taste
½ cup olive oil

1. Preheat the oven to 350°F.

2. Cut the tomatoes crosswise in half and squeeze out the seeds. Cut out the pulp, leaving only a firm shell. Mash the pulp and place it in a strainer set over a bowl.

3. Combine the bread crumbs and milk in a small bowl and stir together. Mix in the drained tomato pulp, basil, and garlic. Add the egg yolks, Parmesan, salt, and pepper. Divide the mixture among the tomatoes and place them in an oiled baking dish. Drizzle a little oil over each tomato. Bake until the tomatoes are tender but still hold their shape, 35 to 40 minutes. Serve 2 halves per person, hot or at room temperature.

SERVES 6

SPAGHETTINI
WITH GOLDEN
VALENCIA TOMATOES

This may be the ultimate pasta "side" for broiled uptown cuts of steak. It was created for a tomato festival by chef John Chiakulas at Chicago's Scoozi restaurant. He uses sweet golden Valencia tomatoes. If not available, substitute chopped cocktail tomatoes or tomatoes on the stem.

1 teaspoon chopped fresh rosemary
    leaves or ¼ teaspoon dried
    rosemary
1 teaspoon chopped fresh thyme
    leaves or ¼ teaspoon dried
    thyme
2 tablespoons chopped fresh basil
    leaves
½ tablespoon finely chopped garlic
½ teaspoon salt
¼ teaspoon freshly ground black
    pepper
½ cup olive oil, preferably extra
    virgin
4 cups seeded and coarsely chopped
    golden Valencia tomatoes
1 pound spaghettini
4 ounces Boursin garlic and
    herb cheese

1. Combine the rosemary, thyme, basil, garlic, salt, and pepper in a large bowl. Stir in the olive oil, then add the tomatoes. Stir and set aside at room temperature for about 1 hour.

2. Cook the pasta in lots of boiling salted water until *al dente,* about 12 minutes. Drain and add the hot pasta to the bowl with the tomato mixture. Toss to mix, then crumble the cheese over the top. Toss again to coat the pasta with cheese. Serve at once.

SERVES 4 TO 6

DAD'S DAY
GRILLED VEGETABLES

Grilling food on Father's Day is a win-win situation, to cite an inescapable cliché of the moment. If Dad wants to work the grill, let him try his hand at this spicy vegetable combination. If he demands "his" day off, cook it for him. I used to grill seasoned eggplant without any other vegetables. My friend John Pisto suggested adding more, as he always does. This is the result, introduced on Father's Day.

■■■■■■■■■■■■■■■■■■■■■■■

1 medium eggplant
2 medium green bell peppers
1 medium red bell pepper
3 medium zucchini
1 medium red onion
8 medium firm-ripe tomatoes, preferably Romas
Spicy seasoning mix such as Cajun Magic or Pisto's Sensational Seasoning, to taste
¼ cup olive oil
1 tablespoon red wine vinegar
1 tablespoon balsamic vinegar
Salt, to taste

1. Prepare coals for grilling.

2. Cut the eggplant into 1-inch cubes and set aside. Core and seed the bell peppers, cut them into 1½-inch chunks, and place in a medium-size bowl. Cut the zucchini on the bias into ½-inch slices. Cut the onion crosswise into ½-inch-thick slices. Transfer both to the bowl with the bell peppers. Cut the Roma tomatoes lengthwise in half or regular tomatoes into 3 pieces and place in the bowl. Add 2 tablespoons of the seasoning mix and toss well. Add the oil and toss again until all the vegetables are coated. Add the eggplant cubes, which will immediately soak up any excess oil.

3. When ready to cook, arrange the vegetables in a hinged grill basket or on a grill rack with narrow slots and place over medium coals. Cook until the vegetables are soft, turning as necessary, about 6 or 7 minutes. There will be flare-ups due to the oil, but some char on the vegetables is desirable.

4. Return the cooked vegetables to the bowl. Sprinkle the red wine and balsamic vinegars over them and toss. Season with salt or additional seasoning mix, if desired. Transfer to a platter and serve lukewarm or at room temperature.

SERVES 6 TO 8

AFTER THE STEAK

Common sense might dictate that what should come after the steak is nothing. And, from time to time, in certain company, or at the end of a family meal, that may be the appropriate choice. But for me, indulgence invites further indulgence, and a final mealtime indulgence is a ten-letter synonym for dessert. So what follows are dessert treats: pies, shortcake, refreshing fruit preparations, and the all-too-easy-to-swallow liquid dessert called the Hummer.

Those who are devotees of summertime grill cooking will enjoy surprising (and delighting) guests by cooking dessert on the grill with Tuttaposto's Dessert Pizza recipe. In chilly weather, use the oven instead and bake the satisfying Rich Raisin Bread Pudding. It's one of the great comfort food desserts.

TUTTAPOSTO'S
GRILLED DESSERT PIZZA

As popular as grill-cooking is, it takes a real grill aficionado such as Tony Mantuano, chef-owner of Chicago's Tuttaposto restaurant, to make an entire meal on one. A pioneer in pan-Mediterranean cooking, he will grill vegetables for a first course, prepare a marinated steak for the entrée, and finish the meal with this dessert pizza. It's not just a conversation piece. The fresh-grilled taste of the pizza sets off the sweet fruit beautifully.

■ ■

2 tablespoons warm water
1 package active dry yeast
2 tablespoons honey
1 teaspoon salt
*1 tablespoon (packed) light brown
    sugar*
Olive oil
4 cups all-purpose flour
1/4 cup whole-wheat flour
*1/2 cup grappa (Italian brandy)
    or kirsch (cherry liqueur)*
1/4 cup granulated sugar
*2 cups mixed fresh berries, washed
    and hulled as necessary*
*1 1/2 tablespoons shredded fresh
    mint leaves*
1 cup heavy (or whipping) cream
*2 tablespoons confectioners'
    sugar*

1. Combine the warm water, yeast, honey, salt, brown sugar, and 2 tablespoons of the oil in a large bowl. Let stand until bubbling, about 10 minutes. Add the all-purpose and whole-wheat flours to the yeast mixture and slowly stir in 1 to 1 1/4 cups of water. When the dough is well mixed, cover the bowl and put it in a warm place to rise until doubled in volume, about 1 hour.

2. Meanwhile, combine the grappa and granulated sugar in a small saucepan and heat until the sugar dissolves. Cook for 1 minute, then add the berries and remove the pan from the heat. When cool, stir in the mint and set aside.

3. Whip the cream to soft peaks, adding the confectioners' sugar in the final stage. Refrigerate the whipped cream until needed.

4. Prepare coals for grilling until the surface heat is medium (see page 26).

5. Punch down the dough, cut it into 8 pieces, and roll each piece into a thin circle 8 inches in diameter. Brush the dough on both sides with oil. Place the pizzas on the

grill in batches of three or four and cook until the undersurface begins to brown, 2 to 3 minutes. Turn and cook the second side 2 to 3 minutes more. Remove from the heat. Repeat until all are done.

6. To serve, spoon fruit over each pizza crust and garnish with large dollops of whipped cream.

SERVES 8

BANANAS CLARENCE

A fifteenth-century Duke of Clarence has been inescapably linked with Madeira ever since his brother, King Richard III, drowned him in a cask of Malmsey. Untainted Malmsey, one of the sweet Madeira wines, is a favorite of mine for cooking as well as sipping. So, with the duke and the justly famous New Orleans creation Bananas Foster in mind, and a glass of Madeira in hand, I concocted the following quick dessert.

■■■■■■■■■■■■■■■■■■■■■■■■

1 tablespoon unsalted butter
¼ cup honey
4 teaspoons fresh lemon juice
½ teaspoon freshly grated nutmeg
½ teaspoon ground ginger
¼ teaspoon finely ground black
  pepper
½ cup Madeira wine, preferably
  Malmsey
4 firm-ripe bananas, each peeled and
  cut into 8 pieces
8 small scoops vanilla ice cream
  (about 1 pint)

1. Melt the butter in a 10- or 12-inch skillet over low heat. Add the honey, lemon juice, nutmeg, ginger, and pepper. Stir until the honey liquefies and the ingredients are well blended. Add the Madeira, bring to a boil, and simmer for 5 minutes. (Recipe may be done ahead to this point. Reheat sauce before continuing.)

2. Add the banana pieces to the simmering sauce. Cook them, basting and turning, until they begin to soften, about 3 minutes.

3. Meanwhile, place 2 scoops of ice cream in each of 4 bowls or soup plates. Spoon the hot bananas and sauce over the ice cream and serve at once.

SERVES 4

WARM
STRAWBERRY GRATIN

With strawberries available virtually year round, this dessert can be prepared at any season. Just remember to leave the broiler on after the steak comes out. When peaches are in season, use half strawberries and half ripe peaches, peeled, pitted, and sliced.

■ ■

1½ teaspoons unsalted butter
1½ pints fresh strawberries, cleaned,
*   hulled, and cut in half if large*
*   (about 4 cups)*
2 large eggs
⅓ cup heavy (or whipping) cream
¼ cup ground almonds
¼ cup sugar
2 tablespoons Cointreau or Grand
*   Marnier (optional)*

1. Preheat the broiler and set the broiler rack 4 inches from the heat source. Butter the bottom and sides of a 10-inch gratin pan or shallow baking dish, reserving any extra butter. Dry the strawberries and arrange them in the pan.

2. Combine the eggs, cream, almonds, sugar, and Cointreau, if using, in a bowl. Beat until light and lemon colored. Pour the egg mixture over the berries and dot the top with the remaining butter. Place the pan under the broiler and cook until the top is well browned, about 5 minutes. Allow the gratin to cool to warm or to room temperature. The interior will have the consistency of a sauce.

SERVES 4

SUMMER

FRUIT COBBLER

S ummer surely says steak to anyone who possesses a charcoal grill or out-door gas barbecue. Just as surely, when the time is right, summer says fresh fruit desserts. This one, a traditional American cobbler, is a particular favorite because the filling can be varied through the summer to feature fruits that are at the peak of ripeness.

*1 pint blueberries, washed and picked
    over*
*8 ounces apricots, pitted, peeled, and
    sliced*
8 ounces nectarines, pitted and sliced
$1/4$ cup granulated sugar
$1^1/2$ tablespoons cornstarch
*1 teaspoon grated lemon zest
    (optional)*
$1^2/3$ cups all-purpose flour
*3 tablespoons (packed) dark brown
    sugar*
$1^1/2$ teaspoons baking powder
$1/4$ teaspoon salt
*6 tablespoons ($3/4$ stick) unsalted
    butter, cold*
$3/4$ cup heavy (or whipping) cream

1. Preheat the oven to 350°F.

2. Combine the fruits in a medium-size bowl. You should have about 5 cups. Add the granulated sugar, cornstarch, and lemon zest, if using. Mix gently but thoroughly. Set aside.

3. Combine the flour, brown sugar, baking powder, and salt in anoth-er bowl. Mix well. Add the butter in table-spoon-size pieces and  use a pastry blender or 2 forks to cut in the butter until the mixture resembles crumbs. Add the cream and stir briefly to moisten the dough evenly.

4. Push or roll out the dough on a lightly floured surface to a $1/2$-inch-thick circle. Cut $2^1/2$-inch shapes as desired with cookie cut-ters. Reassemble scraps and roll out to cut more shapes. Use all the dough.

5. Transfer the fruit mixture to a $1^1/2$-quart baking dish. Arrange the cut-out dough on top of the fruit. Bake until the topping is browned and the juices are bubbling, about 30 minutes. Serve warm or at room temperature.

SERVES 6

BERRY SHORTCAKE

hat could be more American than steak and potatoes? Steak, **potatoes**, and strawberry shortcake! This recipe makes enough for a **party,** but it may be halved or some of the biscuits may be frozen.

Biscuits

4 cups all-purpose flour

⅓ cup granulated sugar

2 tablespoons baking powder

½ teaspoon salt

1 cup (2 sticks) unsalted butter, cut into tablespoon-size pieces, cold

1½ cups cold buttermilk

Fruit

2 quarts rinsed berries, such as strawberries, hulled and sliced, blueberries, blackberries, or raspberries, or a combination

½ to ⅔ cup granulated sugar

2 teaspoons balsamic vinegar or fresh lemon juice

Topping

2 cups heavy (or whipping) cream

¼ cup confectioners' sugar

1 teaspoon vanilla extract

1. Preheat the oven to 400°F.

2. Prepare the biscuits: Combine the flour, sugar, baking powder, and salt in a mixing bowl. Stir briefly to mix. Add the butter pieces and cut them into the flour mixture with a pastry blender or a fork until the mixture is crumbly. Add the cold buttermilk and mix just until well moistened. Form into a dough with your hands.

3. Pat out the dough on a lightly floured surface into a flattened disk ½-inch thick. Cut 3-inch round biscuits using a biscuit cutter dipped into flour. Transfer biscuits to an ungreased baking sheet. Push dough scraps together and repeat until all the dough is used.

4. Bake the biscuits until golden, about 15 minutes. Cool on a wire rack. (Biscuits are best when served slightly warm.)

5. Prepare the fruit while the biscuits are baking: Combine the berries with the sugar, adding only as much sugar as needed to sweeten the fruit without oversweetening. Sprinkle the fruit with vinegar and stir to mix. Set aside at room temperature or refrigerate if serving later.

6. Prepare the topping just before serving: Beat the cream until softly whipped. Add the sugar and vanilla, beating just until the whipped cream holds soft peaks.

7. To assemble, cut the biscuits horizontally in half. Place the bottoms on 12 plates. Spoon a generous portion of the berry mixture onto the shortcake bottoms and top with a spoonful of whipped cream. Cover with the biscuit tops and another spoonful of whipped cream. Serve immediately.

SERVES 12

BROWNIE NUT PIE

Here's a classic fudgy, nutty brownie baked in a cake pan. It cuts up easily into pie-shaped wedges and can be served à la mode with your favorite ice cream or frozen yogurt scooped on top.

■ ■

4 ounces bittersweet or semisweet chocolate
8 tablespoons (1 stick) unsalted butter
2 large eggs
½ cup sugar
1 tablespoon vanilla extract
⅔ cup all-purpose flour
1 cup chopped walnuts or pecans

1. Preheat the oven to 325°F. Grease an 8-inch round cake pan.

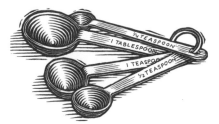

2. Coarsely chop the chocolate and cut the butter into tablespoon-size pieces. Melt together in the top of a double boiler over simmering water, or in a microwave oven. Stir until smooth and set aside.

3. Beat the eggs with the sugar in a mixing bowl until lightened in color and fluffy. Stir in the vanilla and the flour. Stir in the melted chocolate mixture and blend well. Stir in the nuts.

4. Pour the batter into the prepared cake pan. Bake until a toothpick inserted in the center comes out almost clean, about 30 minutes (do not overbake or the brownie will be too dry). Cool in the pan on a wire rack. Cut into wedges and serve.

SERVES 6 TO 8

MISSISSIPPI MUD PIE

A steak house dessert tradition, mud pie can be as simple as chocolate ice cream on a cookie crust or as enticing as the combination of coffee ice cream, peanut butter, chocolate, and whipped cream which follows.

1½ cups Oreo cookie crumbs
  (use the whole cookie)
2 tablespoons unsalted butter,
  melted
1½ quarts coffee ice cream
1 cup chunky peanut butter
8 ounces semisweet chocolate,
  cut into pieces
2 cups heavy (or whipping)
  cream

1. Preheat the oven to 350°F.

2. Combine the cookie crumbs and melted butter in a medium bowl. Stir until well blended. Press the crumb mixture over the bottom of a 10-inch springform pan. Bake until firm, 15 minutes. Transfer the pan to the freezer for 15 minutes to chill the crust.

3. Meanwhile, soften the ice cream in a large bowl. When the ice cream is soft enough to stir, but not melted, blend in the peanut butter. Spoon the mixture into the chilled crust, pressing it down onto the crust to eliminate any air pockets in the ice cream. Return the pan to the freezer and freeze until firm, 2 hours.

4. Combine the chocolate pieces and ½ cup of the cream in the top of a double boiler or in a mixing bowl set over a pan of simmering water. If using a mixing bowl, be careful to keep the water below the lip of the bowl. Slowly heat the mixture, stirring occasionally, until the chocolate is completely melted. Set the sauce aside if not serving right away. Rewarm before serving.

5. Beat the remaining 1½ cups of cream until stiffly whipped. To serve the pie, release the springform sides, cut the frozen pie into wedges, and transfer to serving plates. Drizzle the warm chocolate sauce over each slice and spoon whipped cream on top. Serve immediately.

SERVES 12

RICH RAISIN
BREAD PUDDING

What you see is what you get: comfort food at its most comforting. An unabashed hedonist is likely to ask for some Bourbon Caramel Sauce (recipe follows) to pour over the pudding. Don't discourage it, join in.

5 large eggs
2 cups heavy (or whipping) cream
1 cup sugar
8 tablespoons (1 stick) unsalted butter, melted
1 tablespoon vanilla extract
1½ teaspoons ground cinnamon
1 loaf (1 pound) raisin-nut bread, preferably unsliced

1. Preheat the oven to 350°F.

2. Beat the eggs with the cream, sugar, butter, vanilla, and cinnamon in a medium bowl until well mixed. Pour this mixture into a 1½-quart baking dish.

3. Cut the bread into ½-inch-thick slices, then cut each slice in half on the diagonal. Transfer the bread triangles to the baking dish and immerse them as far as possible in the custard (see Note). Let stand for 10 minutes. Turn the slices over and immerse the second side in the custard. Let stand for 10 minutes more.

4. Heat water in a tea kettle. Place the baking dish in a larger roasting pan, transfer the pans to the oven, then pour hot water into the roasting pan to come halfway up the sides of the baking dish. Bake until the custard is set, about 1 hour. Cover with aluminum foil and bake for 30 minutes more.

5. Remove the dish from the water bath and place on a wire rack to cool. Serve warm, at room temperature, or chilled.

SERVES 6

Note: Arrange the slices leaning against one another on a slant so as much bread as possible is submerged in the custard.

BOURBON
CARAMEL SAUCE

Here is one of the handiest homemade convenience items in my kitchen. If I'm stuck for a dessert, I merely pour a couple of tablespoons of this sauce over ice cream or pound cake. Even if there isn't any on hand, it takes only five minutes to make. Keep it in mind, as well, as a topping for bread pudding or dessert soufflés.

■■■■■■■■■■■■■■■■■■■■■■■■

4 tablespoons (½ stick) unsalted
  butter
¼ cup (packed) dark brown sugar
¼ cup granulated sugar
¼ cup heavy (or whipping) cream
2 tablespoons bourbon

1. Combine the butter, brown and granulated sugars, and cream in a small saucepan. Place the pan over medium heat and bring to a boil while stirring. Allow the mixture to boil without stirring for 2 minutes.

2. Remove from the heat and stir in the bourbon. Set aside to cool to room temperature. The sauce will have the consistency of a glaze. Cover, but if using within 24 hours, do not refrigerate.

MAKES ABOUT ¾ CUP

THE HUMMER

A goodly number of steak lovers also are dessert lovers and after-dinner drink lovers, as the owner of any successful steak house will testify with a smile. For them, in the interest of efficiency as well as pleasure, I am offering a dessert that is a drink, or perhaps it's a drink that is a dessert. I was introduced to the Hummer at the late London Chop House in Detroit. But it was concocted elsewhere in the same city, at the Bayview Yacht Club, in 1968. The author was Jerome Adams, who still commands the club's bar. He says the name comes not from the blender noise, but from a customer who said, "These things really make me want to hum!"

■ ■

2 tablespoons white rum, preferably
  Bacardi
2 tablespoons Kahlúa
²/₃ cup vanilla ice cream
½ cup crushed ice

Pour the rum and Kahlúa into an electric blender. Add the ice cream and the ice. Cover the blender and blend until the ingredients have combined and adhere to the outside of the blender, leaving a funnel in the center. Pour and scrape into a large brandy glass and serve at once.

SERVES 1

BLACK
IRISH COFFEE

From time to time a steak dinner menu is just so rich in flavor and taste that there is no room for a traditional dessert. I find, however, that after a pause almost everyone is game to sip a liquid dessert or nibble on a chocolate. One evening it occurred to me to combine the two and the Black Irish Coffee was born. I make it with fresh brewed coffee, Irish whiskey, freshly whipped cream, and semi-sweet chocolate.

■ ■

1½ ounces semi-sweet chocolate
½ cup heavy (or whipping)
  cream
4 cups hot strong coffee
6 tablespoons sugar
12 tablespoons Irish whiskey
4 cinnamon sticks (3 inches long;
  optional)

1. Melt the chocolate in the top of a double boiler placed over simmering water. Set aside.

2. Whip the cream to stiff peaks in a large bowl. There will be about 1 cup. Gently fold the melted chocolate into the cream until well incorporated.

3. Pour 1 cup of coffee into each of 4 mugs. Add 1½ tablespoons sugar and 3 tablespoons whiskey to each mug and stir to dissolve the sugar. Top each mug with ¼ cup cream, garnish with a cinnamon stick, if using, and serve at once.

SERVES 4

231

MAIL-ORDER STEAKS

As gifts, or for steak lovers who live far from metropolitan markets, call the 800 numbers listed for a catalog, price information, or to order. Most of the steaks are shipped frozen and should arrive frozen. This makes them convenient to order, store, and serve. Small orders make less sense than large ones because of the shipping and handling charges.

Boyle Meat Company, Kansas City, MO
(800) 821-3626.
Specialty: "Combo" box of filets and strip steaks.

Burgers' Smokehouse, California, MO
(800) 624-5426.
Specialty: Steaks and country ham.

Classic Steaks, Omaha, NE
(800) 288-2783.
Specialty: A dozen 4-ounce filet mignon steaks.

Double-J Limousin Beef, McCoy, CO
(800) 544-5893.
Specialty: Lean beef.

Gold Trophy by Bruss, Chicago, IL
(800) 835-6607.
Specialty: Angus beef, 6-ounce filets mignons, six-pack of 8-ounce strip steaks.

Great Plains Meats, Wisner, NE
(800) 871-6328.
Specialty: 12-ounce boneless strip steaks.

Harry and David, Medford, OR
(800) 547-3033.
Specialty: Filet mignon and New York strip.

Maverick Ranch, Denver, CO
(800) 947-2624.
Specialty: Lean beef.

Morton's of Chicago, Chicago, IL
(800) 260-0111.
Speciality: Filet mignon, porterhouse.

Omaha Steaks International, Omaha NE
(800) 228-9055.
Specialty: 5-ounce filets mignons, shipped six to an order.

Palm Pak, Inglewood, CA
(800) 388-7256.
Specialty: Prime Palm restaurant steaks, four different cuts, including four-packs of 1-pound sirloin strips.

Pfaelzer Brothers, Burr Ridge, IL
(800) 621-0226.
Specialty: Filet mignon.

Prime Access, White Plains, NY
(800) 314-2875.
Specialty: 10-ounce boneless prime strip steaks, two to a package, shipped fresh.

CONVERSION CHART

U.S. WEIGHTS AND MEASURES

1 pinch = less than 1/8 teaspoon (dry)

1 dash = 3 drops to 1/4 teaspoon (liquid)

3 teaspoons = 1 tablespoon = 1/2 ounce (liquid + dry)

2 tablespoons = 1 ounce (liquid + dry)

4 tablespoons = 2 ounces (liquid + dry) = 1/4 cup

5 1/3 tablespoons = 1/3 cup

16 tablespoons = 48 teaspoons

32 tablespoons = 16 ounces = 2 cups = 1 pound

64 tablespoons = 32 ounces = 1 quart = 2 pounds

1 cup = 8 ounces (liquid) = 1/2 pint

2 cups = 16 ounces (liquid) = 1 pint

4 cups = 32 ounces (liquid) = 2 pints = 1 quart

16 cups = 128 ounces (liquid) = 4 quarts = 1 gallon

1 quart = 2 pints (dry)

8 quarts = 1 peck (dry)

4 pecks = 1 bushel (dry)

TEMPERATURES:
°Fahrenheit (F) to °Celsius (C)

-10°F =	-23.2°C	(freezer storage)
0°F =	-17.7°C	
32°F =	0°C	(water freezes)
50°F =	10°C	
68°F =	20°C	(room temperature)
100°F =	37.7°C	
150°F =	65.5°C	
205°F =	96.1°C	(water simmers)
212°F =	100°C	(water boils)
300°F =	148.8°C	
325°F =	162.8°C	
350°F =	177°C	(baking)
375°F =	190.5°C	
400°F =	204.4°C	(hot oven)
425°F =	218.3°C	
450°F =	232°C	(very hot oven)
475°F =	246.1°C	
500°F =	260°C	(broiling)

APPROXIMATE EQUIVALENTS

1 quart (liquid) = about 1 liter

8 tablespoons = 4 ounces = 1/2 cup = 1 stick butter

1 cup all-purpose presifted flour = 5 ounces

1 cup stone-ground yellow cornmeal = 4 1/2 ounces

1 cup granulated sugar = 8 ounces

1 cup brown sugar = 6 ounces

1 cup confectioners' sugar = 4 1/2 ounces

1 large egg = 2 ounces + 1/4 cup = 4 tablespoons

1 egg yolk = 1 tablespoon + 1 teaspoon

1 egg white = 2 tablespoons + 2 teaspoons

CONVERSION FACTORS

If you need to convert measurements into their equivalents in another system, here's how to do it.

ounces to grams: multiply ounce figure by 28.3 to get number of grams

grams to ounces: multiply gram figure by 0.0353 to get number of ounces

pounds to grams: multiply pound figure by 453.59 to get number of grams

pounds to kilograms: multiply pound figure by 0.45 to get number of kilograms

ounces to milliliters: multiply ounce figure by 30 to get number of milliliters

cups to liters: multiply cup figure by 0.24 to get number of liters

Fahrenheit to Celsius: subtract 32 from the Fahrenheit figure, multiply by 5, then divide by 9 to get Celsius figure

Celsius to Fahrenheit: multiply Celsius figure by 9, divide by 5, then add 32 to get Fahrenheit figure

inches to centimeters: multiply inch figure by 2.54 to get number of centimeters

centimeters to inches: multiply centimeter figure by 0.39 to get number of inches

INDEX